VACATIONS CAN BE MURDER

VACATIONS CAN BE MURDER

A TRUE CRIME LOVER'S TRAVEL GUIDE TO NEW ENGLAND

VOLUME 1

DAWN M. BARCLAY

LEVEL
TRU

First edition

ISBN: 978-1-68512-910-1

Cover art by Level Best Designs

This book was professionally typeset on Reedsy.
Find out more at reedsy.com

To my mother, Sophie Bernice "Bunny" Barclay, who taught me that you don't have to know anything, you just have to know where to look. And to all the librarians at historical societies throughout New England who helped me do precisely that.

Contents

Praise for Vacations Can Be Murder — Volume 1: New England

"The perfect reference book for the U. S. crime traveler. Barclay rounds up a collection of known and obscure crimes, arranged by geographic area, that features museums, cemeteries, hotels, prisons, and private properties. She even offers itineraries, murder tours, a location-specific list of true-crime books, victim resources, and some ghost stories. This travel guide is a gem. Be packed and ready before you start reading because you'll want to go explore."—Katherine Ramsland, author of *Darkest Waters*, *The Nutcracker Investigations*, and *How to Catch a Killer*

Introduction

There's no denying the public's recent fascination with true crime. Books, podcasts, and television shows abound. There's also been a concurrent boom in dark tourism. Niche travel captivates the curious and adventurous—whether tourists are seeking out crime sites, tombstones, prisons, or sightings of paranormal activity. And there's nothing I like better than learning about various subcultures and then helping the obsessed indulge.

Bouchercon is a mystery writer and fan conference. When I attended the 2022 event in Minnesota, I first came upon the idea for this series of books. I took a true crime tour of Minneapolis and St. Paul and wondered if a resource existed listing all such tours around the world. I found there wasn't—and whenever I happen upon a topic that I can't believe hasn't been covered in book form before, I spring into action and start querying. (Okay, truth is, I'm a serial querier, and it doesn't take much for me to put fingers on keyboard.) Luckily, Shawn Reilly Simmons at Level Best Books appreciated the idea of filling this gap in true crime literature, and here we are.

There are plenty of true crime books that focus on the Who, What, When, and Wow. Sometimes, they even cover the Why (I love the Why—it's why I write psychological thrillers as D.M. Barr). This is the first of a series of books that focuses on the *Where*. For those who want to get closer to the story, follow the path that killers and victims followed, see the spot where they met their demise, this will take you there. For those who want to pay their respects, I tell you where many of the victims and perpetrators are buried (unless they were cremated, buried privately, or buried out at sea, which was true of many of the victims of the 2023 mass shooting in Maine).

I've included hotels and restaurants that were once jails or courthouses; prisons with infamous inmates; and attractions, including museums, which involve crime and justice. Crime tours are listed where available, but also ghost walks and reportedly haunted hotels/restaurants, because if a spirit is not at rest, there's probably a good reason why. Best of all, I bring all these elements together in the itineraries that I publish at the end of each chapter.

Anyone who knows me knows I'm an all-or-nothing girl. (That's a nice way of saying I've got some OCD issues.) Which means, when I took this project on, one thing that worried me was that I was going to leave something out. Now, after months of writing this first volume, I realize that, unfortunately, there's way too much crime out there to include it all. The book is, therefore, filled with interesting and noteworthy information and yet is far from comprehensive. I'm sure your favorite serial killer or haunted venue may have escaped my notice, and I apologize. I tried to include the biggest stories but also those that piqued my interest for other reasons, like how Deborah Gaines, when chased at gunpoint from a Brookline, Mass. abortion clinic by shooter John Salvi III, was left with terrible PTSD and never returned. She ended up carrying her fetus to term and then filed a "wrongful life" lawsuit, claiming the clinic should have offered better protection. I also tended to focus only on those crimes that left readers with places to visit since this is, after all, a travel guide.

And even though the title of this series is *Vacations Can Be Murder*, I've included other types of crimes as well—large thefts, grifts, bombings, and the like. For personal reasons, I've left out church scandals and anything related to war. I've also omitted street numbers for private homes out of consideration for those who live there now. Not off-limits, however, and therefore, included, are exact locations (where available) for businesses, attractions, even apartment buildings where crimes occurred.

I limited the amount of information I shared in each crime summary, mostly due to space constraints. What I've included are really snippets, not the complete story. I'm assuming this will serve as a review for true crime aficionados and a primer to interest novices enough to continue their research—which is why, in each chapter, I've included a list for further reading.

I'm also a stickler for accuracy (remember that all-or-nothing admission?), but I have to acknowledge that I didn't go out and research each of these crimes myself. Variations exist in the references I used, especially when it came to victims' ages. Street names change over the years, companies relocate. Prisoners are transferred between prisons or released early. Though I researched extensively, my details are only as good as the reference materials available. In some cases, using the websites at my disposal, I was able to deduce locations not included in old newspapers. That kind of detective work enthralled me. But where there are mistakes, again, I apologize.

Likewise, where I mention places that are haunted, I am not guaranteeing ghosts, or that ghosts really exist (even if I happen to believe they do). Some restaurants and hotels may be considered haunted by ghosthunters, while the venues themselves may deny any paranormal activity. Consider the "haunted" headings to really read "Supposedly or Reportedly Haunted."

I'm also a nut about uniformity, but unfortunately, it relies on the information that's available. Some restaurants' and hotels' websites included email addresses; others only included an online form for communication. There are tours that are only given seasonally, or on certain days of the week and don't list suggested minimum ages for participants. So, where such information may be omitted herein, it's not out of sloppiness. With the itineraries. I tried to provide routes that didn't backtrack. Out-of-the-way locations, usually prisons or gravesites that don't easily fit into the flow of the trip, are listed at the end of the Itineraries section as "omitted." You may choose to add them back in, or leave out other locations, or reorder your own tour entirely. Have at it.

Finally, before you embark on any journey, recognize that things change, and occasionally, fingers slip on keyboards. Even with verifying information twice, inaccuracies in times, prices, phone numbers, email addresses, tour departure spots, even attraction locations, may exist. And places close, often without notice. Before venturing out, be sure to verify details. Head off disappointment before it occurs.

Travel has been a major part of my life, and I can't picture an existence without it. I hope this series brings you joy as you explore the destinations that feed into your fancies.

– Dawn M. Barclay

Disclaimer

Although the publisher and the author have made every effort to ensure that the information in this book was correct at press time, and while this publication is designed to provide accurate information in regard to the subject matter covered, the publisher and the author assume no responsibility for errors, inaccuracies, omissions, or any other inconsistencies herein, and hereby disclaim any liability to any party for any loss, damage, or disruption caused by errors or omissions, whether such errors or omissions are the result of negligence, accident, or any other cause.

This publication is meant as a source of valuable information for the reader. However, it is not meant as a substitute for verifying travel details directly. Likewise, the inclusion of any venue, tour, or service in this guide should not be construed as an endorsement. If such a level of assistance or recommendation is required, the services of a competent professional, such as a travel agent, should be sought.

Finally, please be aware that the Victims Resources pages were completed before the new administration was inaugurated on 1/20/25 and were accurate up until that date. Some programs may have been altered or eliminated since.

General Travel Information About New England

The term "New England" conjures up many images in the minds of potential visitors: world-renowned colleges and universities like Harvard and MIT: summers spent sunbathing on the pristine beaches of Cape Cod or perhaps whale watching off the coast; the bright, colorful foliage of autumn; the ski slopes in winter. People think of the unique nasal accent, best characterized by expressions about "paahking their caah in Haahvard Yaahd" and commercials that remind you that "Pepperidge Faaahm remembers." And, of course, they drool while discussing the food: Maine lobsters; creamy white clam chowder; Johnnie cakes (pancakes made with cornmeal); pure maple syrup; Toll House chocolate chip cookies; whoopie pies; and Boston cream pie. What they probably don't think about is crime.

This guide will change all that. While there are numerous tomes on bookstore shelves that will go into far more depth on the basics of New England travel (and far less on the murders), here are a few general pointers for travelers from far-off locales:

Peak Travel Season: Expect the largest crowds between May and October, though in college towns like Boston, Cambridge, Holyoke, Amherst, and others, hotels can fill up quickly during Homecoming, football season, graduation (late May/early June), as well as Open House weeks when high school juniors are visiting prospective colleges.

Weather: Temperatures can range from 12 degrees Fahrenheit or colder in winter to around 80 degrees in the summer. Remember, New England encompasses a 640-mile area from the northern tip of Maine to Greenwich,

CT, so expect the lower end of this range the further north you travel.

Time Zone: All of New England runs on Eastern Standard Time (GMT -5).

Major Airports: Most flights come into Portland and Bangor in Maine, Boston, MA; Hartford, CT; and Providence, RI, but many smaller airports also operate.

Tipping: Figure 15%-20%

Differences in vernacular:

(You can tell I went to boarding school and college in New England, based on the food and liquor references listed!)

Blinkers and **directionals** are a vehicle's turn signals.

Carriages are shopping carts.

Frappes are milkshakes (with ice cream), milkshakes are milk and syrup.

Grinders and subs are what people from other areas call heroes, hoagies, or grinders.

Jimmies are what people from other areas call "sprinkles "and go on top of ice cream.

Package stores or **packies** are liquor stores.

That's just a start. For more, check out this USA Today article: 50 New England Words and Phrases the Rest of Us Probably Don't Get (at https://www.usatoday.com/picture-gallery/travel/2019/08/07/things-they-say-in-new-england-that-the-rest-of-us-probably-dont-get/39900209/).

The most important tip I can give you is to enjoy yourself! This guide will get you as close to the crimes of New England as you can get, while still breathing.

Chapter 1: Vacations Can Be Murder in Connecticut

Connecticut Crime Statistics

Summary of serial killings, mass shootings, mob hits, and other crimes
(listed alphabetically by location)

For those traveling throughout Connecticut, here is just a sampling of true crime that occurred in the state. Should you wish to visit these cities, exact addresses, where available, are listed in the "Itineraries" section at the end of the chapter:

Bridgeport: Emanuel Lovell Webb, also known as the "East End Killer" or the "Bridgeport Killer," is a former security guard who strangled and, in most cases, mutilated 4-5 women in Bridgeport's East End between 1990 and 1994. Of the murders he was charged with, he left 34-year-old Elizabeth "Maxine" Gandy's body on the floor of a former pool hall, stabbed Minnie Sutton (37) in her home, and abandoned 39-year-old Sharon Cunningham's corpse in a car that he'd set afire. He was already serving time in Georgia for violating parole when DNA evidence linked him to these Bridgeport cold cases. In 2008, he pleaded no contest to the charges, and a judge sentenced him to 60 years in prison, currently being served at the MacDougall-Walker Correctional Institute in Suffield.

Frank Piccolo, aka "Frankie Cigars" or "the Attorney," was the Gambino's Capo in Connecticut, at least until September 19, 1981. On that date, he was gunned down while using a phone booth on Main Street. The ambitious 58-year-old, who was perhaps best known for his involvement in a conspiracy to extort funds from entertainers Wayne Newton and Lola Falana, had angered Gambino godfather Paul Castellano by encroaching on Genovese family territory and upsetting relations between the two families. Gustave "Gus" Curcio of a rival family was later charged with conspiracy to commit murder.

Cheshire is the site of the highly publicized home invasion murders by Steven (now Linda) Hayes and Joshua Komisarjevsky. On July 23rd, 2007, they destroyed the lives of Dr. William Petit, his wife, Jennifer Hawke Petit, and their daughters, Hayley (17) and Michaela (11). Hayes and Komisarjevsky claimed they initially intended only to rob the family. But after beating and imprisoning William in the basement, they forced Jennifer to withdraw $15,000 from the Bank of America branch in Cheshire and then once home again, raped her and her youngest daughter Michaela. Next, they tied the two daughters to their beds, doused them with gasoline, and lit a match. The girls died of smoke inhalation, the mother from strangulation. William, the father, survived. The assault led to the death penalty for the perpetrators, later commuted to six consecutive life sentences plus 106 years after Connecticut abolished capital punishment.

Derby was the home of the "Derby Poisoner," Lydia Sherman, and one of her three husbands, Horatio (though at one time, she worked as a nurse in Stratford and married a farmer in Litchfield). Between 1864 and 1871, Sherman poisoned all three spouses and as many as eight children and stepchildren, in part, for the insurance money. In 1873, in a New Haven courtroom, she was convicted of second-degree murder and given a life sentence. In 1877, she escaped from Wethersfield State Prison but was recaptured in Providence, RI. She died in prison in 1878.

Fairfield: Jonathon Edington, a patent attorney, stabbed his neighbor, Barry James on August 26th, 2006, after his two-year-old daughter told her mother, Christina, that the man had repeatedly molested her. The ensuing police investigation revealed no evidence of the alleged molestation. Edington pleaded guilty to first-degree manslaughter and was sentenced to 12 years in prison, followed by five years of probation.

A separate fact: Fairfield participated in Witch Trials that predated those in Salem by nearly four decades. One notable victim was Goodwife Knapp who, in 1653, was tried and hanged in a field in what's now the Black Rock section of town.

Greenwich: In the Belle Haven section of Greenwich, on October 30th, 1975, fifteen-year-old Martha Moxley was bludgeoned and then stabbed to death with a six-iron golf club. Her neighbor, Michael Skakel, a member of one of America's wealthiest families—with Kennedy connections to boot—was later convicted of the crime. He was sentenced to 20 years to life in prison. He served a little over eleven of those years and then was released, thanks to the repeated appeals that big money can apparently afford to file and litigate. In 2018, the Connecticut Supreme Court reinstated the conviction, but in 2020, prosecutors announced they would not seek a retrial.

Griswold: Rapist and eight-time killer Michael Bruce Ross was born in Putnam and attended Killingly High School in Dayville. Several of his victims from his 1981-1984 reign of terror were from Griswold, including Wendy Baribeault (17), Leslie Shelley (14), April Brunais (14), and Debra Smith Taylor (23). Another of his victims, Robin Dawn Stavinsky (19), was from Norwich.

Hartford may be considered one of Connecticut's most dangerous cities, but its suburbs have seen their fair share of crime over the years.

The Hartford Witch Trials occurred between 1647 and 1663. In all of Connecticut, there were 43 trials and 16 executions, many in Hartford and three in Wethersfield. On May 26, 1647, Alice (Alse) Young of Windsor was the first to be executed. Servant girl Mary Johnson was the first to confess to witchcraft in Connecticut but was likely coerced by extensive torture. She was executed somewhere between 1648 and 1650 (reports vary).

In 1839, The *Amistad* criminal and civil cases were tried at Old Statehouse in Hartford. The case revolved around a mutiny by, and subsequent charging of, 53 Mende African men, women, and children who had been captured and were being transported between Sierra Leone and Havana, Cuba, aboard the ship to serve as slaves. The story was the subject of the Steven Spielberg film *Amistad*. Several other Connecticut locations connected to the trial can be found at https://www.nps.gov/subjects/travelamistad/visit.htm.

Joseph "Mad Dog" Taborsky was a murderer sentenced to death after a string of brutal robberies and murders in Hartford and West Hartford in the 1950s. He was sentenced twice to be executed for two different crimes, but the first conviction was overturned due to the mental competency of a witness, his brother Albert, testifying against him. (Albert was later declared insane.) In December 1956, a little over a year after his release from prison, Taborsky launched a 14-month murder spree that killed gas station attendant Edward Kurpewski and customer Daniel Janowski, package store owner Samuel Cohn, shoe store customers Bernard and Ruth Speyer, and pharmacy owner John M. "Jack" Rosenthal. The second conviction stuck, and he died in the electric chair in 1960, the last execution in Connecticut until that of Michael Bruce Ross in 2005.

In 2004, Matthew Steven Johnson was convicted of the 2000 and 2001 slayings of three female sex workers he murdered—Rosali Jimenez (33), Aida Quinones (33), and Alesia Ford (37)—who were all found dead in the Asylum Hill neighborhood of Hartford. Each of the women had drugs in their system and were found with their bodies stomped upon, strewn with Johnson's semen, and with their pants pulled down around one leg. Johnson was found guilty and sentenced to three consecutive 60-year sentences at the Cheshire Correctional Institution.

Lazale Ashby became one of the youngest prisoners on Connecticut's death row for kidnapping, raping, burglarizing, and murdering his neighbor Elizabeth Garcia in 2002 when he was just 18. He was suspected of another Hartford rape, as well.

Ashby has actually been tried and sentenced three times for Garcia's murder, the final time in 2023, when he confessed to the crime. Now that Connecticut has abolished the death penalty, he's been sentenced to 46.5 years in prison. In addition, he was convicted and received a 25-year sentence for the 2003 fatal shooting of 22-year-old Nahshon Cohen of Manchester, whose body was found on a street in the city's North End.

Speaking of Manchester, in August of 2010, the city became the location of a mass shooting at a beer distribution company, Hartford Distributors. Disgruntled former employee Omar Thorton, forced to resign after video evidence revealed he'd been stealing and reselling the company's beer, fatally shot eight coworkers and injured two others. He then committed suicide on site. Those who knew him cited racism as the reason for his upset, but these allegations were disputed by the firm and not substantiated by the investigation that followed.

William Devin Howell's rape and murder spree, which started on New Year's Day in 2003, took place in Seymour, West Hartford, and Wethersfield, as well as New Britain. Triggered by a fight with his girlfriend, Howell succumbed to years-long rape fantasies, Referring to himself as the "Sick Ripper," he would lure female drug addicts, unlikely to be missed, into his "murder mobile." There, he would rape them, often videotaping bizarre sex acts, before murdering them and disposing of the bodies in a seldom frequented area behind a strip mall in New Britain which he called his "garden." He was arrested in North Carolina and plea-bargained his way into a fifteen-year sentence for the manslaughter of Mary Jane Menard. However, new evidence that surfaced while he was already in jail earned him six consecutive life sentences (360 years in prison) to be spent at the Cheshire Correctional Institution.

In 1986, at the Jamaican Progressive League, a club in Hartford's North End, Bonnie Foreshaw stopped to get a beer and ended up committing a murder that bought her the longest jail sentence ever handed down to a woman in the state. Having endured a lifetime of sexual and spousal abuse, when Hector Freeman offered to buy her a drink and wouldn't let up when she turned him down, the encounter triggered her. She drew her handgun to fire a warning shot, but Freeman protected himself by using a pregnant woman, Joyce Amos, as a human shield. Foreshaw's bullet killed her accidentally.

Foreshaw spent the majority of her jail time at the York Correctional Institution in Niantic, where author Wally Lamb taught a writing class for prisoners. Lamb took up her cause, believing she'd been over-sentenced, and thanks to his help, Foreshaw was granted clemency after serving just 27 years of a 49-year sentence. Once released, she changed her name to Bonnie Jean Cook and helped other ex-convicts adjust to life on the outside until her death in 2022.

All of these murders pale in comparison to the crimes of Amy Archer-Gilligan. While she was charged with five deaths (though only tried for one), she may have killed as many as one hundred. Archer-Gilligan ran the Archer Home for Elderly People and Chronic Invalids in the Hartford suburb of Windsor, where countless older residents were bilked out of money and then poisoned by arsenic, including the murderer's own husbands. Other locations tied to Archer-Gilligan include Newington, where she and her first husband, James Archer, lived with John Seymour until he died, and then they transformed the home into Sister Amy's Nursing Home for the Elderly. In 1917, she was convicted of the murder of Franklin Andrew and sentenced to death by hanging, but she appealed. During a second trial in 1919, she pleaded insanity and was convicted of second-degree murder, earning her a life sentence. In 1924, she was transferred to the Connecticut General Hospital for the Insane in Middletown, where she remained until her death in 1962. The play *Arsenic and Old Lace* is loosely based on her story.

Also in Hartford, the Circus Fire that killed 168 persons and injured 412-700 others through trampling and asphyxiation occurred on July 6, 1944 ("The Day the Clowns Cried") and is considered one of the country's worst fire disasters. The Big Top Tent was coated in paraffin plus gasoline or kerosene for waterproofing; therefore, it was highly flammable. On top of that, some of the exits were blocked by animal chutes. Arson was suspected; others blamed a carelessly tossed lit cigarette. A mentally ill man named Robert Dale Segee, 21, of Circleville, OH, confessed to setting the fire, as well as up to 30 other blazes in Maine, New Hampshire, and Ohio. He later recanted his confession and was never tried in Connecticut. However, Segee was indicted and convicted in Ohio on two charges of arson and served eight out of a four-to-forty-year jail sentence. He died in 1997.

Finally, on May 18, 1988, Billy "Hot Dog" Grant, a bookie who was in charge of Connecticut safe houses for New York's five families, was reportedly murdered in the parking lot of the Westfarms Mall in Farmington. Grant, who had owned Augie and Ray's Hot Dog and Hamburger shop in East Hartford, and later the South End Seaport restaurant on Franklin Avenue, was suspected of having given up details of the hiding spot of the brother of a mafia boss. He is supposedly buried underneath a Farmington residence.

New Canaan: In May of 2019, 51-year-old author and blogger Jennifer Farber Dulos disappeared after dropping her kids off at New Canaan Country School. Jennifer came from money with family connections to the founders of Liz Claiborne, Inc. She was in the middle of a contentious divorce from Fotis Dulos, a man in serious debt who would gain custody of their five children and their combined trust fund, worth millions, in the event of her death. Despite the lack of a body, enough evidence was found to arrest Dulos and his girlfriend, Michelle Troconis, in January 2020. Less than three weeks later, he killed himself. In early March 2024, Troconis was convicted of conspiracy to commit murder.

New Haven: On February 6, 2021, Kevin Jiang, a 26-year-old Yale grad student, was allegedly killed by Qinxuan Pan, an MIT AI researcher and jealous wannabe boyfriend of Jiang's fiancé, grad student, Zion Perry. Pan was accused of shooting Jiang multiple times in the face, chest, and limbs before fleeing and spending the night at a Best Western Hotel under a false name. Pan was fingered for the murder after a police officer discovered incriminating evidence in a towed car Pan had rented, including an Arby's paper bag and blood stains and residue that appeared to match that of Jiang. The bag was significant because police had received a call from an Arby's worker who had found a tote behind their dumpster containing a gun, ammunition, and identifying clothing. Pan was captured after fleeing to Alabama, and bail was set at $20 million. In late February 2024, He pled guilty to murder, and, in April, received a 35-year sentence as part of his plea agreement.

A slew of mob hits have occurred in New Haven. While Eric Miller—a boxer, mob enforcer, and drug dealer—was found shot in Hartford on Dec 27, 1988, it's likely the hit was triggered by an earlier altercation with New England mafia underboss Billy Grasso outside of Grasso's New Haven restaurant, Franco's. Johnny "Slew" Palmieri was blown up by an explosive device hidden in the trunk of his car on November 10, 1974. And on or around March 20, 1951, Ralph Mele, an infamous member of the Genovese crime family, was found shot to death on the side of the road in East Rock Park after drinking with two major Mafia figures at Lip's Bar and Grill.

Newington: Matthew Beck worked at the headquarters of the Connecticut Lottery for several years. He took off four months between November 1997 and late February 1998 due to stress-related medical issues. When he returned, he found that his request for backpay to cover his job change 18 months earlier, from number-crunching to software testing, had been rejected. Beck returned to the office on March 6th with a semi-automatic handgun and a butcher knife and killed four of his supervisors before turning the gun on himself.

Newtown is the site of the horrific Sandy Hook Elementary School shootings on December 14, 2012, by 20-year-old Adam Lanza, who killed his mother in their home before traveling to the school and tragically taking the lives of twenty children and six employees. He then committed suicide on site. The incident was, at the time, the second-deadliest mass shooting in the United States after "the 2007 shooting at Virginia Tech, [where] a gunman killed 32 students and teachers before committing suicide."[1] Following the tragedy, the school was demolished and replaced. A memorial to those who perished stands in the woods adjacent to the location of the new school.

Also in Newtown, the November 1986 murder of Danish flight attendant Helle Crafts by her husband inspired the woodchipper scene in the movie *Fargo*. Her husband, Richard Crafts, a philandering airline pilot with a temper, used such a device to dispose of his late wife's body. At the time, they were pursuing a divorce. The "Woodchipper Murder," as it was called, was the first in which a murder conviction in the state of Connecticut was handed down without locating a corpse. The evidence they did find sufficed: proof of purchases for a freezer, a chainsaw, and a woodchipper rental, and witness statements detailing grapefruit-sized blood stains on a bedroom carpet that was later removed. A chainsaw was ultimately recovered in Lake Zoar, covered in hair and blood that matched Helle's. The first trial, held in New London, ended with a mistrial due to a hung jury. When the case was retried in Norwalk, Crafts was found guilty, and, in 1990, was sentenced to serve 50 years in state prison. In 2020, he was released early for good behavior, transferred to the Isaiah House, a halfway house in Bridgeport, and was last reported living in a homeless shelter for veterans.

Prospect: One of the worst mass murders in the history of Connecticut occurred on July 22nd, 1977, when Lorne J. Acquin killed his foster brother's wife, along with her seven children and her niece (all aged 4 to 12) with a tire iron and then burnt down their house. Acquin's previous criminal record included convictions for burglary and attempted jailbreak. While awaiting trial, Acquin spent time at the Whiting Forensic Institute, a state mental hospital in Middletown, where he was diagnosed with possible schizophrenia or epilepsy. At his trial in Waterbury in 1979, he declared himself not guilty—despite having signed a confession—and because some of the bloody handprints found at the scene were not his, it's possible he had an accomplice. He was ultimately convicted on all nine murder counts, along with an arson charge, and was sentenced to 25 years to life at the MacDougall-Walker Correctional Institution in Suffield. He died in 2015 from a severe brain bleed at the UConn Health Center in Farmington.

Redding: Talk about a landlord from hell. When Geoffrey Kent Ferguson had rent issues with three of his tenants who lived at his Redding rental house, he tossed their belongings onto the lawn, except for $3,000 worth of their items that he kept for himself. When they pressed charges, he shot all three tenants and two of their friends on April 18, 1995, before setting the house—and the tenants—on fire. One tenant, Scott Auerbach, survived and fingered Ferguson for the crime. He was convicted to life in prison without possibility of parole and committed suicide in 2003 after spending nearly five years behind bars.

Wethersfield: William Beadle and his wife Lydia moved from London to Stratford, Connecticut, in 1762 and then to Wethersfield in 1773. By 1776, they were a family of six, with one son. Ansell, and three daughters—Elizabeth, Lydia, and Mary. Beadle made his fortune in Wethersfield as a merchant and enjoyed an elite social life. But his fortunes turned during the American Revolution, when he chose not to charge more for his wares as the continental paper currency lost value. He did not take well to his new, less privileged life, and after three years of contemplation, when Congress devalued the currency to one-fortieth of its March 1780 value, he decided that neither he nor his family should face life without the security of wealth. On December 10th, he sharpened his large carving knife, and early the next morning, after sending the maid away, he ax-murdered his wife as she lay sleeping in their bed, slit her throat with his knife, and placed a handkerchief over her face. Then he did the same to each of his four children, laying the girls on the floor side by side before slitting their throats. Tracking their blood on his shoes, he went down to the lower level, sat in a Windsor chair, picked up two pistols, and blew his brains out.

Woodstock: Judith M. Nilan (44), a middle school social worker, went jogging on the afternoon of December 12, 2005, and was never seen alive again. Her corpse—arms tied behind her back, jogging pants pulled down, and head bloody from a beating—was found the next day in a shed on a property owned by Caroll Spinney, who played Big Bird and Oscar the Grouch on *Sesame Street* and was in no way connected to this incident.

Spinney's caretaker and handyman, Scott J. Deojay (36), was arrested and charged with kidnapping. He claimed he hit Nilan in an automobile accident, panicked, and hid her body where it was later found. He said he bound her with rope only to hoist her into the shed. The wounds Nilan suffered were inconsistent with his claims. It later turned out Deojay had a criminal record going back to the 1980s. He pled guilty to kidnapping and murder and was sentenced to life at the Corrigan Correctional Center in Uncasville without the possibility of parole. An additional 20 years were later added to his prison sentence for first-degree sexual assault in an incident dating back to 2004.

If the above didn't satisfy your appetite for Connecticut true crime, find more at https://murderpedia.org/usa/connecticut.htm.

Read Before You Leave: A Sampling of Connecticut True Crime Books

(listed alphabetically by author)

Note: Some of these books may cover crimes not discussed elsewhere in this guide.

- Barthel, Joan. *A Death in Canaan*. Open Road Media, 2016.
- Belkin, Lisa. *Genealogy of a Murder: Four Generations, Three Families, One Fateful Night*. W. W. Norton & Company, 2023.
- Benson, Michael. *Murder in Connecticut*. Rowman & Littlefield, 2008.
- Boynton, Cynthia Wolfe. *Connecticut Witch Trials: The First Panic in the New World*. The History Press, 2014.
- Bruno, Joe. *The Mysterious Murder of Martha Moxley*. Self-published, 2017.
- Demeusy, Gerald J. *Ten Weeks of Terror: A Chronicle of the Making of a Killer*. Gerald Demeusy, 2002.
- Dove, Pete. *Mad Dog & Meatball*. Self-published, 2020.
- Dumas, Timothy. *Greentown: Murder and Mystery in Greenwich, America's Wealthiest*. Arcade Publishing, Inc., 1998.
- Elliott, Martha J. H. *The Man in the Monster: Inside the Mind of a Serial Killer*. Penguin Books, 2016.
- Ethier, Bryan. *True Crime: New York City*. Stackpole Books, 2010.
- Herzog, Arthur. *The Woodchipper Murder*. Self-published, 2001.
- Holliday, Lillie. *The Voice of Omar Shariff Thornton*. Self-published,

2016.

- Howard, Anne K. *His Garden*. WildBlue Press, 2018.
- Hudson, Ashley. *United States of True Crime: Connecticut*. True Crime Publishing Company LLC, 2023.
- Jurmain, Suzanne. *The Forbidden Schoolhouse: The True and Dramatic Story of Prudence Crandall and Her Students*. Houghton Mifflin, 2005.
- Lamb, Wally, and Women of York Correctional Institution. *Couldn't Keep It to Myself: Testimonies from Our Imprisoned Sisters*. Harper Perennial, 2004.
- Margolick, David. *The Predator Priest* (Kindle Single). Self-published. 2011.
- Massey, Don, and Rick Davey. *A Matter of Degree*. Willow Brook Press, 2001.
- McConnell, Virginia A. *Arsenic under the Elms*. U of Nebraska Press, 2005.
- Meyer, Peter. Yale Murder: The Compelling True Narrative of the Fatal Romance of Bonnie Garland and Richard Herrin. Empire Books, 1982.
- Murphy, Kevin J. *Lydia Sherman*. Self-Published, 2013.
- Phelps, M. William. *Devil's Rooming House*. Rowman & Littlefield, 2011.
- Sherman, Lydia. *Lydia Sherman: Confession of the Arch Murderess of Connecticut*. Gale, 2010. Originally published 1873.
- Skidgell, Michael. *The Hartford Circus Fire: Tragedy under the Big Top*. The History Press, 2014.
- Williamson, Elizabeth. *Sandy Hook*. Penguin, 2022.

Accommodations and Restaurants that are Crime/Justice-Related or Haunted

Crime and Justice-Related Accommodations

Litchfield

There are plans in place to transform the approx. 18,000-square-foot, granite-block Litchfield Courthouse at 15 West Street into a 20-room boutique hotel, with the second floor turned into an upscale restaurant with a rooftop lounge. Stay tuned.

Haunted Accommodations

While I couldn't find (currently open) hotels in Connecticut that are renovated prisons or courthouses, or locations of previous crimes, the following accommodations are rumored to be haunted:

Norfolk

Blackberry River Inn
538 Greenwoods Road W, Norfolk
860-542-5100
BRI@BlackberryRiverInn.com
https://www.blackberryriverinn.com
Built in 1763, haunted by a 'white lady" who hangs out on the second floor or visits the empty house at the back of the property.

Old Saybrook

Saybrook Point Resort & Marina
2 Bridge Street, Old Saybrook
860-395-2000
info@saybrook.com
https://www.saybrook.com
The resident ghost apparently enjoys weddings and sometimes attends, even posing for photos with guests.

Poquetanuck/Preston

Captain Grant's B&B
109 Route 2A, Poquetanuck Village, Preston
860-303-8748
stay@captaingrants.com
http://www.captaingrants.com
Built in 1754, set between two historic cemeteries. The spirits of a woman and two children have been spotted in the Adelaide Room.

Woodbury

1754 House and Restaurant (formerly Evergreen Inn & Tavern)
506 Main Street S, Woodbury
203-405-3735
info@1754house.com
https://www.1754house.com
A spirit named Betty haunts Room 16.

Crime and Justice-Related Restaurants

Litchfield

The Market Place Tavern at the Old Litchfield Jail
7 North Street, Litchfield
860-361-9930
https://mptavern.com/litchfield/about

As per their website, the Tavern is "the oldest public building in town and one of the oldest penal facilities in the state. It was built in 1812 to serve as a jail for British prisoners during the War of 1812. A cell block and a three-story wing with additional cell blocks, now part of the restaurant's bar area, were added in 1846. The jail closed in 1992 and was used as a treatment center for men serving prison sentences. It shut down again in 1993 and reopened in 1994 as a rehabilitation center for women facing incarceration. When that center closed, the state decided to sell it. "The jail cells overlooking the three-story bar are still intact, as are the bars on the windows that face the Litchfield Green."[2]

Middletown

Harrie's Jailhouse
51 Warwick Street, Middletown
860-788-2450
heather@harriesjailhouse.com
https://www.harriesjailhouse.com

Now a restaurant but was a jail back in the 1850s. It's also rumored to be haunted.

Newtown

NewSylum Brewing
36 Keating Farms Avenue, Newtown
203-491-2038
markl@newsylumbrewing.com
https://www.newsylumbrewing.com

This property was formerly a section of the Fairfield State Hospital, later renamed Fairfield Hills Hospital. It was a psychiatric facility from 1930-1995 and housed the criminally insane from throughout the state.

Putnam

The Courthouse Bar and Grille
121 Main Street, Putnam

860-963-0074

james@courthousebarandgrille.com

https://www.courthousebarandgrille.com

In 1889, this restaurant was the town's courthouse. Puns on the menu allude to its former life.

Haunted Restaurants

Derby

The Twisted Vine

285 Main Street, Derby

203-734-2462

mike@twistedvinerestaurant.com

http://www.twistedvinerestaurant.com

Was named one of Food Network's "Most Haunted Restaurants in Every State." Offers a Paranormal Dinner & Tour each month, as well as Spiritual Nights.

East Windsor

Roberto's Real American Tavern

31 South Main Street, East Windsor

860-370-9888

robertostavern@gmail.com

https://www.robertosct.com

Formerly the location of the haunted Jonathan Pasco House, built in 1784. Pasco is still said to haunt the building.

Mystic

The Captain Daniel Packer Inne

32 Water Street, Mystic

860-536-3555

https://danielpacker.com

While living here, Packer's great-great-niece, Aida, died of scarlet fever and is said to haunt the building.

New London

1902 Tavern and Lighthouse Inn

6 West Guthrie Place, New London

860-709-7883

1902tavern@gmail.com

https://www.lighthouseinn.us

A bride allegedly fell down a winding staircase and broke her neck at her husband's feet. and she's been haunting the building ever since.

Plainville

J. Timothy's Taverne

143 New Britain Avenue, Plainville

860-747-6813

https://jtimothys.com

Dates back to 1789. The ghost is speculated to be the wife of the original owner.

Weatogue (a village in Simsbury)

Abigail's Grille & Wine Bar

4 Hartford Road, Simsbury

860-264-1580

events@abigailsgrill.com

https://abigailsgrill.com

The building dates back to 1780, when it served as a stagecoach stop. It was named after Mrs. Abigail Pettibone, who used to have affairs here when her husband, a whaling captain, was out of town. He murdered her when he found her in bed with another man. She now haunts the building.

Crime Tours and Paranormal Tours

(listed alphabetically by city)

Milford

Spirits of Milford Ghost Walks: 90 minutes, from $18-$23 in advance, $28 walk-up (limited)

Spirits of Milford Haunted Pub Crawls, held during the December holidays. 21+. Advance tickets required.

For more information on either tour, contact http://spiritsofmilfordghostwalks.com, 203-214-7554, milfordspirits@gmail.com.

Mystic

Downtown Mystic Ghost Tour: 2 hours, from $30-$35

Mystic Ghosts of Christmas Past Downtown Walking Tour: just under 2 hours, from $30

My Bloody Valentine Downtown Mystic Ghost Tour: 2 hours, from $30

Moonlit Mystic Graveyard Ghost Tour: up to 2 hours, ages 11+, from $30-$35

Paranormal Pub Crawl: Beer tour, up to 2.5 hours, 21+, from $65

Spirits of Mystic: Cocktail Pub Crawl: up to 2.5 hours, 21+. from $85

For more information, contact: Seaside Shadows Haunted History Tours LLC, 855-957-1272, info@seasideshadows.com, https://www.seasidesha

dows.com.

New Haven

Taste of New Haven Food and Drink Tours: Murder Mystery Cocktail Tour:

4-5 hours from 2pm, progressive dinner, from $150

For more information, visit https://tasteofnewhaven.com/tours or email dan@tasteofnewhaven.com, or contact 888-975-8664

Ghosts of New Haven: 90 minutes, $25, departs 7:30 p.m. from 1070 Chapel Street in front of Starbucks. Offered Fridays and Saturdays; private tours can be arranged for other days, inquire.

For more information, visit https://ghostsofnewhaven.com/new-haven-ghost-walk or contact 202-780-7169, realscarytours@gmail.com

All prices are per person. Tour offerings, prices, times, age restrictions, and meeting locations are subject to change.

Police/Crime/Prison/Courthouse Museums and Other Attractions

East Granby

Old New-Gate Prison and Copper Mine
  115 Newgate Road, East Granby
  860-653-3563
  Newgate.museum@ct.gov
  https://portal.ct.gov/DECD/Content/Historic-Preservation/04_State
  _Museums/Old-Newgate-Prison-and-Copper-Mine
  This former prison and mine site also houses the first-ever Re-entry Hall
of Change, a place to honor formerly incarcerated men and women who
have made a great positive impact in their communities. Open seasonally,
May to September. Check the exact dates before visiting during those
months.

East Haddam

Gillette Castle State Park
  Mailing address: 67 River Road, East Haddam
  860-526-2336
  https://www.reserveamerica.com/tourParkDetail.do?contractCode=
  CT&legacy=true&parkId=101150

The castle was built in 1919 as the retirement home of William Gillette, the author who wrote the first authorized play adaptation of the Sherlock Holmes novels. Gillette starred onstage as the famous detective for 33 years, created the image of Sherlock Holmes that we know today, and reportedly coined the expression "Elementary, my dear Watson." Tours are offered seasonally, May-October. Check the exact opening and closing dates before visiting during those months.

Meriden

Connecticut State Police Museum
  The Leo J. Mulcahy Complex
  294 Colony Street, Meriden
  203-440-3858
  https://www.cspaaa.com/museum
  Open Saturdays 12:00 p.m. - 4:00 p.m.
Features the department's rich history, dating back to 1903, as well as the history of law enforcement in Connecticut from its early days until today.

Tolland

Old Tolland County Court House Museum
  52 Tolland Green, Tolland
  860-870-9599
  https://tollandhistorical.org/old-tolland-county-courthouse
  Open Memorial Day through September 1 p.m. - 4 p.m.
  Tours available by appointment. Voicemail answered once per week.

Old Tolland County Jail and Museum
  Also at 52 Tolland Green, Tolland
  860-870-9599
  https://tollandhistorical.org/old-tolland-county-jail-and-museum-2

Open Sundays, 1 p.m. - 4 p.m., from Memorial Day through September. Tours are available by appointment. Voicemail answered once per week. Open Memorial Day through September 1 p.m.- 4 p.m.

The museum is also the headquarters for the Tolland Historical Society. It features a cellblock that dates back to 1856, and the attached jailer's home from 1893.

Winsted

American Museum of Tort Law
  654 Main Street, Winsted, CT
  860-379-0505
  tortmail@tortmuseum.org
  https://www.tortmuseum.org
  Winter hours (Jan-Mar): Friday and Saturday 10:00 a.m. - 5:00 p.m., Sunday 11:00 a.m. - 4:00 p.m. Call for hours during other months.

Developed by Ralph Nader, this was the first law museum in the United States.

Note: Many attractions are open seasonally. Check before traveling.

State and Federal Prisons of Note in Connecticut

Cheshire

Cheshire Correctional Institution
  900 Highland Avenue, Cheshire
  Infamous past/present inmates include Earl Bradley, the worst pedophile in American history at the time of conviction, now incarcerated in Delaware; Raymond J. Clark III, a Yale laboratory technician who murdered Yale doctoral student Annie Marie Thu Le in a campus research building on September 8, 2009, five days before she was to be wed; and both William Devin Howell and Matthew Johnson, whose crimes are described earlier in this chapter.

Danbury

The Federal Correctional Institution, Danbury (FCI Danbury)
  33 1/2 Pembroke Road, Danbury
  A low-security United States federal prison.
  Infamous past/present inmates include hotelier Leona Helmsley (tax evasion); the Reverend Sun Myung Moon of the Unification Church (tax evasion); singer and actress Lauryn Hill (income tax issues); Piper Kerman, author of *Orange is the New Black* (money laundering); reality

star Teresa Giudice (bankruptcy and tax fraud); fertilizer manufacturer Alexander Salvagno (environmental crime); and Mafia boss Michael Mancuso (orchestrating a murder).

Newtown

Garner Correctional Institution
   50 Nunnawauk Road, Newtown
   Infamous past/present inmates include Phillip Giordano, the former Waterbury mayor and convicted pedophile, and both Geoffrey Ferguson and Michael Skakel, whose crimes are described earlier in this chapter.

Niantic

York Correctional Institution
   201 W. Main Street, Niantic
   Connecticut's only state prison for women.
   Infamous past/present inmates: Bonnie Foreshaw (whose crimes were described earlier). She caught the eye of novelist Wally Lamb when he taught writing prison workshops to inmates. He then published anthologies of their work.

Suffield

MacDougall-Walker Correctional Institution
   1153 East Street South, Suffield
   A high-end, maximum-security level prison for adult males.
   Infamous past/present inmates include Jesse Velez, a pedophile, and Emanuel Lovell Webb, Lorne J. Acquin, and Richard Crafts, whose crimes were described earlier in this chapter.

Somers

Osborn Correctional Institution (formerly known as the Connecticut Correctional Institution—Somers)

335 Bilton Road, Somers

A medium-security state prison with a high-security mental health unit for men. Osborn once housed the state's execution chamber and held death row inmates until 1995, when they were transferred to the nearby Northern Correctional Institution. Infamous past/present inmates include Francis Clifford Smith, the oldest living and longest-serving inmate in Connecticut, and possibly the country. He murdered a nightwatchman during a robbery at a yacht club, but after 70 years and 31 days, he was paroled and moved to a nursing home in 2020. Also, Michael Bruce Ross, whose crimes were described earlier in this chapter.

Uncasville

Corrigan Correctional Center

986 Norwich-New London Turnpike, Uncasville

This medium-security state prison is where Scott J. Deojay is reportedly incarcerated.

Notable Crime-and-Justice-Related Burial Sites

Plot locations included where available. Not all burial sites are included in itineraries.

Some burial sites are for persons not mentioned earlier in the guide but may be of interest.

Bloomfield

Mountain View Cemetery
30 Mountain Avenue, Bloomfield
Burial Site of Nahshon Bradshaw Cohen, victim of Lazale Ashby.

Bridgeport

Lakeview Cemetery
885 Boston Avenue, Bridgeport
Burial site of murderer Lydia Sherman, the Derby Poisoner.

Columbia

Columbia Burying Grounds
CT-87, Columbia
Burial site of Robin Dawn Stavinsky, victim of Michael Bruce Ross.

Derby Oak Cliff Cemetery

72 Hawthorne Avenue, Derby
   Burial site of Horatio Nelson Sherman, the husband and final victim of Lydia Sherman, the Derby Poisoner.

Fairfield

1n 1653, Goodwife Knapp was tried and hanged in the Black Rock section of town, near 2470 Fairfield Avenue.

Oak Lawn Cemetery
   1530 Bronson Road, Fairfield
   Burial site of Barry Charles James, murdered by Jonathon Edington based on a rumor that James molested Edington's daughter.

Greenwich

Putnam Cemetery
   35 Parsonage Road, Greenwich
   Burial site of Martha Elizabeth Moxley (Moxley family plot).

Griswold

Pachaug Cemetery
   Route 138 at the intersection of Campbell Road, Griswold
   Burial site of Leslie Ann Shelley and April Dawn Brunais, victims of Michael Bruce Ross.

Hartford

Beth Israel Cemetery
  119 Affleck Street, Hartford
Burial site of John Marcus Rosenthal, victim of Joseph "Mad Dog" Taborsky.

Meriden

Meriden Hebrew Cemetery
  136 Corrigan Avenue, Meriden
Burial site of Bernard J. "Buster" Speyer and Ruth A. Speyer, victims of Joseph "Mad Dog" Taborsky.

Middletown

Saint John's Cemetery
  65 Johnson Street, Middletown
Burial Site of Amy "Sister" Duggan Archer-Gilligan.

Connecticut State Veterans Cemetery
  317 Bow Lane, Middletown
Burial site of Kevin Jiang, victim of Qinxuan Pan (Section 67, Row A, Site 25).

New Canaan

Lakeview Cemetery
  352 Main Street, New Canaan
Lakeview Cemetery contains the grave of Kitty Genovese (Section U, Lot 119), who was murdered on the street in Kew Gardens, NY, in 1964. The story claimed that she begged for help, but 38 witnesses never came to her aid. The New York Times covered the story, and the phenomenon was

later coined the "Bystander Effect." As described by Psychology Today, the Effect occurs when "the presence of others discourages an individual from intervening in an emergency situation against a bully or during an assault or another crime. The greater the number of bystanders, the less likely it is for any one of them to provide help to a person in distress."[3] In later years, the Times' coverage was "criticized for numerous factual errors and accused of contriving a social phenomenon for sensationalistic purposes."[4]

New Haven

Evergreen Cemetery
   92 Winthrop Avenue/769 Ella T Grasso Blvd., New Haven
   Burial site of Mary E. Hart, also known as Midnight Mary (Evergreen Avenue, Plot 50, Grave 4). According to folklore, she was thought to have been accidentally buried alive, and tried to claw her way out of her grave.

Norwich

Sacred Heart Cemetery
   260 Harland Road, Norwich
   Burial site of Wendy Lynn Baribeault, victim of Michael Bruce Ross.

Plainville

West Cemetery
   180 North Washington Street, Plainville
   Burial site for Jennifer Lynn Hawke Petit and her daughters Haley Elizabeth and Michaela Rose, murdered by Steven (now Linda) Hayes and Joshua Komisarjevsky.

Redding

Benedictine Grange Cemetery
   45 Dorethy Road, Redding
   Burial site for rapist and eight-time killer, Michael Bruce Ross.

Roxbury

Roxbury Center Cemetery
   North Street (Route 67), Roxbury
   Burial site of Manfred Bennington Lee, half of the team that wrote the Ellery Queen novels.

Stratford

Saint John the Baptist Orthodox Cemetery
   2610 Nicols Avenue, Stratford
   Burial Site for Sharon Cunningham, victim of Emanuel Lovell Webb (East End Killer/Bridgeport Killer).

Trumbull

Gregory's Four Corners Burial Ground
   91-99 Spring Hill Rd., Trumbull
   Burial site of Hannah Cranna Hovey, known as the "Wicked Witch of Monroe." It is rumored she killed her husband, and her home burned to the ground after her burial.

Wethersfield

Piaterer Verein Society Cemetery
   623-629 Jordan Lane, Wethersfield
   Burial site of Samuel H. Cohn, victim of Joseph "Mad Dog" Taborsky

(Plot E19).

Emanuel Synagogue Cemetery
    Jordan Lane, Wethersfield
    Burial site of mob enforcer Eric J. Miller (Section 6, Plot 103, Grave 8).

Windsor

There are memorial bricks for both Alse (Alice) Young and Lydia Gilbert, two women executed for witchcraft in Connecticut in the 1600s. You'll find the bricks in a small plaza in a green area downtown, at the intersection of Central Street and Broad Street near the post office.

Saint Joseph's Cemetery
    1747 Poquonock Avenue, Windsor
    Burial site of James Henry Archer, husband and possible victim of Amy Duggan Archer-Gilligan.

Windsor Locks

Saint Mary's Cemetery
    233 Spring Street, Windsor Locks
    Burial site of Michael W. Gilligan, husband and possible victim of Amy Duggan Archer-Gilligan.

Putting It All Together: Itineraries

Itinerary: True Crime Tour of Fairfield County

This tour starts at the southwest corner of the state and heads east, and then north, before swinging back west.

We begin in **Greenwich** where Martha Moxley was bludgeoned and then stabbed to death on the 0-100 block of Walsh Lane in the Belle Haven district, across the street from Michael Skakel and his family. Continue northeast to **New Canaan.** where Jennifer Farber Dulos was last seen dropping her kids off at the New Canaan Country School on Frogtown Road, after leaving her home on the 0-100 block of Welles Lane. Also in New Canaan, stop by the Lakeview Cemetery on 352 Main Street to pay your respects to Kitty Genovese.

Next, travel southeast to **Fairfield**, where Jonathon Edington repeatedly stabbed his neighbor, Barry James, on the 100-block of Colony Street. James is buried at the Oak Lawn Cemetery at 1530 Bronson Road. Also visit 2470 Fairfield Avenue in the Black Rock section, where Goodwife Knapp was hanged for witchcraft.

From there, continue to **Bridgeport**, where Emanuel Lovell Webb strangled and mutilated his victims. His last known addresses are where he lived with his girlfriend, Jadee Hanson, in the apartments on Smith Street and later at 537 Carroll Avenue. One of his victims, Minnie Sutton, was found stabbed in her home on the 0-100 block of Webster Avenue. The body of another victim, Sharon Cunningham, was abandoned in a burning vehicle at the corner of Crescent and Bunnell Streets. Elizabeth Gandy's corpse was found in an abandoned building at the corner of Stratford Avenue and Fifth Street. A fourth murder for which he was suspected but never charged, was that of Sheila Etheridge (29), who was killed in her apartment at 695 Bishop Avenue. Webb worked for J&B Construction at 2240 East Main Street.

While in Bridgeport, visit the corner near Main Street and Jewett Avenue, where Frank Piccolo was gunned down by a rival crime family outside a phone booth. You can also visit the Lakeview Cemetery at 885 Boston Avenue to see the burial site of Lydia Sherman, the Derby Poisoner. And in 2020, following his early release from prison, 82-year-old murderer Richard Crafts was moved to the Isaiah House, a halfway house located at one of three possible locations:112, 120, or 405 Clinton Avenue, for three months before being transferred to a Bridgeport homeless shelter for veterans.

From there, travel north to **Trumbull** to visit the grave of Hannah Hovey, aka "Hannah Cranna, the Wicked Witch of Monroe," at Gregory's Four Corners Burial Ground at 91-99 Spring Hill Road. Next stop: northwest to **Newtown** to visit the memorial at 28 Riverside Road for those who perished at Sandy Hook Elementary. While in Newtown, you can drive past the Garner Correctional Institution at 50 Nunnawauk Road, which once housed Geoffrey Ferguson and Michael Skakel, and then visit the 0-100 block of Newfield Lane, former home to philandering and murderous pilot Richard Crafts, who disposed of his wife Helle's body using a woodchipper. Catch a beer at NewSylum Brewing, formerly a hospital for the criminally insane, at 36 Keating Farms Avenue. If you take a side trip to the northeast into **Southbury**, you can visit Lake Zoar where Craft dumped his wife's remains. There's a boat launch at 210 Scout Road.

Swinging west, drive to **Danbury** and pass the Federal Correctional Institution (FCI Danbury) at 33 ½ Pembroke Road, which once housed the likes of Leona Helmsley, Lauryn Hill, and Rev. Sun Myung Moon. Finally, drive southeast to **Redding** to make two stops. The first is 166 Portland Avenue in the Georgetown section. This is the site of the home Geoffrey Kent Ferguson rented out and later burned down, along with the tenants he shot, all because they were late on their rent payments. Second stop: the burial site for eight-time killer Michael Bruce Ross at the Benedictine Grange Cemetery at 45 Dorethy Road.

Itinerary: True Crime Tour of New Haven County

This tour starts toward the center of New Haven county and heads northeast before swinging west and south. Start in **Milford** to enjoy a ghost walk or haunted pub crawl. Then head northeast to **New Haven**. On Lawrence Street between Nicoll and Nash in the East Rock neighborhood, you can stand where Kevin Jiang was gunned down by Qinxuan Pan. You can also drive by (or even overnight) at the Best Western at 201 Washington Avenue, where Pan stayed under a false name, or stop by the Arby's at 267 Washington Avenue in North Haven, behind which Pan dumped a bag containing firearms, ammunition, and identifying clothing.

Drive down Franklin Avenue, site of mobster Billy Grasso's restaurant Franco's, where he had an altercation with Eric Miller which led to his murder in Hartford. Bella Vista at 339 Eastern Street is where Johnny Palmieri left his apartment before a bomb blew up his car. If you drive by the former location of Lip's Bar and Grill at 100 Church Street, you can imagine Ralph Mele's last meal before he was shot, and his body abandoned in the East Rock Park section of town.

If thoughts of that meal pique your appetite, sign up for one of Taste of New Haven's Food and Drink Tours, where you can help solve a yet-unsolved Victorian mystery. Or, if you're more a fan of the paranormal, consider taking a Ghosts of New Haven walking tour. Finally, drop by Evergreen Cemetery at 769 Ella T Grasso Blvd., to tour the grave of Mary Hart (aka Midnight Mary) who, according to folklore, was accidentally buried alive at that spot and tried to claw her way free.

From New Haven, drive northeast to the top of the county, and visit the Connecticut State Police Museum at 294 Colony Street in **Meriden**. Follow that with a stop at the Meriden Hebrew Cemetery at 136 Corrigan Avenue to pay respects to Bernard J Speyer and Ruth Speyer, both victims of Joseph "Mad Dog" Taborsky. Then head southwest to 300 Sorghum Mill Drive in **Cheshire**, where a memorial garden honors the Petit family, whose lives were destroyed by a home invasion. You can also drive by the Cheshire Correctional Institution at 900 Highland Avenue, where several infamous prisoners include William Devin Howell and Matthew Johnson.

From Cheshire, continue further west to **Prospect**, where Lorne J. Acquin killed his foster brother's family and burnt down their house on Cedar Hill Drive at the corner of Route 68. Finally, head further south to **Derby**, where Lydia Sherman, the Derby Poisoner, wiped out three husbands and as many as ten children. At the Oak Cliff Cemetery (72 Hawthorne Avenue), you can visit the burial site for one of her husbands, Horatio Nelson Sherman. You can also catch a bite at the haunted Twisted Vine Restaurant at 285 Main Street before ending your tour.

Itinerary: True Crime Tour of Hartford County

This will definitely be the longest of the tours. We start in **West Hartford** at 407 New Park Avenue, where in 1950, Joseph Taborsky fatally shot his first victim, Louis Wolfson, at what was then Cooper's Package Store. Head southwest to **Farmington**, where Billy "Hot Dog" Grant, a bookie who worked for the Mafia, was supposedly murdered, or at least abducted from the parking lot of the Westfarms Mall. The remains of William Devin Howell's victim, Marilyn Gonzalez from Waterbury, were found behind the same mall. I've seen the address listed as both 500 W. Farms Mall, Farmington, which is their mailing address, and 1500 New Britain Avenue in West Hartford, which is their GPS address.

Drive south to **New Britain,** where Joseph "Mad Dog" Taborsky shot attendant Edward Kurpewsky and his customer Daniel Janowski at Kup's Tydol Gasoline Station, reportedly at the intersection of Stanley Street and Eddy Glover Boulevard. Also in New Britain, William Devin Howell buried his victims in his "garden" behind the strip mall at 593 Hartford Road. Those murdered included Diane Cusack, Joyvaline Martinez, Mary Jane Menard, and Nilsa Arizmendi, whose remains were finally found and identified in 2015.

Continue northeast to 85 Alumni Road in **Newington**, where Matthew Beck shot his Connecticut Lottery immediate supervisors and then killed himself. The Lottery has since relocated to Wallingford. Also, in Newington at 4 Chapman Street, the apartments stand on what was once the home of John Seymour, later converted into Sister Amy's Nursing Home for the Elderly by serial murderer Amy Archer aka Amy Archer-Gilligan.

Head west to **Wethersfield** where William Beadle and the family he slaughtered lived at 47-49 Hartford Avenue, now partially occupied by McCue Gardens, a wholesale plant supplier. There's also a park on the banks of the Connecticut River where the Wethersfield Prison once stood, and where Joseph Taborsky and others were executed. Other inmates included Amy Archer-Gilligan, Lydia Sherman, and Gerald Chapman, who was a Prohibition-era gangster and murderer. The Stop and Shop at 1380 Berlin Turnpike is assumed to be the last location where Janice Roberts (formerly Danny Lee Whistant) and sex worker Nilsa Arizmendi were seen in 2003 before William Devin Howell murdered them in separate incidents. Mob enforcer Eric Miller is buried at the Emanuel Synagogue Cemetery on Jordan Lane, and at 623-629 Jordan Lane, Samuel H. Cohn, victim of Joseph "Mad Dog" Taborsky, is buried at the Piaterer Verein Society Cemetery.

Drive north to **Hartford**, where the Amistad civil case was tried at the Old Statehouse at 800 Main Street, also the site near where Alice (Alse) Young may have been executed (now known as Meeting House Square, though the execution might have happened on a hill near Albany Avenue or on the site that is now part of Trinity College).

Also in Hartford, Joseph Taborsky shot John (Jack) Rosenthal, owner of Rosenthal's Drug Store, which was located at 4 Maple Avenue. He's buried at the Beth Israel Cemetery at 119 Affleck Street. Matthew Steven Johnson was convicted of murdering three sex workers in the Asylum Hill neighborhood of Hartford: Aida Quinones's body was found near an Interstate 84 overpass adjacent to Laurel Street; Rosali Jimenez was discovered in the basement of an abandoned building at 50-52 Cedar Street; and the body of Alesia Ford was found next to the loading dock of an abandoned building at 1 Myrtle Street. Johnson was also suspected of the 1999 murder of LaDawn Roberts (28), found on the back porch of 272 Garden Street, and the death of Rosalind Casey (32), whose body was found beneath a railroad bridge at the intersection of Sigourney Street and Homestead Avenue.

Lazale Ashby raped and murdered his neighbor, Elizabeth Garcia, in an apartment at 147 Zion Street, and shot Manchester resident Nahshon Cohen in the head while he sat in his car on Charlotte Street in the North End. Also in the North End: the Jamaican Progressive League at 1120 Albany Avenue, the club where Bonnie Foreshaw shot pregnant Joyce Amos when she meant to kill Hector Freeman.

Mob enforcer Eric Miller was found dead after being fatally shot in his Chevy Blazer outside 237 Ledyard Street.

Finally, the Hartford Circus Fire that killed 168 persons and injured as many as 700 others in 1944, is commemorated by the memorial at 350 Barbour Street behind the Wish School, the site of the actual fire. It was dedicated on July 6, 2005.

East Hartford is the town where three more of Joseph Taborsky's victims perished: Samuel Cohn, the owner of a package store located at 72 ½ Pleasant Street; and Bernard and Ruth Speyer at Caso's Drive-in Shoe Store, then located at 449 Washington Avenue. Also, Mafia big wig Billy "Hot Dog" Grant owned Augie & Ray's Drive-in Hot Dog and Hamburger restaurant at 314 Main Street, and then later the South End Seaport restaurant at 458 Franklin Avenue in Hartford, before being murdered.

Head east to **Manchester**, where disgruntled former employee Omar Thorton murdered eight coworkers at Hartford Distributors at 131 Chapel Road. Then northwest to **Windsor**, where Amy Archer-Gilligan killed at least sixty of her clients who resided at The Archer Home for Elderly People and Chronic Invalids at 37 Prospect Street. In downtown Windsor, you'll find the memorial bricks for Alse (Alice) Young and Lydia Gilbert near the post office, in a green area at the intersection of Central Street and Broad

Street. And James Henry Archer, husband and possible victim of Amy Archer-Gilligan, is buried at Saint Joseph's Cemetery at 1747 Poquonock Avenue. A side trip east takes you to Roberto's Real American Tavern at 31 South Main Street in **East Windsor**, where you can lunch with an apparition. Next stop: northwest to the top of the state. MacDougall-Walker Correctional Institution at 1153 East Street South in **Suffield** is where current inmates include Emanuel Lovell Webb, and previously, both Lorne J. Acquin and Richard Crafts. (Acquin died in 2015, and in 2020, Crafts was released early for good behavior.)

The tour ends south in **East Granby** at the Old New-Gate Prison and Copper Mine at 115 Newgate Road.

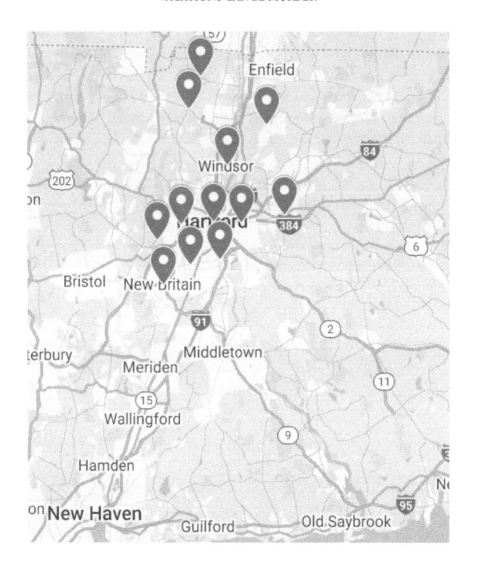

Itinerary: True Crime Tour of Litchfield County (Mini-Tour)

A true crime tour of northwestern Connecticut may be short, yet interesting. Start at **Roxbury** at the Roxbury Center Cemetery on North Street (Route 67) and pay your respects to Manfred Bennington Lee, half of the duo who penned the Ellery Queen novels. From there, head due east to **Woodbury** where the 1754 House (formerly the Evergreen Inn & Tavern) at 506 Main Street South is rumored to be haunted.

Next, drive north through Bethlehem and Morris to **Litchfield**, where the Old Litchfield Jail at 7 North Street has been transformed into a shopping mall and a restaurant called The Market Place Tavern. Grab a bite to eat before driving northeast to the **Winchester's** unincorporated community of **Winsted**, where you can visit the American Museum of Tort Law at 654 Main Street. Finish up further northwest, close to the top of the state in **Norfolk**, perhaps with an overnight at the Blackberry River Inn at 538 Greenwoods Road West (US Route 44), which is also thought to harbor spirits.

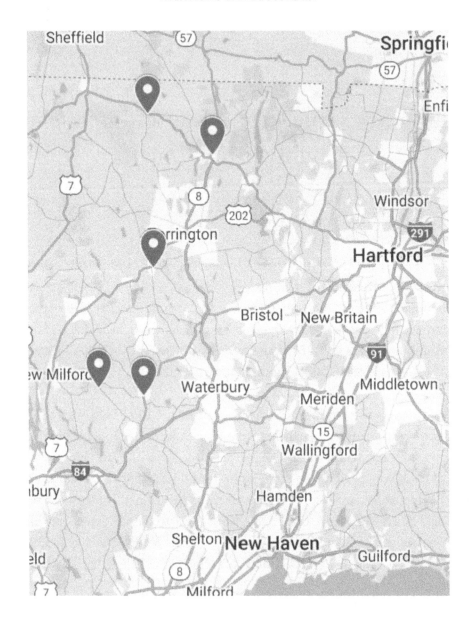

Itinerary: True Crime Tour of Middlesex County (Mini-Tour)

Another short tour: Start in **Old Saybrook** where the Saybrook Point Resort & Marina at 2 Bridge Street is said to be haunted. Head northwest to **East Haddam**, to Gillette Castle State Park, at 67 River Road. (That's the mailing address). Northwest of East Haddam, you can grab lunch at Harrie's Jailhouse at 51 Warwick Street in **Middletown**. While there, you can visit Kevin Jiang's burial site at the Connecticut State Veterans Cemetery. located at 317 Bow Lane, as well as the burial site of Amy Archer-Gilligan, situated at the Old St. John's Cemetery at 65 Johnson Street.

Itinerary: True Crime Tour of New London and Windham Counties (Mini-Tour)

Start in **Mystic** and take one of the numerous ghost tours that are offered. Enjoy a meal with some apparitions at The Captain Daniel Packer Inne at 32 Water Street, or drive west to **New London**, and dine with ghosts at the 1902 Tavern and Lighthouse Inn at 6 West Guthrie Place. Next, head northwest to 986 Norwich-New London Turnpike in **Uncasville/Montville**, where the Corrigan Correctional Center is now home to murderer Scott Deojay. Drive northeast to visit the ghosts at Captain Grant's B&B at 109 Route 2A in **Poquetanuck** (in the town of **Preston**). Further north, **Norwich** was once home to Robin Dawn Stavinsky, killed by Michael Bruce Ross, and where Wendy Baribeault is buried at the Sacred Heart Cemetery at 260 Harland Road.

To the northeast, **Griswold** was home to many of Michael Bruce Ross's victims, including Debra Smith Taylor. Wendy Baribeault, Leslie Shelley, and April Brunais. Both Shelley and Brunais are buried at the Pachaug Cemetery on Route 138, at the intersection of Campbell Road. Next stop is north to **Plainfield**, where Scott Deojay lived in the 0-50 area of Texas Heights Road. Then. further north to **Putnam**, for a bite at the Courthouse Bar and Grille at 121 Main Street. Continue northwest to **Woodstock**, where Deojay abducted Judith M. Nilan as she was jogging on Redhead

51

Hill Road near her home in the 0-50 area of English Neighborhood Road. Nilan's body was found the day after her murder in a shed on the 900 block of Brickyard Road in Woodstock, near the Southbridge town line.

Itinerary: True Crime Tour of Tolland County (Mini-Tour)

Only two stops on this tour, starting in **Tolland**, where you can visit the Old Tolland County Court House Museum, and the County Jail and Museum, both located at 52 Tolland Green. Both are open seasonally. End the tour by continuing northwest to **Somers**, where you can drive by the Osborn Correctional Institution (formerly the Connecticut Correctional Institution) at 335 Bilton Road, once the prison home of Michael Bruce Ross and others on death row before capital punishment was abolished in the state.

Some attractions do not work within these set itineraries, but you still may want to visit them. Not included in these tours: Burial sites for the Petit family and J. Timothy's Taverne in **Plainville**; Robin Dawn Stavinsky (**Columbia**); Nahshon Cohen (**Bloomfield**); and Michael W. Gilligan (**Windsor Locks**). Also omitted: The York Correctional Institution in **East Lyme**; Abigail's Grille & Wine Bar in **Weatogue**.

Connecticut Victim Resources

This is a noncomprehensive summary of services available to victims of crime in Connecticut. Information was taken directly from their websites. Visit/contact agencies for complete information and note that some programs offered by certain contractors focus on specific geographic areas. Some resource categories and content may overlap. Inclusion does not equate to recommendation.

Office of Victim Services

- Office of Victim Services: Programs include Victim Compensation (financial help for victims of violent crimes and their families); Victim Notification (confidential notification about the status of a criminal court case); Victim Advocacy; QVS Helpline (information on crime victim rights, referrals to state and community agencies and more); Sexual Assault Forensic Examiners Program; Victim Resources, 800-822-8428, OVS@jud.ct.gov, https://www.jud.ct.gov/crimevictim/. Find an extensive list of OVS contractors and their programs at https://www.jud.ct.gov/crimevictim/OVS_Contractors.pdf.
- VINE: various resources, see https://vinelink.vineapps.com/search/providers;siteRefId=CTSWVINE;serviceCategory=VICTIM_ASST;stateServed=CT.

Crime-centric List of Resources

Child Abuse

- Department of Children and Families (DCF): Statewide 24-hour toll-free Careline: 1-800-842-2288. Receives and processes reports of alleged child abuse and neglect. See https://portal.ct.gov/dcf.

Civil Legal Help for People with Low Incomes

- Statewide Legal Services: Toll-free: 1-800-453-3320, M-F 9 a.m. to 3 p.m. Apply online: https://slsct.org/get-help. Provides legal advice, advocacy, referrals, and information on numerous issues, such as legal issues for domestic violence victims. Anyone may apply, and services are free. Eligibility depends on your income, family size, assets, and the legal issue involved. Also see CtLawHelp.org, but note that the network does not provide legal help for criminal cases.

Domestic Violence

- Connecticut Coalition Against Domestic Violence (CCADV): Statewide 24-hour toll-free Hotline: 1-888-774-2900 (English); 1-844-831-9200 (Spanish). CCADV has 18 domestic violence member programs throughout Connecticut to help victims of domestic violence by providing counseling services, shelters, advocacy, referrals, and support groups. All services are free and confidential. See https://www.ctcadv.org.
- National Domestic Violence Hotline: Nationwide 24-hour toll-free Hotline: 1-800-799-7233. The National Domestic Violence Hotline provides free and confidential 24-hour support through advocacy, safety planning, and resources. See https://www.thehotline.org.
- Domestic Shelters: List of resources, see https://www.domesticshelters.org/help.

Drunk Driving Victims

- Mothers Against Drunk Driving (MADD) - Connecticut Chapter Office: 203-764-2566, Hotline: 877-MADD-HELP (877-623-3435).MADD provides advocacy, information, and referrals for victims of impaired or drunk drivers, see https://madd.org/connecticut.

Elder Abuse

- Department of Social Services, Protective Services for the Elderly (PSE): Statewide toll-free Referrals: 1-888-385-4225. PSE helps people 60 years of age or older who are being physically, mentally, or emotionally abused, neglected, abandoned, and/or have been financially abused and exploited. See https://portal.ct.gov/dsshome?language=en_US.

Fraud

- Annual Credit Report Request Service from Annual Credit Report.com: see https://www.annualcreditreport.com/protectYourIdentity.action
- National Consumers League Fraud Center (not limited to Connecticut): see https://fraud.org.

General

- United Way of Connecticut (211) Statewide 24-hour toll-free hotline: 211(when calling from CT) or 1-800-203-1234 (when calling from outside the state). 211 is a free service that helps callers find programs and services in their area. See https://www.211ct.org.

Identity Theft

- Federal Trade Commission (FTC), Consumer Information: Identity Theft: Nationwide toll-free Hotline: 1-877-438-4338. The FTC has an

Identity Theft Hotline and Resource Center that provides information on identity theft crimes. See https://consumer.ftc.gov/features/ident ity-theft.

Online Criminal Case Status, Inmate Status, and Sex Offender Registry

- Connecticut Department of Correction (DOC), Offender Information Search: The Offender Information Search is an online tool that allows users to access information on inmates, including prison location, status of the criminal case, sentence, and estimated release date, see http://www.ctinmateinfo.state.ct.us.
- Connecticut Judicial Branch, Online Case Lookup: The Case Lookup is a tool that allows users to access information about Supreme and Appellate, civil, family, criminal, motor vehicle, housing, and small claims court cases, see https://www.jud.ct.gov/jud2.htm.
- Connecticut Sex Offender Registry: Search for information on a published registered sex offender, including offenders living near your home, work, or school. You may also register on this website for e-mail alerts when a published registered sex offender registers within one mile of the address you provided, see https://www.communitynotific ation.com/cap_office_disclaimer.php?office=54567.
- National Organizations for Victim Assistance (NOVA): NOVA provides online resources, information, and links to state and local victim assistance programs. See https://trynova.org.

Sexual Assault

- Connecticut Alliance to End Sexual Violence (formerly CONNSACS): Statewide 24-hour toll-free Hotline: 1-888-999-5545 (English); 1-888-568-8332 (Spanish). The Alliance has nine member centers throughout the state that help adult and child victims of sexual assault by providing crisis intervention, advocacy services, information, support groups, and referrals. See https://endsexualviolencect.org.

- National Sexual Assault Hotline: Nationwide 24-hour toll-free Hotline: 1-800-656-4673. Confidential 24-hour online Hotline:https://hotline.rainn.org, see https://rainn.org/about-national-sexual-assault-telephone-hotline.

Survivors of Homicide

- Survivors of Homicide (SOH) Office: 860-257-7388. SOH provides support and advocacy for surviving family members and friends of homicide victims, see https://www.survivorsofhomicide.com.

Victim Advocacy

- The Office of Victim Services (OVS) has compassionate and caring victim services advocates at courthouses throughout the state and at the Board of Pardons and Paroles (BOPP) to help victims of personal injury crimes, family members of homicide victims, and people who need help filing a civil protection order. Videos available, see https://www.jud.ct.gov/crimevictim/advocacy.htm.

Victim Compensation

- The Victim Compensation Program provides help with the application and claim process. 888-286-7347, OVSCompensation@jud.ct.gov, see more, including a series of videos at https://www.jud.ct.gov/crimevictim/compensation.htm.

Victim Notification

- Connecticut Statewide Automated Victim Information and Notification (CT SAVIN): 24-hour Services: 1-877-846-3428. Provides crime victims and the public with information about an offender's upcoming court case, changes in an inmate's status, and when a court order of protection is issued, changed, or ends. Notifications are provided in English, Polish, Portuguese, and Spanish. See https://jud.ct.gov/external/news/press400.htm.

- Department of Correction, Victim Services Unit (DOC) Accused Status Notification Program and Post-Conviction Notification Program: Statewide toll-free phone number: 1-888-869-7057. The DOC Victim Services Unit has two notification programs: the Accused Status Notification Program, which provides notification on changes in the status of a pre-sentenced inmate (accused), and the Post-Conviction Notification Program (Helpline: 1-800-822-8428), which provides notification when an inmate is released, escapes, or is scheduled for a sentence review, modification, and/or parole hearings. See https://portal.ct.gov/doc.
- Psychiatric Security Review Board (PSRB): Office: 860-566-1441. Crime victims and their survivors or representatives may receive notification when a defendant, found not guilty by lack of capacity because of mental disease or defect (acquittee), is scheduled for a hearing, escapes, or is released. See https://portal.ct.gov/psrb.

Victim Rights and Services Complaints

- Office of the Victim Advocate (OVA): Statewide toll-free: 1-888-771-3126 or 860-550-6632. The OVA advocates for victims who believe their constitutional rights were violated and/or have complaints about the service received from a state or non-profit agency. See https://portal.ct.gov/ova.

Victim Services Videos

- OVS has an informational video series for victims, service providers, and other professionals who work with crime victims. The video series includes an OVS overview, information on the Victim Compensation

Program, the adult criminal court process, and the difference between a family restraining order and a civil protection order. To view the videos, see https://jud.ct.gov/crimevictim/videos.htm.

Programs subject to change or end without notice.

Chapter 2: Vacations Can Be Murder in Maine

Maine Crime Statistics

In 2022, FBI data revealed that Maine had the lowest rate of violent crime in the nation; at 103.3 incidents per 100,000 residents (or 1.03 per 1,000), it's less than a third of the national average (380.7). According to NeighborhoodScout.com, the chance of being the victim of a violent crime in Maine during 2023 was 1 in 968. Of the state's 1,431 violent crimes, there were 30 murders, 444 rapes, 139 robberies, and 818 assaults. Maine also experienced 16,811 property crimes, a rate of 12.13. The website ranks the five safest cities in Maine as Palermo-Freedom, Winterport, Eastport, Liberty-Montville, and Richmond. Conversely, FBI data ranked the five riskiest places in 2024 as Augusta, Waterville, Biddeford, Skowhegan, and Bangor.

Summary of serial killings, mass shootings, mob hits, and other crimes
(listed alphabetically by location)

For those traveling throughout Maine, here is just a sampling of true crime that occurred in the state. Should you wish to visit these cities, exact addresses, where available, are listed in the "Itineraries" section at the end of the chapter:

Amity: On June 22nd, 2010, Thayne Ormsby (20) of **Ellsworth** went to the home of Jeffrey Ryan (55), where Ryan was at home with his ten-year-old son Jesse and family friend, Jason Dehahn (30). Ormsby stabbed all three to death, killing Ryan in the woodshed and Dehahn at the end of the driveway as he fled. Then he murdered Jesse in a back bedroom before driving Ryan's truck to Bancroft Road in Weston and setting it on fire to cover up the crimes. His rationale: his belief that Ryan was a drug dealer and the other two were collateral damage. A fingerprint on a beer bottle and DNA collected from a cigarette butt linked Ormsby to the crimes, and police arrested him in Dover, NH. He confessed but then pleaded not guilty by reason of insanity. Nevertheless, a jury convicted him of murder, and the judge sent him to Maine State Prison in Warren to serve three life terms.

For those interested in looking deeper into Ormsby's past, two years prior, he worked for John Frary's congressional campaign. Frary gave him room and board in his home and in turn, Ormsby took over some campaign duties and even accompanied Frary to St. Stephen's Traditional Anglican Church, where he officiated as an acolyte upon occasion. Frary later wrote that he detected no homicidal tendencies.

Augusta: Late on July 8, 1806 (or early on the morning of July 9th), Captain James Purrington (also sometimes written as Purrinton), a farmer and Revolutionary War veteran, reportedly ax-murdered his wife Elizabeth (Betsey) and six of his children: Polly (19), Benjamin (12), Anna (10), Nathaniel (8), Nathan (6), and Louisa (18 months). The house showed signs of a struggle. He was reportedly feeling suicidal due to crop failure brought on by a drought. His 17-year-old son, James, survived the attack and ran to the neighbors for help. His 15-year-old daughter, Martha, also survived, though she died from her wounds three weeks later. To end the onslaught, Purrington slit his own throat with a razor and was found dead at the scene.

Bangor: Late on August 12, 2012, drug dealers Nicholas Sexton (31) and Randall Daluz (34) picked up three passengers, who were likely clients, in a rented 2001 white Pontiac Grand Prix to sell cocaine and smoke marijuana. The passengers, Lucas Tuscano (28), Daniel Borders (26), and Nicolle Lugdon (24), could never have imagined how badly the drive would end. A comment from Borders angered Daluz, who didn't need much to set him off because he was already angry with Borders for switching to a different drug dealer. Daluz started smacking him repeatedly on the head with a .380 caliber handgun. When the gun went off accidentally, killing Borders, everyone panicked. Daluz ended up also shooting Tuscano.

With Lugdon hysterically screaming and crying in the back seat, Sexton fueled the car at a friend's house in Dedham and then drove to a remote area in Hermon. Daluz wrenched Lugdon from the car, forced her to take a handful of pills, then shot her dead. Sexton dropped Daluz off at a Ramada Inn back in Bangor and then set the car containing the three bodies on fire at an industrial park just before dawn. Video surveillance captured Sexton running from the car and later coming in and out of the hotel. Daluz was later sentenced to three life terms in prison for murder plus 20 years for arson, while Sexton was sentenced to 70 years for murder and 20 years for arson.

Bath: On September 4, 1883, 38-year-old Englishman and prison escapee Daniel Wilkinson, along with his accomplice John Ewitt, shot Constable William Lawrence (63) in the head with a .32 caliber revolver during an interrupted robbery at the D.C. Gould Ship Chandlery and Provision Store. He was arrested, supposedly in Bangor, less than a week later, though some accounts say the two men were discovered while hiding in Murderer's Cave in Bath. Ewitt escaped to England, but Wilkinson was charged with, and convicted of, first-degree murder at the Bath Superior Court. His hanging took place at Maine State Prison in Thomaston on November 21, 1885. He was the last person ever executed by the State of Maine.

Benedicta: In July of 2015, Anthony Lord, a registered sex offender with a long criminal history, burned down the barn of Kim Irish, the mother of Lord's ex-girlfriend Brittany Irish, and the grandmother of Lord's recently deceased six-month-old son. (Irish later claimed the barn burning was retribution for her reporting Lord's sexual assault two days prior.) Next, Lord visited his friend's uncle, Kary Mayo, who lived in Silver Ridge

Township, hit the man on the head with a hammer, ordered him inside, stole a shotgun and a .22 caliber revolver with ammunition, and barricaded him in the basement. After shooting into his brother's house, Lord returned to Kim Irish's house, wounded Kim, shot Brittany's current boyfriend, Kyle Hewitt (22) eight times (he later died), and wounded and kidnapped Brittany. He attacked others before driving into a lot on Winn Road in **Lee** and shooting two men dropping off a load of wood: 58-year-old Kevin Tozier, who died, and Clayton McCarthy (54), who survived. Following a string of robberies and a massive 18-hour manhunt, Lord was finally apprehended at his uncle Carl Lord Jr's home in Houlton. He confessed to murder and was sentenced to life in prison.

Bowdoin: On April 18, 2023, just days after being released from the Maine Correctional Center in Windham for aggravated assault, Joseph Eaton (34) allegedly killed four people and then began randomly shooting motorists on Interstate 295 in Yarmouth, alleging they were law enforcement. A family of three in one car were injured, but there were no other fatalities. In Eaton's home, police found the corpses of his mother, Cynthia (62), and family friends Robert (72) and Patricia Eger (62). Joseph Eaton's father David (66) was found shot dead in a barn. Eaton was accused of also killing the family's dog. He had been held at the Two Bridges Regional Jail, and though he'd confessed to the murders, he changed his plea to not guilty by reason of insanity, and then, on July 1, 2024, pleaded guilty to all charges. Eaton was sentenced to life in prison. He is currently incarcerated at Maine State Prison.

Carmel: The first disappearance of someone connected to James Rodney Hicks occurred on July 19, 1977, when his wife, Jennie Lynn Hicks, vanished from their Carmel trailer. The couple lived there with their two children, Veronica (6) and Sean (2), in a volatile marriage filled with infidelity, unexpected pregnancies, and plans for divorce. The second disappearance occurred in 1982, when Hicks was seen leaving the Gateway Lounge in Newport with Jerilyn Tibbetts-Towers, who was never seen again. In 1983, though neither woman's body had been found, Hicks was arrested, and in 1985, he was convicted of fourth-degree homicide of his wife. He served six out of a ten-year sentence at the Maine State Prison in Thomaston (since moved to Warren). By May of 1996, Hicks was living with Lynn Willette, 40, a colleague from a motel job in Brewer, and he eventually moved into her apartment. Then, she went missing, too.

Hicks himself disappeared for a bit but resurfaced in Texas in April of 2000. That's when June Moss, a 67-year-old woman from Lubbock, accused him of forcing her at gunpoint to give him a check, sign over her car title, and then write a suicide note. She claimed he'd tried to force her to drink cough syrup, so she'd fall asleep before he drowned her, but she'd escaped. Hicks was indicted and then convicted of aggravated assault. He received a 55-year prison sentence.

Terrified of the prospect of serving time in Texas, Hicks confessed to the murders of the three women who vanished in Maine and led state police and forensic experts to their remains. In six-inch-deep graves behind a shed at Hicks' former homestead, they discovered Jennie Hicks' skull embedded in cement, and one hundred feet away, Tibbetts-Towers' dismembered body. Willette's partial remains were found entrenched in cement-filled buckets on a swampy site along Route 2A in Forkstown Township. Hicks is currently serving a life sentence for the three murders at Maine State Prison.

Houlton: Stephen Alexander Marshall was a 20-year-old American Canadian dishwasher from a broken home, living in North Sydney, Nova Scotia. He had recently converted to Christianity, and among his dislikes—which included women and authority—was a hatred for pedophiles. At age 15, he had already been charged with aggravated assault.

In the spring of 2006, Marshall traveled to Houlton to visit his father, Ralph, bringing with him a list of 29 of the 34 sex offenders on the Maine registry. Late on April 15th or in the wee hours of April 16th, he borrowed his father's 2002 silver Toyota Tundra and drove off with his laptop and three of his father's firearms: two handguns and a .223 Colt Sporter semi-automatic rifle. He traveled 2.5 hours south to Milo, where he shot Joseph Gray (57), who had served time for raping a child under 14. Then, he drove to Corinth and murdered William Elliott (24) in the doorway of his mobile home. Elliott had been convicted of the statutory rape of a girl a few days shy of her sixteenth birthday, when such intimacies would have been legal.

Following the shooting, Elliott's girlfriend snapped a photo of Marshall's license plate as he drove off. He abandoned the truck behind a Bangor skating rink and boarded a Vermont Bus Lines coach bound for Boston. Police boarded Marshall's bus as it approached South Station, prompting Marshall to commit suicide by shooting himself in the head. His laptop revealed he had visited the homes of four other sex offenders between the two murders, but those stops ended without incident.

Kittery: Stephen Howard Oken (25) came to Kittery in November of 1987 after shooting and killing two women in Maryland: Dawn Marie Garvin (20) of White Marsh, where he left a condiment bottle protruding from her vagina; and then a fortnight later, his sister-in-law, Patricia Antoinette Hirt (43), whom he sexually assaulted and murdered in her home. At his hotel, the Coachman Motor Inn in Kittery, he killed desk clerk Lori Ward (25) in a room behind the check-in desk. Oken was convicted in Maine of first-degree murder and robbery with a firearm, for which he was sentenced to life in prison. Then, he was extradited to Maryland, where he was tried and convicted for the first two killings. In 2004, at the age of 42, Oken was executed in Maryland by lethal injection.

Lewiston: On October 25, 2023, Army reservist and firearms instructor Robert Card (40) from Bowdoin, opened fire at the Just-in-Time Recreation bowling alley, and soon afterward, at a restaurant called Schemengees Bar & Grille. His rampage cost eighteen people their lives—fifteen men, two women, and a fourteen-year-old boy—and injured 13 others. After the shootings, authorities found his car abandoned at a boat ramp, and two days later, Card himself was found dead from a self-inflicted gunshot wound in a trailer parked in the lot of a recycling company in Lisbon Falls, where he used to work as a commercial driver. Thus ended an intensive two-day search during which the townspeople sequestered themselves in their homes. Up until that date, there had only been 29 murders in Maine in all of 2022, but Card's assault counted as the thirty-sixth mass killing in the United States in 2023.

The prior summer, Card had been training with the Army Reserve's 3rd Battalion, 304th Infantry Regiment in West Point, NY, when his behavior became erratic, and he complained of hearing voices making violent threats. He was committed to the Keller Army Community Hospital and evaluated for two weeks. A note at a home associated with Card, addressed to his son, left no specific motive but did include the passcodes to his phone and bank account numbers.

In March 2024, the post-mortem analysis of Card's brain by Boston University's CTE Center revealed "significant evidence of traumatic brain injuries at the time of the shooting." Such damage could stem from exposure to training blasts in the military, a study found.[1]

New Sweden: On April 27, 2003, sixteen members of the sixty regular worshippers at the Gustaf Adolph Lutheran Church became violently ill after partaking in coffee and doughnuts following services. The next day, Walter Reid Morrill (78), church caretaker and usher, died from arsenic poisoning. Others were in critical condition, but thanks to arsenic antidotes shipped from Portland, they survived. It was later confirmed that someone had intentionally added arsenic to the brew. On May 2nd, Daniel Bondeson (53), a substitute teacher and nurse from neighboring Woodland, died of what was determined to be a self-inflicted gunshot wound to the chest. He left behind a suicide note that took responsibility for the poisoning but insisted that he acted alone. The contents of the note were never made public. Many questioned the motive behind the attack and whether others were involved, but nothing more was ever resolved.

Newry: Christian Charles Nielsen rented a room for several months at the Black Bear Bed and Breakfast and worked as a cook at the Sudbury Inn in Bethel. On September 1st, 2006, he murdered James Whitehurst (50) of Batesville, Arkansas, who had been receiving free lodging in exchange for handyman services. Nielsen later described Whitehurst as "objectionable." The next day, he burned the body, cut it in half, and dumped it in the woods in Upton. His Labor Day murder spree had just begun. To hide that crime and take over the property, on September 3rd, he shot and killed the B&B owner, Julie Bullard (65), and the next day, Julie's daughter Selby (30) and her friend Cindy Beatson (43). He dismembered all three bodies, using an ax, a hacksaw, and a chainsaw. He also killed three dogs.

On the Sunday of that weekend, after killing four people, Nielsen showed up for work for his line-cook shift as if nothing had happened. On Labor Day evening, he phoned his father and told him he was running the inn in Julie Bullard's absence. His father found this suspicious and called the police. They found Nielsen's handgun on the premises, and he confessed to the killings. He gave no motive, other than saying murder was something he'd considered for years. However, there is speculation that Bullard and Whitehurst may have been trying to evict Nielsen for non-payment of rent. Bullard had actually decided to sell the B&B, finding it hard to make ends meet. It's one of the reasons she'd rented the room to Nielsen in the first place. There had been a For Sale sign outside since February.

It was later discovered Nielsen suffered from schizoid personality disorder and a mild form of autism.

Those who want to probe into Nielsen's past can check out various venues in Farmington where he lived prior to moving to Newry: The University of Maine. where he studied English in spurts without earning a degree; Devaney Doak & Garrett Booksellers, where he was a frequent customer; and the Family Fare Restaurant, where he worked as a cook. Nielsen is currently serving a life sentence at Maine State Prison in Warren.

Old Orchard Beach: On February 20, 2008, 21-year-old University of Maine student Matthew Paul Cushing drove home to his family's residence. As each of his family members arrived home—starting with his stepbrother Joshua (15), followed by his mother and stepfather, Carol and Chris

Bolduc—he incapacitated them with a stun gun before stabbing them to death in the face and eyes. He even killed the family dog, Spike. Then he set the house ablaze to hide his actions. Since he'd been seen in town, police quickly zeroed in on Matthew as the killer, and he confessed to the crimes.

Because he pled guilty, there was no trial, and his motives remain unclear, but there is speculation that his upset stemmed from the fact his stepfather was gay and planned to leave his mother to live with his lover in South Carolina. Cushing was reportedly also upset that his parents wouldn't support his plan to drop out of school and backpack through Europe. The house has since been leveled, and a memorial stands in its place. Their family business, Blustery Day Flags, is now the site of Christina's Classic Cookies. The victims' names are also inscribed on the Maine Murder Victims' Memorial in Augusta Holy Family Cemetery. Cushing is serving a life sentence at Maine State Prison in Warren.

Portland: Serial killer John Joseph Joubert IV came from a broken Massachusetts home with a domineering mother. They moved to Portland in 1974. While a strong student, he was often bullied at school and didn't defend himself. Later psychological profiles revealed that in his teens, he entertained fantasies of torture and murder. He assaulted local children by stabbing or slashing them but never got charged. His first murder was that of Richard Stetson (11) in August 1982, when the boy disappeared while jogging on the Back Cove trail. His body was found the next day, with stab wounds and human bite marks.

The case went cold until 1984, when a 20-year-old enlisted radar technician from the Offutt Air Force Base in Nebraska was arrested and charged with the abduction and killings of Christopher Walden (12) and paper delivery boy Danny Joe Eberle (13). Their murders resembled aspects of the Stetson killing in Maine, including matching hair samples and tooth impressions. Thanks to witness sightings of his car, Joubert was eventually arrested, and DNA evidence helped convict him of Stetson's murder. He was later diagnosed with obsessive-compulsive disorder, sadistic tendencies, and schizoid personality disorder. However, he was deemed not to have been psychotic at the time of the murders. He was sentenced to life imprisonment in Maine, but Nebraska appealed that sentence and requested his return. They executed him by electric chair on July 17, 1996.

Smuttynose Island (Isles of Shoals): Smuttynose Island is one of the Isles of Shoals, part of the town of Kittery in York County. This is where Louis Wagner allegedly killed two women. However, because part of the story occurred in New Hampshire, and tours to the Island leave from Portsmouth, the story is covered in that chapter of this book.

Waldoboro: On July 21st, 2012, Arline Lawless (25), who also went by the name Arline Seavey, shot her boyfriend of four months, Norman Benner Jr., in the back of the head while he slept. She then shot herself in the face, but not fatally so. Lawless later claimed she shot him because she feared Benner was going to leave her for being too clingy. In fact, he had gone home that day to end the relationship, according to Benner's mother, Dawn.

Lawless stayed in the bedroom with Benner for at least a day before they were discovered on July 23rd by Benner's father, mother, and sister. She was arrested on August 15th as she was leaving the Spring Harbor Treatment Center in Westbrook. Lawless plea-bargained herself into a 35-year sentence at the Maine Correctional Center in Windham, where she remains today.

Waterville/Fairfield Center: Constance Margaret (Sirois) Fisher was an often anxious and depressed housewife plagued by hallucinations, visions, and periods of mental weakness. While it wasn't really a "thing" in the 1950s, she probably also suffered from postpartum depression.

On March 8, 1954, her husband Carl discovered the bodies of their three children—Richard (almost 7), Daniel (5), and Deborah Kay (1)—who had been drowned in the family bathtub in their Waterville home. Fisher, who had attempted to commit suicide by downing a bottle of shampoo, left a note claiming she'd drowned them to protect them from evil. She was diagnosed with paranoid schizophrenia, at trial, found not guilty by reason of insanity, and committed to the Augusta State Hospital (since renamed Augusta Mental Health Institute).

Five years after the incident, Fisher was found fit enough for release. The couple moved to Fairfield and had three more children, whom Fisher drowned on June 30, 1966—Kathleen Louise (6), Michael Jon (4) and Natalie Rose (9 months). Again, she tried to kill herself, this time with a pill overdose. She was rushed to Thayer Hospital in Waterville and later, sent back to the psychiatric hospital, where she was to be confined for the rest of her natural life. Fisher remained there until 1973, when she escaped and drowned herself in the Kennebec River. Duck hunters found her bloated body nine days later in the Kennebec River in Gardiner.

York: The second woman ever to be hanged in Maine was Patience Sampson (23), aka Patience Boston, a Native American who, in her short life, served as a servant to several families. Sampson considered herself to be evil. At age twelve, she attempted to burn down her master's house three times, and after marriage, confessed more than once to murdering children, though two of her children died after birth without her involvement. Sampson drank heavily, committed adultery, and when she was sold to Benjamin Skillin of Casco Bay in Falmouth (now Portland), a master she didn't like, she followed the "wicked oath" she'd made to herself. She drowned his grandson, Benjamin Trot, in a well in the woods on July 9, 1734. While in prison, she gave birth and converted to Christianity. Some questioned whether Benjamin fell into the well accidentally, and Patience claimed she drowned him out of a sense of responsibility for his well-being. Nevertheless, she was hanged in York in July of 1735 and buried in an unmarked grave.

Read Before You Leave: A Sampling of Maine True Crime Books

(listed alphabetically by author)

Note: Some of these books may cover crimes not discussed elsewhere in this guide.

- Boston, Patience, Samuel Moody, Joseph Moody, Samuel Kneeland, and Timothy Green. *A Faithful Narrative of the Wicked Life and Remarkable Conversion of Patience Boston Alias Samson;* https://quod.lib.umich.edu/cgi/t/text/text-idx?c=evans;cc=evans;view=toc;idno=N03473.0001.001, 1738.
- Briggs, Bob. *The Constance Fisher Tragedy*. Author House, 2011.
- De Wolfe, Elizabeth A. *The Murder of Mary Bean and Other Stories*. True Crime History, 2007.
- Duffin, Allan, and Darryl Kimball. *Takedown*. Duffin Creative, 2015.
- Flagg, Pat. *The Disappearance of Amy Cave*. Down East Books, 1991.
- Loughlin, Joseph K, and Kate Clark Flora. *Finding Amy*. UPNE, 2011.
- Pesha, Ronald. *The Great Gold Swindle of Lubec, Maine*. Arcadia Publishing, 2013.
- Robinson, J. Dennis. *Mystery on the Isles of Shoals*. Simon and Schuster, 2014.
- Scee, Trudy Irene. *Tragedy in the North Woods*. Arcadia Publishing, 2009.
- Spooner, Emeric. *In Search of Mattie Hackett*. Self-published, 2010.

- ———. *In Search of Melissa Thayer*. Self-published, 2008.
- ———. *In Search of Sarah Ware*. Self-published, 2008.
- Wight, Eric. *Life and Death in the North Woods*. Down East Books, 2014.
- Young, Christine Ellen. *A Bitter Brew: Faith, Power, and Poison in a Small New England Town*. Berkley Books, 2005.

Accommodations and Restaurants that are Crime/Justice-Related or Haunted

Crime/Justice-Related Accommodations

Portland

The Press Hotel
119 Exchange Street, Portland
207-808-8800
info@ThePressHotel.com
https://thepresshotel.com

It's not where the crimes happened, but where they may have been written about. The former Portland Herald Press building is now a boutique hotel.

Haunted Accommodations

While there are no crime-related hotels in Maine, and no jails converted into accommodations, the following hotels are rumored to be haunted. And where there are souls not at rest, perhaps foul play caused their demise?

Bar Harbor

Coach Stop Inn
715 State Highway 3, Bar Harbor
207-288-9886

info@coachstopinn.com

https://www.coachstopinn.com

This may be the oldest house still standing in the area, having survived the Fire of 1947. Abbe, a child spirit, makes her presence known.

Dedham

The Lucerne Inn

2517 Main Road, Dedham

207-843-5123

reservations@lucerneinn.com

https://www.lucerneinn.com

Site of a murder/suicide; the spirits of both individuals hung around the place—chatting, playing the piano, turning televisions on and off, and opening doors.

Fryeburg

Admiral Peary Inn

27 Elm Street, Fryeburg

207-935-1269

info@admiralpearyinn.com

https://www.admiralpearyinn.com

Unexplained shadows and footprints might be attributable to the ghosts of Nathan and Abigail, two spirits that live on the second floor.

Greenville

Greenville Inn at Moosehead Lake

40 Norris Street, Greenville

207-695-2206

https://www.greenvilleinn.com

Guests report unexplained voices, tape dancing, and the ghost of a beautiful lady.

Kennebunk

The Kennebunk Inn and Tavern
45 Main Street, Kennebunk
207-985-3351
info@thekennebunkinn.com
https://www.thekennebunkinn.com
Built in 1799, this former private residence is home to at least one ghost, reportedly the former nightwatchman and auditor, Silas Perkins, who likes to move dishware and make noise.

Kennebunkport

Captain Fairfield Inn, aka James Fairfield House
8 Pleasant Street, Kennebunkport
207-967-4454
stay@kennebunkportcaptains.com
https://www.larkhotels.com/hotels/kennebunkport-captains-collecti on
Former owner, Captain James Fairfield, who died of pneumonia, has been seen floating in the basement and reportedly acts friendly toward guests.

Nathaniel Lord Mansion

6 Pleasant Street, Kennebunkport
207-967-3141
stay@kennebunkportcaptains.com
https://www.larkhotels.com/hotels/kennebunkport-captains-collecti on/rooms/chid_86/nlm-nathaniel-lord-suite
Formerly the Captain Lord Mansion, the captain's wife has appeared in spirit form in the Lincoln bedroom, her perfume scenting the air.

The Tides Beach Club

930 Kings Highway, Kennebunkport
800-572-8696
stay@tidesbeachclubmaine.com

www.tidesbeachclubmaine.com

Emma Foss, a former owner, is said to still reside here, spending most of her time in Room 25.

Poland

Poland Spring Resort

640 Maine Street, Poland

207-998-4351

info@polandspringresort.com

https://polandspringresort.com

The first owner is said to walk the halls. There's also a female spirit dressed in white.

Rockland

The Lindsey Guest House

5 Lindsey Street, Rockland

207-466-9015

stay@lindseyguesthouse.com

https://www.lindseyguesthouse.com

Guests have seen faces in furniture, along with unexplained handprints and seat impressions.

LimeRock Inn

96 LimeRock Street, Rockland

207-594-2257

info@limerockinn.com

https://www.limerockinn.com

The ghosts are thought to be former patients of the doctor who practiced from home.

Tenants Harbor

The East Wind Inn

21 Mechanic Street, Tenants Harbor

207-372-6366

info@eastwindinn.com

https://eastwindinn.com

A woman, once stabbed here, frequents the upper floor and the attic. Her anger evokes intense emotions from visitors, who have seen furniture and objects move. Some claim to have been held down in their beds or pushed out of bed by her. Guests have also heard late night crying and witnessed windows shatter. On lower floors, some have observed a gray spirit ascending the stairs and smelled the scent of tobacco. This less-hostile presence is thought to be the ghost of a sea captain.

Please note: Some hotels are open seasonally.

Crime/Justice-Related Restaurants

Skowhegan

The Miller's Table

42 Court Street, Skowhegan

207-612-5322

millerstable@mainegrains.com

https://www.millerstable.com

This farm-to-table restaurant is located inside the former garage bay of the renovated Somerset County jail. It was reborn as a grist mill before it became a restaurant.

Haunted Restaurants

Cape Elizabeth

Inn by the Sea

40 Bowery Beach Road, Cape Elizabeth

207-799-3134

info@innbythesea.com

https://innbythesea.com

Lydia Carver haunts the Inn; she was killed in a shipwreck right before her wedding day and took up residence here, where she stacks dishes that have been set out on tables the night before.

Freeport

Jameson Tavern

115 Main Street, Freeport

207-865-4196

Thejamesontavern@gmail.com

https://www.jamesontavern.com

Built in 1779, the tavern is haunted by both a man in a top hat and a little girl who died in a fire but whose spirit runs between rooms.

Portland

DiMillo's On the Water

25 Long Wharf, Portland

207-772-2216

restaurant@dimillos.com

https://www.dimillos.com

A maintenance worker saw apparitions during the three decades he worked here. He said the ghosts were always turning lights on and off and were quite talkative.

Empire Chinese Kitchen and Empire Live (formerly Empire Dine and Dance)

575 Congress Street Portland

207-747-5063

https://www.portlandempire.com

This Cantonese restaurant, with entertainment offered upstairs, has gone through many iterations, dating back to 1916. A manager used to block his door to ignore the spirits outside his office.

Note: There's also a restaurant at the haunted Kennebunk Inn in Kennebunk.

Crime Tours and Paranormal Tours

Augusta

Capital City Shivers Haunted History Tour: 90-120 minutes, $25, ages 13+, meets at Waterfront Park on Front Street. Offered by Kennebec Creeps & Crawl, 207-542-3701, kennebeccreepsandcrawls@gmail.com, https://kennebeccreepsandcrawls.com.

Bar Harbor

- Bar Harbor Ghost Tour: 60-90 minutes, $12-$24, departs 8:00 p.m. nightly from the Abbe Museum Courtyard at 26 Mount Desert Street.
- Monsters by Moonlight: 1 hour, $12-$24, departs 9:00 p.m. nightly from the Abbe Museum bench in front of the gift shop at 26 Mount Desert Street.

Both of the above-listed tours are offered through Bar Harbor Ghost Tours, 207-404-4113, https://www.barharborghosttours.com.

Bar Harbor Ghost Walk: 90 minutes, from $25, departs 6:30 p.m. from Agamont Park Gazebo near the Shore Path by the cannons. Offered by American Ghost Walks, 1-833-GHOST13, info@americanghostwalks.com, https://www.americanghostwalks.com.

Boothbay Harbor

Boothbay Harbor Ghost Walk: 90 minutes, from $25, departs from 15 Oak Street.

Offered by American Ghost Walks, 1-833-GHOST13, info@americang hostwalks.com, https://www.americanghostwalks.com

Hallowell

- Granite City Ghosts: 90-120 min, $25, ages 13+, departs from the Hubbard Free Library at 115 Second Street.
- "Grave Secrets" Tour of the Hallowell Village Cemetery: 90-120 min, $30, ages 13+. Departs from Hallowell Village Cemetery at 27 Water Street.

Both offered by Kennebec Creeps & Crawls, 207-542-3701, kennebeccree psandcrawls@gmail.com, https://kennebeccreepsandcrawls.com.

Kennebunkport

Kennebunkport Ghost Walk: 90 minutes, from $25, departs from White Columns at 8 Maine Street. Offered by American Ghost Walks, 1-833-GHOST13, info@americanghostwalks.com.

https://www.americanghostwalks.com/tour/kennebunkport-ghost-w alk.

Portland

Portland Maine Hidden Histories Tour: 2 hours, from $42, departs from 389 Congress Street. Offered by Portland by the Foot, 207-200-5885, hi@portlandbythefoot.com. https://www.portlandbythefoot.com. Tour includes some crime, but it is not the sole focus.

A Comedy of Haunted History: 75 minutes, $25-$35, departs usually at 8:00 p.m. from Bell Buoy Park, 60 Commercial Street (between Flatbread and Casco Bay Lines). Offered by Wicked Walking Tours, 207-730-0490, info@wickedwalkingtours.com, https://www.wickedwalkingtours.com.

Wiscasset

Wiscasset Ghost Walk: 90 minutes, from $25, departs from the front of the Lincoln County Courthouse at 32 High Street. Offered by American Ghost Walks, 1-833-GHOST13, info@americanghostwalks.com, https://www.americanghostwalks.com/tour/wiscasset-ghost-walk.

York Beach

Ghostly Tours of York: 60 minutes, $10-$15, children six and under free. The tour departs at 8:00 p.m. in front of Molly'O's Restaurant, 2 Main Street, York. The tour runs from the third Friday in June until the Saturday of Labor Day weekend. Between Labor Day and Halloween, the company will accommodate groups of 10 or more, $150 minimum.

Contact the operator at 207-363-0000, https://www.haunts.com/ghostlytoursyorkmaine.

Haunted York Village: ages 17+, $20, Offered on very limited dates.
roxiezwicker@gmail.com, 603-343-7977; https://newenglandcuriosities.com/haunted-york-village.

Please note: some tours may be seasonal. All prices are per person. Tour offerings, prices, times, age restrictions, and meeting locations are subject to change.

Police/Crime/Prison/Courthouse Museums and Other Attractions

Bangor

Museum of Law Enforcement (Bangor Police Department Museum)
  240 Main Street, Bangor
  207-947-7384
  bangor.police@bangormaine.gov
  https://www.facebook.com/bangormainepolice
  Call anytime Monday through Friday, 8 a.m. to 5 p.m., to make an appointment.

Author Stephen King's Former Home (Exterior)
  47 West Broadway, Bangor

Dresden

The Pownalborough Court House
  23 Court House Road, Dresden
  207-882-6817
  https://www.lincolncountyhistory.org/visit/museums
  Dates back to 1761 and still stands on its original site on the banks of the Kennebec River.

Open Saturday, Sunday, and Thursday from 10:00 a.m. until 4:00 p.m. Admission $15 per adult, children are free.

Thomaston

Maine State Prison Showroom (crafts made by maximum security prisoners)

358 US Highway 1 (Main Street), Thomaston

207-354-9237

https://www.facebook.com/MSPShowroom

Open 9:00 a.m. until 4:00 p.m., seven days a week. Park behind the store and look to your right. The large open park is the site of the former grounds of the State Prison. It was demolished in 2002, but a plaque remains. The corner of the 35-acre site contains one remaining piece of the massive wall that surrounded the building, as well as the cemetery, which lacks grave markers identifying the prisoners. As per the Thomaston Historical Society, the grounds will soon be partially filled by a medical clinic and the renovated fire station, but around nine acres will remain parkland.

Wiscasset

1811 Old Lincoln County Jail (aka Old Jail, 1811 Old Jail)

Lincoln County Museum

133 Federal Street, Route 218, Wiscasset

207-882-6817

www.lincolncountyhistory.org

The Old Jail (and Maine State Penitentiary from 1820-1824) includes tours of the cells.

Visitors can see graffiti left by 19th century French or British sailors imprisoned here, as well as the original locks, keys, shackles, and jailer's log from 1800-1954. Not open every day.

Open from Memorial Day to Indigenous Peoples Day on Saturdays and Sundays from noon until 4:00 p.m. Admission is $15 for adults, children admitted free.

York

Old York Historical Society
  3 Lindsay Road, York
  207-363-1756 (Visitor Services)
  https://oldyork.org
Open seasonally, normally starting at the end of May. Check the website for exact dates and times.

The Royal Gaol (Jail) was a colonial prison dating back to 1656. Sections from 1719 incorporate parts of the original jail, which was in operation until 1879 when it was converted into a warehouse, and then eventually, a museum. Patience Sampson (aka Boston) was imprisoned here.

State and Federal Prisons of Note in Maine

Charleston

Mountain View Correctional Facility (aka Charleston Correctional Facility)
  1182 Dover Road, Charleston
  Known for its baking, composting, agriculture, and local food operations.

Warren

Maine State Prison
  807 Cushing Road, Warren
  Notable prisoners include Thayne Ormsby, Joseph Eaton, Christian Charles Nielsen, and Matthew Paul Cushing.

Bolduc Correctional Facility
  516 Cushing Road, Warren

Windham

Maine Correctional Center and Southern Maine Women's Reentry Center
  17 Mallison Falls Road, Windham

Notable Crime-and-Justice-Related Burial Sites

Plot locations included where available, burial sites not always included in itineraries.

Argyle

Hoyt Brook Cemetery (aka Spencer Cemetery)
  Main 116 N., Argyle
  Burial site of Nicolle Ashley Lugdon, murdered by Nicholas Sexton.

Auburn

Gracelawn Memorial Park
  980 Turner Street, Auburn
  Burial site of Jennie Lynn Cyr Hicks, killed by her husband James.

Augusta

Maine Veterans Memorial Cemetery
  163 Mount Vernon Road, Augusta
  Burial site for Joseph Lewis Gray, murdered by Stephen Alexander Marshall (Section D, Row 21, Site 13)

Mount Vernon Cemetery
  Winthrop Street, Augusta
  Burial site of Captain James Scales Purrington Sr., plot close to the highway near intersection of Winthrop and High Streets. Also buried here, his victims: wife Elizabeth Clifford Purrington, and his children Polly, Benjamin, Anna, Nathaniel, Nathan, and Louisa.

Bath

Oak Grove Cemetery
  Oak Grove Avenue, Bath
  Burial site of Constable William Lawrence, murdered by Daniel Wilkinson (5 West, Lot 5).

Brownville

Brownville Village Cemetery
  9 Stickney Hill Road, Brownville
  Burial site of Walter Reid Morrill, poisoned by arsenic at a church function by Daniel Bondeson.

Brunswick

Pine Grove Cemetery
  Just off Bath Road and Pine Street, Brunswick
  Burial site for William Frank "Billy" Brackett, murdered by Robert Card.

New Sweden

New Sweden Cemetery (aka Capitol Hill Cemetery)
  116 Station Road, New Sweden
  Burial site of Daniel S. Bondeson, suspected of murder.

Newry

Sunday River Cemetery
  610-678 Sunday River Road, Newry
  Burial Site of Selby Ellen Bullard, murdered by Christian Charles Nielsen.

Orrington

Oak Hill Cemetery
  Oak Hill Road (directly off Dow Road at Orrington Center), Orrington
  Burial site of Lynn Ann Hincks Willette, murdered by James Hicks.

Rome

Rome Cemetery
  (No street address available), Rome
  Burial site for Jerilyn Leigh Tibbetts-Towers, murdered by James Hicks.

Sabattus

Pleasant Hill Cemetery
  150 Pleasant Hill Road, Sabattus
  Burial site for Jason Adam Walker, murdered by Robert Card.

Saint Albans

Maloon Cemetery
  Grant Road, Saint Albans
  Burial site for William Robert Elliott, murdered by Stephen Alexander Marshall.

Springfield

Springfield Village Cemetery (aka Springfield Corner Cemetery)
    32 North Road, Springfield
    Burial site of Kevin Ray Tozier, murdered by Anthony Lord.

South Portland

Calvary Cemetery
    1461 Broadway, South Portland
    Burial site of Carol Lee Griffin Bolduc, Christopher Scott Bolduc, and
their son Joshua Richard Bolduc, all murdered by Matthew Paul Cushing.

Forest City Cemetery

232 Lincoln Street, South Portland
    Burial site for Richard "Ricky" Stetson, murdered by John Joseph Joubert
IV (Section 2, Lot 211).

Thomaston

Thomaston State Prison Cemetery
    358 Main Street, Thomaston (Park in back of prison store. To the right
are the former grounds of the prison, including the cemetery with its
unmarked graves.)
    Burial site of Daniel Wilkinson, murderer.

Waterville

Saint Francis Catholic Cemetery
    78 Grove Street, Waterville
    Burial site of Constance Margaret (Sirois) Fisher, who murdered her
six children (Lot 0937W, Grave 6). Also buried here: her children Natalie

Rose Fisher (Lot 1022W, Grave 1). Michael Jo Fisher (Lot 1022W, Grave 2), Deborah Kay Fisher (Lot 1022W, Grave 3), Kathleen Louise Fisher (also listed as Lot 1022W, Grave 3), Daniel B. Fisher (Lot 1022W, Grave 4), Richard N. Fisher (Lot 1022W, Grave 5).

York

Old Burying Yard of York
    23 Lindsay Road (Corner of York St—Rt 1A—and Lindsay Road), York
    Burial site of Mary Nasson, accused of being a witch.

Putting it All Together: Itineraries

Note: Where the word "likely" is used in conjunction with an address, the street was confirmed through newspaper or Internet research, but the street number or range of numbers was determined through the author's own investigation.

Itinerary: True Crime Tour of Southern Maine

Our true crime tour of southern Maine starts in **Kittery,** where Stephen Howard Oken murdered motel clerk Lori Ward at the Coachman Motor Inn at 380 U.S. 1 in a room behind the check-in desk. **Smuttynose Island**, where Louis Wagner killed two Norwegian women in 1873 (see the New Hampshire chapter) is also part of Kittery, but tours depart from Portsmouth, NH).

Travel northeast to **York**, where you can visit the Royal Gaol at 3 Lindsay Road (part of the Old York Historical Society) where Patience Boston (aka Patience Sampson) was imprisoned. At the nearby Old Burying Yard at 23 Lindsay Road, you can see the burial site of accused witch Mary Nasson. And Ghostly Tours of York offers a sixty-minute tour of paranormal York for those with otherworldly interests.

Continue following the coastline north to **Kennebunk** to sleep or dine with ghosts at the Kennebunk Inn at 45 Main Street. Then head southeast to **Kennebunkport**, where three inns are rumored to be haunted: the Nathaniel Lord Mansion at 6 Pleasant Street, Captain Fairfield Inn at 8 Pleasant Street, and the Tides Beach Club at 930 Kings Highway. On to **Old Orchard Beach,** where Matthew Paul Cushing murdered his brother, mother, and stepfather, one by one, as they arrived home at 15 Birkdale Circle. The house has been leveled, but a memorial stands in its place. Their family business, Blustery Day Flags, is now Christina's Classic Cookies at 39 Old Orchard Street.

Drive further northeast to **Cape Elizabeth** if you'd like to visit ghosts at the Inn by the Sea at 40 Bowery Beach Road, then north to **South Portland**, where Matthew Cushing's family, the Bolducs, are buried at Calvary Cemetery at 1461 Broadway. The Forest City Cemetery at 232 Lincoln Street is the burial site of Richard "Ricky" Stetson, one of the victims of John Joseph Joubert IV. Stetson was allegedly abducted while jogging on the Back Cove trail in **Portland**. His body was found on a grassy triangle off Interstate 295 near Tukey's Bridge.

Also, in Portland proper, you can enjoy the Comedy of Haunted History walking tour. You can also stay at The Press Hotel at 119 Exchange Street, a converted former newspaper building where crime news was once written, and then dine at one of two haunted restaurants: DiMillo's On the Water at 25 Long Wharf. and the Empire Chinese Kitchen at 575 Congress Street.

Just outside Portland in **Westbrook** is where murderer Arline Lawless (Seavey), was arrested as she was leaving the Spring Harbor Treatment Center at 123 Andover Road.

Further north in **Yarmouth,** on Interstate 295 between Exits 15 and 17/East Main Street, is where Joseph Eaton began randomly shooting at innocent motorists. And at the Pine Grove Cemetery in **Brunswick** (Bath Road and Pine Street), you can pay your respects to William Frank "Billy" Brackett, killed by Robert Card in the Lewiston mass shooting. To the northeast in **Freeport**, you can dine with apparitions at the Jameson Tavern at 115 Main Street. Then continue further east to **Bath**, so you can stand where prison escapee Daniel Wilkinson shot Constable William Lawrence at the D.C. Gould Ship Chandlery and Provision Store, which is now 105 Front Street, home to Bath Savings Institute (the building is also known as the Hyde Block.) Lawrence is buried at Oak Grove Cemetery on Oak Grove Avenue.

To the northeast, in **Wiscasset**, Joseph Eaton was held at the Two Bridges Regional Jail at 522 Bath Rd, and you can visit the 1811 Jail at the Lincoln County Museum, 133 Federal Street (Route 218). Be sure to check ahead because it's not open every day. You can also take a ghost tour offered by American Ghost Tours.

Drive southeast to visit **Waldoboro**, where Arline Lawless (Seavey), shot her boyfriend on the 2100-block of Friendship Road. And further north in **Warren**, you can drive by Maine State Prison at 807 Cushing Road, where notable prisoners have included Thayne Ormsby, Joseph Eaton, Christian Charles Nielsen, and Matthew Paul Cushing. The Bolduc Correctional Facility is down the road at 516 Cushing Road. The State Prison moved from **Thomaston,** where you can still visit their showroom to purchase crafts made by maximum security prisoners. It's located at 358 Main Street.

If you park behind the store and look to your right, the large open park is the site of the former grounds of the State Prison. It was demolished in 2002, but a plaque remains. The corner of the 35-acre site contains one remaining corner of the massive wall that surrounded the building, as well as the cemetery, which lacks grave markers identifying the prisoners, including Daniel Wilkinson.

Still further northeast in **Rockland** are two more haunted hotels, the LimeRock Inn at 96 LimeRock Street and the Lindsey Guest House at 5 Lindsey Street.

The tour now turns northwest to **Augusta,** where you can visit the Maine Murder Victims' Memorial at the Augusta Holy Family Cemetery at 197 Civic Center Drive. At the Maine Veterans Memorial Cemetery at 163 Mount Vernon Road (aka New Maine Veterans Memorial Cemetery), you can visit the burial site of Joseph Lewis Gray, murdered by Stephen Alexander Marshall.

At the Mount Vernon Cemetery on Winthrop Street, you can pay respects to Captain James Scales Purrington Sr. and the family he murdered before committing suicide. The Purrington family lived on a farm on Belgrade

Road.

The Riverview Psychiatric Center (once named the Augusta State Hospital and later the Augusta Mental Health Institute), where Constance Fisher was committed after drowning her children, is part of a campus of buildings encompassing 67 Independence Drive and 250 Arsenal Street. There's also a Kennebec Creeps & Crawls tour of Augusta for you to enjoy.

Drive slightly southwest to **Hallowell** for the Granite City Ghosts Tour and/or the Grave Secrets Cemetery Tour. South of Hallowell in **South Gardiner** is where Constance Fisher's body washed up along the banks of the Kennebec River. Then head southeast to **Dresden** to visit the Pownalborough Court House at 23 Court House Road. To the southwest to the 1400 block of Augusta Lane in **Bowdoin**, Joseph Eaton killed his parents and the Egers, two of his parents' friends.

Mass murderer Robert Card was found dead from a self-inflicted gunshot wound to the southwest in nearby **Lisbon Falls** by the Androscoggin River. It's about eight miles southeast of where his second shooting occurred (see below) and is connected by a walking trail along the waterway to where he abandoned his Subaru. Authorities found his body near the sliding door of an unlocked trailer in the overflow parking lot of the Maine Recycling Corp. at 61 Capital Avenue, across the street from the main facility. Northwest in **Lewiston** is where Card unleashed fire at the Just-in-Time Recreation bowling alley at 24 Mollison Way and then Schemengees Bar & Grille at 551 Lincoln St.

To the west in **Auburn**, the Gracelawn Memorial Park at 980 Turner Street is the burial site of Jennie Lynn Cyr Hicks, murdered by her husband James. To the southwest in **Poland**, you can greet the resident ghosts at the Poland Spring Resort (640 Maine Street) before heading northwest to **Newry,** where Christian Charles Nielsen's murder spree took place at the Black Bear Inn at 829 Sunday River Road. Down the way at 610-678 Sunday River Road. Selby Ellen Bullard, one of Nielsen's victims, was laid to rest at the Sunday River Cemetery.

If you want to walk more extensively in Nielsen's shoes, you can head northeast to **Farmington**, where he studied English at the University of Maine (224 Main St), shopped often at Devaney Doak & Garrett Booksellers (193 Broadway), and worked as a cook at the Family Fare Restaurant (now closed). He also worked as a cook around six miles south of Newry at the Sudbury Inn at 151 Main St in **Bethel**. You might choose to stay overnight here. Their website for reservations is www.thesudburyinn.mobi.

Note: This tour omits the ghost tours in Boothbay Harbor, and the haunted hotels in Fryeburg and Tenants Harbor, as well as the grave of Jason Walker in Sabattus.

Itinerary: True Crime Tour of Central Maine

This tour starts in **Waterville**, where Constance Margaret (Sirois) Fisher drowned her three children in the family bathtub at their home on the 0-50 block of High Street. After murdering her next three children and attempting suicide, she was rushed to the Thayer Hospital at 149 North Street. She's buried at Saint Francis Catholic Cemetery at 78 Grove Street, along with both sets of three children (six in total) whom she drowned.

Next, drive west to **Oakland**, past St. Stephen's Traditional Anglican Church at 41 Church Street, where murderer Thayne Ormsby functioned as an acolyte upon occasion. From there, head north to **Fairfield Center**, where Constance Fisher killed her second set of three children. (Research suggests it occurred at a bungalow on Ohio Hill Road). Next, drive northwest to **Skowhegan,** where you can dine at The Miller's Table at 42 Court Street, formerly the garage of the Somerset County Jail-turned-grain mill and reborn again as a restaurant.

To the east is the Gateway Lounge in **Newport** (now a Chinese restaurant called Chinaway at 42 N. Main Street), where Jerilyn Towers was last seen leaving with murderer James Hicks before she disappeared. Further east, authorities found Jennie Hicks' skull embedded in cement and the dismembered body of Towers one hundred feet apart in six-inch-deep graves behind a shed at Hicks' former homestead on Route 2 in **Etna**. It's believed the spot is just south of the general store, which is now Etna Village Variety at 239 US Highway 2. And slightly southeast in **Carmel** was the T&N Trailer Court on Route 2 (since condemned and the trailer destroyed), where James and Jennie Hicks once lived and from where Jennie disappeared.

North in **Corinth**, Stephen Alexander Marshall shot statutory rapist William Elliott in the doorway of his mobile home on the 900 block of Main Street. And to the north in **Milo**, Marshall shot Joseph Gray in his home on the 200 block of West Main Street. Take a slight deviation to the northwest to the Brownville Village Cemetery in **Brownville** (Stickney Hill Road off Church Street) if you'd like to pay your respects to Walter Reid Morrill, who was poisoned by arsenic at a church function by Daniel Bondeson.

To the southeast in **Argyle**, Nicolle Ashley Lugdon, murdered by Nicholas Sexton, is buried at the Hoyt Brook Cemetery on Maine 116 North. Next, drive south to **Brewer**, where James Hicks worked with his third victim, Lynn Willette, at the Twin City Motor Inn at 453 Wilson Street (now the Maine Woods Inn/Vacationland Inn). He eventually moved into her apartment on South Main Street before she went missing, too.

At a Boiling Drive apartment to the west in nearby **Bangor**, drug dealers Nicholas Sexton and Randall Daluz met with the three people who eventually became their murder victims. Later, after the killings, Sexton dropped Daluz off at the Ramada Inn at 357 Odlin Road and then drove to 22 Target Industrial Circle before dawn and set fire to the car containing their bodies.

Also in Bangor, you can visit the Museum of Law Enforcement (Bangor Police Department Museum) at 240 Main Street and the exterior of horror and suspense author Stephen King's former home at 47 West Broadway. Sawyer Arena, a skating rink at 107 13th Street in Hayford Park, is where Stephen Alexander Marshall abandoned his truck after murdering two convicted rapists before boarding a bus bound for Boston.

To the southeast is **Dedham**, where the haunted Lucerne Inn at 2517 Main Road was the site of a murder/suicide. The final stop on the tour is **Bar Harbor**, for either a ghost tour offered by Bar Harbor Ghost Tours or a Monsters by Moonlight tour. You might be able to stay with the ghosts themselves at the Coach Stop Inn at 715 State Highway 3.

(Omitted from this tour are Rome (the burial site for Jerilyn Leigh Tibbetts-Towers); St. Albans (the Maloon Cemetery burial site of William Robert Elliott, shot dead by Stephen Alexander Marshall); Springfield Village Cemetery, where Anthony Lord victim Kevin Ray Tozier is buried; the haunted Greenville Inn at Moosehead Lake; and the Oak Hill Cemetery in Orrington, where Lynn Ann Hincks Willette is buried. Also omitted, the Mountain View Correctional Facility in Charleston.

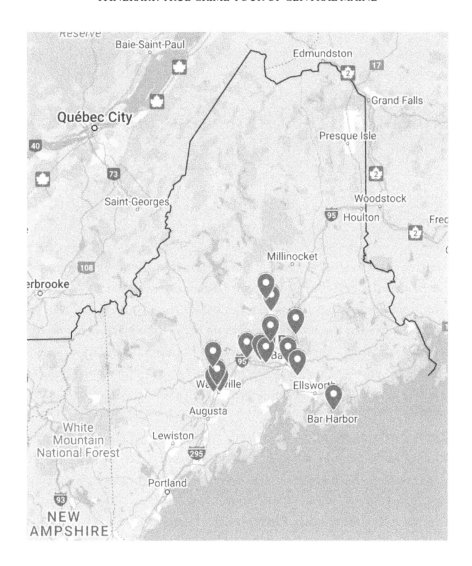

Itinerary: True Crime Tour of Northern Maine

The true crime tour of Northern Maine starts in **Benedicta,** where Anthony Lord burned down the barn of Kim Irish, located on the 100 block of Aroostook Road. Hours later, he assaulted his friend's uncle, Kary Mayo, who likely lived on the 1000-block of Silver Ridge Road in Sherman (**Silver Ridge Township).** returned to Kim Irish's house and killed Kyle Hewitt. During the ensuing murder spree, he drove to a woodlot about 35 miles south to Winn Road in **Lee** and killed Kevin Tozier.

Drive northeast from Lee (or southeast from Silver Ridge) to **Weston,** where Thayne Ormsby drove Jeffrey Ryan's truck to Bancroft Road to set it on fire. Then head north to **Amity,** where Ormsby originally picked up the truck from the home of Jeffrey Ryan, likely on the 100-200 block of U.S. Route 1, after stabbing three people to death.

Continuing north to **Houlton,** Anthony Lord was finally apprehended at his uncle Carl Lord Jr's home, likely located on the 0-100 block of North Street. Also in Houlton, Stephen Alexander Marshall visited his father Ralph's house, likely on the 0-100 block of Court Street, and borrowed his truck and firearms before murdering two sex offenders. And Lynn Willette's partial remains were found embedded in cement-filled buckets on a swampy road site along Route 2A just south of Houlton in **Forkstown Township**.

Finally, a 90-minute drive northwest brings you to **New Sweden** and the Gustaf Adolph Lutheran Church at 48 Capitol Hill Road, where Daniel Bondeson supposedly poisoned the church coffee with arsenic and murdered Walter Reid Morrill. Bondeson is buried at the New Sweden Cemetery at 116 Station Road and he lived in neighboring **Woodland** on Bondeson Road.

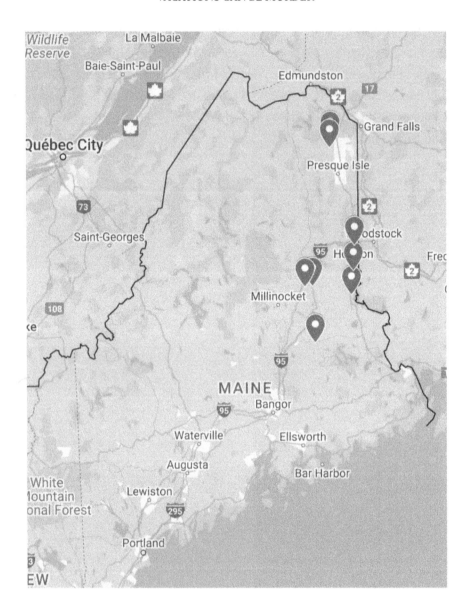

Maine Victim Resources

This is a noncomprehensive summary of services available to victims of crime in Maine. Information was taken directly from their websites. Visit/contact agencies for complete information and note that some programs offered by certain contractors focus on specific geographic areas. Some resource categories and content may overlap. Inclusion does not equate to recommendation.

Child Abuse

- Maine Department of Health and Human Services: see https://www.maine.gov/dhhs/ocfs. Telephone: 207-624-7900. Toll-free hotline to report abuse: 800-452-1999.

Civil Legal Help for People with Low Income

- Maine Volunteer Lawyers Project: The Maine Volunteer Lawyers Project (VLP) coordinates the volunteer efforts of Maine attorneys and community members to help low-income people navigate the civil justice system. They provide free information, brief assistance, and pro-bono legal representation in civil legal matters to qualifying clients. Their volunteers give low-income Mainers the tools and the knowledge to be equal participants in the legal system. See https://www.vlp.org.
- Penquis Law Project: 800-215-4942, info@penquis.org, The Penquis Law Project is a public interest law practice that seeks to create access

to civil legal services for low- and moderate-income residents of Penobscot and Piscataquis counties who would otherwise be without counsel and/or representation. In particular, the Law Project serves clients who have experienced or are experiencing domestic violence, sexual assault, or stalking. Legal assistance is available in the following areas: protection from abuse orders, determination of parental rights and responsibilities, divorce, post-judgment actions, other family matters, and civil matters related to sexual assault and/or stalking. See https://www.penquis.org.

- Pine Tree Legal Assistance: 207-942-8322. Pine Tree Legal Assistance is a nonprofit corporation established in 1966 by private attorneys in Maine to promote access to justice by providing high-quality free legal assistance, responsive to the immediate needs of individual low-income clients, and to address the long-range barriers to justice affecting low-income people in Maine. See https://www.ptla.org.

Domestic Violence

- Domestic Violence Statewide Hotline: Available 24/7 at (866) 834-4357.
- Domestic Shelters: see https://www.domesticshelters.org.
- The Maine Coalition to End Domestic Violence (MCEDV): See https://www.mcedv.org.
- Domestic Violence Resource Centers:
- Aroostook County: Hope and Justice Project: See https://www.hopeandjusticeproject.org.
- Penobscot & Piscataquis Counties: Partners for Peace: See https://www.partnersforpeaceme.org.
- Hancock & Washington Counties: Next Step Domestic Violence Project: See https://www.nextstepdvproject.org.
- Kennebec & Somerset Counties: Family Violence Project: See https://www.familyviolenceproject.org.
- Knox, Lincoln, Sagadahoc & Waldo Counties: New Hope Midcoast:

See https://newhopemidcoast.org.
- Androscoggin, Franklin & Oxford Counties: Safe Voices: See https://safevoices.org.
- Cumberland County: Through These Doors: See https://www.throughthesedoors.org.
- York County: Caring Unlimited: See https://www.caring-unlimited.org.

Drunk Driving Victims

- Mothers Against Drunk Driving Victim Services: 877-MADD-HELP (877-623-3435). See https://madd.org/victim-assistance.

Elder Abuse

- Elder Abuse Institute of Maine: See https://eaime.org.
- Legal Services for the Elderly: LSE provides persons age 60 and over with free legal advice regarding health care, health insurance, Medicare (including Part D), MaineCare (Medicaid), Social Security and other public benefits, pension and retirement benefits, powers of attorney, consumer matters including creditor and bankruptcy problems, physical and financial abuse, guardianship defense, and other issues. See https://mainelse.org.
- Maine Council for Elder Abuse Prevention: The Maine Council for Elder Abuse Prevention (MCEAP) is comprised of over 80 organizations and individuals from across Maine and supports collaborative efforts to combat elder abuse, neglect, and exploitation. See https://elderabuseprevention.info.

Fraud

- Annual Credit Report Request Service from Annual Credit Report.com: see https://www.annualcreditreport.com/protectYourIdentity.actio

111

<u>n</u>.

- National Consumers League Fraud Center (not limited to Maine): see https://fraud.org.

General

- United Way of Maine (long list of Victim Service Providers): See https://www.unitedway.org/find-your-united-way?field_country= 211&field_state=321.

Identity Theft

- Office of Maine Attorney General Consumer Protection: See https://w ww.maine.gov/ag/privacy/identity_theft.shtml .

Online Criminal Case Status, Inmate Status, and Sex Offender Registry

- Maine eCourts: The Maine eCourts system provides access to electronic court records for civil, family, child protection, and protection order cases. The system also allows registered attorneys, firms, and parties to submit and view electronic filings. See https://www.courts. maine.gov/ecourts. More information available at https://www.cou rts.maine.gov/ecourts/access.html#:~:text=own%20case%20docume nts.-,Parties,are%20not%20available%20electronically%20yet.
- Maine Court Inmate Search: https://mainecourtrecords.us/criminal-court-records/inmate/, More information at https://www.maine.go v/corrections/adultinfo.
- Maine Sex Offender Registry: The Sex Offender Registry website is maintained by the Maine State Police, State Bureau of Identification and is intended to provide the public information concerning the location of registered offenders currently within Maine. The registration information contained on the Maine Sex Offender Registry is updated

on a daily basis to reflect the most current information on file with the State Bureau of Identification. See https://apps.web.maine.gov/cgi-bin/sor/index.pl .

Tribal Assistance

• Wabanaki Women's Coalition: The Wabanaki Women's Coalition's mission is to increase the capacity of Tribal Communities to respond to domestic and sexual violence, and influence Tribal, National, and Regional systems to increase awareness, safety, justice and healing for all their relations. See https://www.wabanakiwomenscoalition.org.

Sexual Assault

• Sexual Assault Statewide Hotline: Available 24/7 at 800-871-7741.
• The Maine Coalition Against Sexual Assault (MECASA): see https://www.mcedv.org.
• The Maine Sex Trafficking and Exploitation Network: see https://www.mainesten.org.
• The Maine Network of Children's Advocacy Centers: see https://www.cacmaine.org.
• The Children's Safety Partnership: see https://www.childrenssafetypartnership.org.

Sexual Assault Support Centers:

• AMHC Sexual Assault Services (AMHC) for Aroostook, Hancock & Washington Counties: see https://www.amhcsas.org
• Maine Army National Guard – SARC: The Maine Army National Guard Sexual Assault Prevention and Response Program is designed to help prevent and respond to sexual assault among members of the military in Maine. See https://www.me.ng.mil/MENG-Member-Services/Maine-National-Guard-Resources.

- Rape Response Services (RRS): Penobscot & Piscataquis Counties: See https://www.rrsonline.org.
- Sexual Assault Prevention & Response Services (SAPARS): Androscoggin, Oxford & Franklin Counties & the Towns of Bridgton & Harrison. See https://www.sapars.org.
- Sexual Assault Crisis & Support Center (SAC&SC): Kennebec & Somerset Counties. See https://www.silentnomore.org.
- Sexual Assault Response Services of Southern Maine (SARSSM): Cumberland & York Counties. See https://www.sarssm.org.
- Sexual Assault Support Services of Midcoast Maine (SASSMM): Eastern Cumberland County, Sagadahoc, Knox, Waldo & Lincoln Counties. See https://www.sassmm.org.

Victim Advocacy

- Maine Department of Corrections Victim Services: Provides assistance to victims of crime and can be contacted at (800) 968-6909 or (207) 287-4385. See https://www.maine.gov/corrections/victimservices.
- Maine Crime Victims Rights Law Guide (for professionals): See https://www.mcedv.org/wp-content/uploads/2021/12/Maine-Victim-Rights-Law-Guide-2021_Updated-6.30.2021.pdf.

Victim Compensation

- VOCA-Funded Victim Assistance Program: Maine Department of Health and Human Services, Office of Children and Family Services, Phone: (207) 287-3707. VOCA Victim Compensation formula grants provide funding to supplement state compensation programs awarding financial assistance and reimbursement to victims for crime-related out-of-pocket expenses. See www.maine.gov/dhhs.
- VOCA-Funded Victim Compensation Program: Office of the Maine Attorney General Victims Compensation Program, Phone: 207-624-7882, See: www.maine.gov/ag/crime/victims_compensation/index.

shtml

Victim Notification

- Maine Department of Corrections Victim Services: This website accesses the information provided by the Department of Corrections for victims of crime. The information includes, but is not limited to, sentencing information, anticipated date of release, place of confinement, and restitution status of those convicted of crimes relating to the victim. See https://www.maine.gov/corrections/vic timservices.

Victim Rights and Services Complaints

- The rights of victims of federal crime are defined in the Crime Victims' Rights Act.If you are a victim and believe you have not been accorded your rights under the Crime Victims' Rights Act, you may file an administrative complaint by downloading an administrative complaint form, or you may request one to be mailed or faxed to you. The completed form should be mailed to the United States Attorney's Office, Attn: Todd Lowell, Assistant U.S. Attorney, 100 Middle Street, 6th Floor East, Portland, ME 04104; for more information, see https://www.justice.gov/usao/resources/crime-victims-rights-omb udsman/victims-rights-act.

Victim Witness Services

- The Victim Witness Services Unit for the United States Attorney's Office, District of Maine, provides services, support, and education to victims and witnesses of federal crimes. Services include notification of significant court events, referral to appropriate support services, reasonable protection from the accused, help determining and request-ing restitution and the return of property, and information concerning the conviction, sentencing, imprisonment and release of the offender. See https://www.justice.gov/usao-me/victim-witness-services.

- **Maine Victim Witness Advocates**Victim Witness Advocates work within the criminal justice system to provide support to crime victims in dealing with the inconvenience and anxiety of going to court and understanding the often confusing procedures of the criminal justice process. See https://www.mainecounties.org/district-attorneys.html.

Programs subject to change or end without notice.

Chapter 3: Vacations Can Be Murder in Massachusetts

Massachusetts Crime Statistics

When comparing the fifty states from safest to most risky, Safewise.com reports that Massachusetts ranks as the 19th safest state, meaning its violent crime rate is lower than that of 31 states but higher than that of 18." But, while Massachusetts might see lower crime rates than much of the remainder of the country, according to the FBI, it does harbor the reputation as New England's most dangerous state.

According to NeighborhoodScout.com, in 2023, Massachusetts residents were victims of 21,998 violent crimes (146 murders, 1,910 rapes, 2,560 robberies, 17,382 assaults), a rate of 3.14 per 1,000 residents. There is a 1 in 314 chance of becoming a victim here. Massachusetts residents also endured 77,067 property crimes (a rate of 11,01 per 1,000 residents, or a 1 in 91 chance of becoming a victim).

The Gitnux Marketdata report listed the 2021 most dangerous Massachusetts cities as Fall River, Holyoke, Brockton, Springfield, and New Bedford. Meanwhile, Safewise listed the 2024 safest cities in Massachusetts as Northborough, Wayland, Clinton, Grafton, and Ipswich. Unsurprisingly, these cities are barely mentioned in the chapter that follows.

**Summary of serial killings, mass shootings, mob hits, and other crimes
(listed alphabetically by location)**

For those traveling throughout Massachusetts, here is just a sampling of true crime that occurred in the state. Should you wish to visit these cities, exact addresses, where available, are listed in the "Itineraries" section at the end of the chapter:

Boston: When many people hear the word "murder" coupled with "Boston," they immediately think of the Boston Strangler, who terrorized the city and its suburbs in the early 1960s. He easily gained access to women's apartments, presumably by posing as a detective, motorist in need, building handyman, or other service provider, Once he'd gained access, he usually sexually assaulted and strangled his victims. Some believed multiple perpetrators were guilty of the murders.

Albert DeSalvo was eventually tried and convicted of unrelated sexual assaults and robberies but was never tried for the Boston Strangler murders. However, he later confessed to the murders, describing aspects of the crimes that even some witnesses remembered incorrectly. (The victims are listed in the Itineraries section of this book, along with their locations.)

In 1967, DeSalvo was sentenced to prison. He escaped with two other inmates from Bridgewater State Hospital in February of that year but gave himself up between one and three days later (accounts vary). He was then transferred to the maximum-security Walpole State Prison, where, in November of 1973, he was stabbed to death in the infirmary.

Fast forward forty years: DNA from DeSalvo's nephew was compared to a sample found on the body of one of the Boston Strangler victims, Mary Sullivan. In 2013, DeSalvo's body was exhumed for comparison and conclusively proved he was Sullivan's attacker, and therefore, the Boston Strangler.

More recently, the Boston Marathon Bombings were an act of domestic terrorism perpetrated by two brothers: one, a permanent U.S. resident originally from the Soviet Union, and the other, a naturalized American citizen from Kyrgyzstan. Dzhokhar and Tamerian Tsarnaev, influenced by extremist Islamic beliefs, wanted to protest American military action in Iraq and Afghanistan. The explosions occurred on April 15, 2013, when two homemade pressure cooker bombs detonated around 210 yards apart at the finish line on Boylston Street near Copley Square. Six people were killed—three at the scene: Martin Richard (8) of Dorchester, Lingzi Lu (23) of China, and Krystie Campbell (29) of Arlington. Another three later succumbed to their injuries: MIT police officer Sean Allen Collier (27); Tamerlan Tsarnaev (26, from gunshot wounds, suffered during his escape); and police officer Dennis Simmonds (28), who was injured and subsequently died following a confrontation with the bombers in Watertown post-marathon. At least 16 others lost limbs; hundreds were wounded. After a 100+ hour manhunt, Dzhokhar Tsarnaev was found hiding in David Henneberry's boat in the driveway of his home in Watertown. Tsarnaev is currently incarcerated at ADX Florence, a supermax prison in Colorado, and awaits the death penalty.

As a side note, Tamerlan Tsarnaev might have been responsible for, or at least involved in, a triple homicide that occurred either late on September 11th or early on September 12th, 2011, at an apartment building in Waltham. Three men: Brendan Mess (25), Erik Weissman (31), and Raphael Teken (37)—a known drug dealer—all had their throats cut so severely, they had nearly been decapitated. There were no signs of forced entry and no evidence of robbery; the bodies were found alongside thousands of dollars of cash and marijuana. Tsarnaev had described Mess as his best friend but there had been issues between them.

Two hotels in Boston were crime sites of "The Craigslist Killer," so nicknamed because he met his victims via that online medium. Police determined TCK's identity to be that of Boston University second-year medical student Philip Haynes Markoff. He was later charged with the April 10, 2009, Westin Copley Place Hotel robbery of Trisha Leffler, an escort, and the murder of masseuse Julissa Brisman (26) at the Copley Marriott four days later. Thanks to security camera footage, cell phone activity, and email evidence, police were able to connect Markoff to the crimes. He was arrested on April 20th of that year at a raffic stop on Interstate 95 in Walpole. After three failed suicide attempts, he finally succeeded while incarcerated and awaiting trial at the Nashua Street Jail.

Also in Boston, Kenneth Francis Harrison was nicknamed "The Giggler" because he called the police and giggled after confessing his murderous crimes. His first offense was in April of 1967, when he murdered 6-year-old Lucy Palmarin, a Spanish-speaking girl from Puerto Rico. Her parents sent her out on an errand; her body was later found wedged between some rubbish thrown into the Fort Point Channel. His second attack was against a 31-year-old Marine Corps veteran named Joseph "Joe" Breen. On June 15th, 1969, Breen was drinking in the Combat Zone at the Novelty Bar and played shuffleboard with Harrison. They left together. They later got into an argument over money, and Harrison pushed Breen into a water-filled pit in a construction site and beat him over the head with rocks, followed by a call to the police, riddled with giggles over the location of the body.

Harrison's third victim was Clovis Parker (75), who was found floating in the Fort Point Channel on November 27th, a murder that was originally thought to be an accidental drowning. But it was the death of 9-year-old Kenneth "Kenny" Martin that finally led to Harrison's capture. The killer lured the boy into a tunnel under South Station around December 24th, and then strangled him and covered him with canvas, his body found and identified on January 6th.. After he called his sister to confess, an "anonymous tip" led to Harrison's capture at the Biltmore Hotel in Providence, RI. He confessed to murder and was sentenced to life imprisonment, which ended when he committed suicide in April 1989 by overdosing on anti-depressant medication.

Organized Crime in Boston: James "Whitey" Bulger was a murderer, bank robber, extortionist, gang member, and FBI informant who grew up as a "Southie" in South Boston. In the 1970s and 1980s, he played a major role in Boston's organized crime as part of its largely Irish mob. He also spent sixteen years as a fugitive on the FBI's Most Wanted List, starting in 1994 when he disappeared before his impending arrest. Bulger had ties to the Boston waterfront and engaged in various illegal activities there, including extortion, smuggling, and drug trafficking. As the eventual leader of the Winter Hill Gang, Bulger considered the Lancaster Street Garage to be his "West End headquarters." In 2013, he was convicted at the John

Joseph Moakley Federal Courthouse on multiple charges, including his involvement in eleven murders.

Another organized crime-related spot was the Blackfriars Pub, a tavern that doubled as a late-night disco. On June 28, 1978, five men were executed gangland-style here in what was assumed to be a dispute over cocaine. Four of the five murdered men were known criminals: Charles Magarian (37); Peter Meroth (31); Freddie Delavega (34); and owner Vincent E. Solmonte (35). The fifth victim was John "Jack" Kelly (34), pub manager and a former television and radio investigative reporter, who was known to associate with the other targeted men. The killers were never apprehended but were thought to include James "Whitey" Bulger.

Racial disharmony in Boston: The media afforded minimal coverage to the numerous murders that plagued the Roxbury section of Boston in the wake of the 1970s desegregation of public schools. Between January and May 1979, eleven Black women were found murdered within several miles of one another; at least four different men were charged. Black feminist groups such as the Combahee River Collective connected these deaths to the racial and sexist sentiments of the time.

Victims included: Christine (Chris) Ricketts (15), found January 29 alongside Andrea Foye (17) in trash bags; Gwendolyn Yvette Stinson (15), strangled, with her body dumped in a ditch; Caren Prater (25), beaten and stabbed to death; Daryal Ann Hargett (29), bound and strangled in her apartment; Desiree Denise Etheridge (17), beaten and burned to death in an alley with her skull and jaw shattered; Darlene Rogers (22), stabbed and abandoned naked from the waist down; Lois Hood Nesbitt (31), tied up in bed and strangled with a radio cord; Valyric Holland (19), stabbed in her Dorchester residence; Sandra Boulware (30), found burned and naked; and Bobbie Jean Graham (34), a Dorchester insurance company owner found in an alley after being beaten with a blunt object. Those arrested in connection with these murders include Dennis Jamal Porter (Ricketts and Foye); James Brown (Stinson); Kenneth Spann (Prater); Richard Strother (Nesbitt); Eugene B. Conway (Holland); and Osbourne "Jimmy" Sheppard

(Boulware).

In 2019, a 10-part art installation series called The Estuary Projects, anchored in Roxbury, and created and championed by activist and artist Kendra Rosalie Hicks, went on display to honor the victims. Each installation went up on the anniversary of the woman's death, near where they were found, and came down 24 hours later. One installation jointly commemorated Ricketts and Foye, the two women who were found together.

Theft in Boston: Aside from murder, Boston is also known for its famous swindles and thefts. It's where Italian con artist Charles Ponzi (born Carlo Pietro Giovanni Guglielmo Tebaldo Ponzi) set up the Security Exchange Company in January 1920. Ponzi collectively cheated as many as 40,000 investors out of an estimated $20 million (that's over $300 million in 2025 dollars, according to In2013dollars.com, though some estimate the losses to be far higher. He employed the technique that now bears his name—using the money of new investors to pay off old ones—and it's also how he procured the money to buy a mansion in Lexington.

More theft: On January 17, 1950, in Boston's North End, a group of eleven thieves led by Anthony "Fats" Pino almost pulled off a perfect robbery of security firm Brinks, Inc., making off with nearly $3 million in cash and securities, the largest heist of its time. And in 1990, the Isabella Stewart Gardner Museum fell victim to one of the most notorious art heists in history when two men disguised as police officers made off with thirteen prized paintings valued at up to half a billion dollars, including those by Vermeer, Rembrandt, Manet, and Degas. The perpetrators have never been identified, and a $10 million reward remains in effect for information leading to the safe return of the stolen artwork.

Defrocked priests in and around Boston: Anyone who has seen the movie *Spotlight* is aware of the sex scandals concerning defrocked priests like John Geoghan and Paul R. Shanley. I have made the decision not to elaborate upon them here, other than to include their burial sites in that section of the chapter.

Braintree: April 15, 1920, saw the robbery of the Slater-Morrill Shoe Company factory and the death of two men killed while transporting the company's payroll to the main factory. The perpetrators shot security guard Alessandro Berardelli four times and Frederick Parmenter, a paymaster, twice. The robbers got away with the payroll boxes in a stolen dark blue Buick.

A jury convicted two Italian-born anarchists, Nicola Sacco and Bartolomeo Vanzetti, of the robbery and murders in a highly controversial trial. Purely circumstantial evidence tied the two men to the events, but despite widespread protests and doubts about their guilt, they were sentenced to death in 1921. Outcries from people as disparate as future Supreme Court Justice Felix Frankfurter and Italian dictator Benito Mussolini alleged anti-Italian prejudice, as well as the U.S. treatment of immigrants and political dissidents. Their protests failed to change the verdict. Sacco and Vanzetti were held in their cells at the Charlestown State Prison before being executed by electric chair on August 23, 1927, becoming symbols of injustice and prejudice in the American legal system. More than 20,000 protestors crowded Boston Common the day before the execution, and 10,000 mourners visited the Langone Funeral Home to view Sacco and Vanzetti's open caskets for three days afterward.

Bridgewater: In July of 2002, Alexandra Nicole Zapp (30), traveling south to her Newport, Rhode Island home after a Boston charity event, made a pit stop at a Burger King rest area in Bridgewater. She entered the women's bathroom, and when she tried to leave, sex offender Paul Leahy (40) blocked her exit and, in a totally random and unprovoked attack, proceeded to stab her multiple times in the chest, as well as cut her arms, wrists, hand, and chin as she fought for her life. Off-duty police lieutenant Stephen O'Reilly was too late to save Zapp but arrested Leahy, whom he caught cleaning up after the murder. In 2003, a jury found Leahy guilty of first-degree murder, and the judge sentenced him to life without parole. In her memory, Zapp's mother and stepfather founded the ALLY Foundation to "prevent opportunities for violent sex offenses, to educate the public and advocate for necessary changes in culture, attitude, and policy...and to work for more comprehensive and evidence-based policies to effectively manage sex offenders as they move through the criminal justice system and the community."[1]

Brockton: White supremacist and neo-Nazi Keith Luke (22) had a stated mission: to kill as many Jews, blacks, and Hispanics as he could find before killing himself. But he didn't want to die a virgin. So, he planned a break-in at an apartment in a Clinton Street building where he once lived, now occupied by two women from Cape Verde. On January 21, 2009, Luke murdered Selma Goncalves and then raped, sodomized, and shot her 22-year-old unidentified sister, who ultimately survived and testified against him. As he escaped, he shot a homeless man named Arlindo Goncalves (72, no relation), that he knew from the neighborhood.

When the police caught up with him, Luke fired at them, albeit reluctantly because they were white, and also because he wanted to save his two hundred rounds of ammunition to shoot up a bingo game at Temple Beth Emunah in Stoughton. The police pursued his van, which ultimately crashed. When Luke showed up in court in May of 2009, he had a swastika carved into his forehead. He was convicted and received two consecutive life sentences, then tried three times to kill himself while in prison. On May 16th, 2014, he succeeded, and his mother donated his organs to those who needed them.

Brookline: On December 30, 1994, a teacher told 22-year-old New Hampshire hairdressing student John C. Salvi III, a man with mental health issues and extreme anti-abortion views, that he wasn't ready to cut hair. The comment triggered him, and he subsequently launched attacks at two abortion clinics in Brookline, two miles apart. He first shot up the reception area at a Planned Parenthood office, killing Shannon Lowney

(25) and wounding a medical assistant as well as two people accompanying patients to the clinic. Then he continued on to Preterm Health Services, where he killed receptionist Leanne Nichols (38) and wounded an office worker and a security guard.

The next day, Salvi was arrested in Norfolk, VA, after firing on a clinic there. He eventually committed suicide in 1996 while serving two life sentences in prison. An unusual outcome was that at one of the clinics, Salvi chased pregnant women out of the waiting room, firing after them as they ran. One patient, Deborah Gaines, was so anguished by the event, she never returned to the clinic and ended up carrying her baby to term. Afterward, she sued the clinic in a "wrongful life" case for lacking proper security. The lawsuit was settled out of court.

Cataumet: In the 1860s, Honora Kelley was placed as an indentured servant with the Toppan family of Lowell when she was around seven or eight. While never formally adopted, she took on the name of Jane Toppan and was later known as Jolly Jane because of her happy attitude when attending to patients. Trained as a nurse in Cambridge Hospital, she experimented to see the effects of morphine and atropine on patients' nervous systems.

After a brief stint at Mass General, she was let go and became a private nurse. This is where she developed a unique way of getting the things she wanted, whether it was a job or the potential affections of a man—she poisoned those in her way. She later explained she derived sexual thrills from bringing people close to death, reviving them, and then letting them die. These victims included her Cambridge landlord Israel Dunham and his wife Lovey (1895); her foster sister Elizabeth (1897); and in Cataumet in 1901, the prominent Captain Alden Davis along with his wife Mattie, sister Edna, and Davis's two married daughters. When the remaining family members ordered a toxicology report, morphine was found in their blood.

By 1902, Toppan confessed to thirty-one murders, though many believe the body count to be much higher. She was eventually found not guilty by reason of insanity, perhaps because she claimed her life goal was to "have killed more people—helpless people—than any other man or woman who ever lived." She was committed for life to the Taunton Insane Hospital and died in 1938 at the age of 84.

Danvers: On October 22nd, 2013, Philip Chism, a ninth grader at Danvers High School, cornered his math teacher, Colleen Ritzer (24), in the school toilet. He robbed, sexually assaulted, and stabbed her sixteen times in the neck with a box cutter. He then stuffed her corpse into a recycling barrel and left it in the woods behind the school with a note nearby that read "I hate you all." Then, he treated himself to the movies using her credit card. The murder was apparently an extensively planned event that involved several clothes changes, and yet, ironically, he hadn't bothered to wash her blood from his hands by the next morning when the police found him. Chism was tried as an adult for murder, aggravated rape, and armed robbery and was sentenced to at least forty years. Chism received an additional sentence of 17-20 years following an attack of a clinician at a Worcester Department of Youth Services detention center in 2014, where he was incarcerated until he turned 18 and could be moved to a state prison, currently the Souza Baranowski Correctional Center in Lancaster.

East Weymouth: They called Grayce Asquith "the Merry Widow" because of the frequent parties she threw. But there was nothing particularly merry about the way she died. Police who investigated her summer cottage found blood everywhere. They'd searched because two legs had turned up in two separate burlap bags in Boston Harbor at Jeffery Field (now Logan Airport), and a friend had reported both Grayce and her fiancé, John Lyons, missing. They also found bits of flesh clogging the cottage's bathtub pipes. Asquith's head was later found under the Congress Bridge in Boston.

A bloody footprint matching that of Asquith's handyman, Oscar Bartolini, an Italian immigrant, led to his arrest. In his apartment, police discovered materials similar to those used to wrap the body parts. He was convicted and sentenced to death, but this was later commuted to a life sentence. Then, in 1961, authorities released Bartolini and deported him back to Italy.

Many suspected that Asquith's fiancé, disabled salesperson John Lyons, was the actual murderer and the handyman had merely disposed of the body.

Fall River: What child hasn't jumped rope while reciting the nursery rhyme about Lizzie Borden giving her mother forty whacks and her father forty-one? Here's where it started:

On August 4, 1892, Lizzie Borden's father, Andrew Jackson Borden (worth over $7 million in 2023 dollars at the time of his death), and her stepmother, Abby Durfee Gray Borden, were ax-murdered in their Fall River home. It was a household filled with tension over money and property division and jealousy over property being given to Abby's family. Lizzie Borden, who claimed she was out of the house at the time of the attacks, had contradictory answers to questions posed by the police after the murders were uncovered. She was tried and acquitted. Though ostracized by the locals, she spent the rest of her life in town until she died of pneumonia in 1927 at age 66. Borden's story has morphed into folk legend and has inspired a slew of books, plays, movies, and even songs. Developers have transformed the Borden home into a Bed and Breakfast.

Framingham: There had already been tension in their marriage and on two separate occasions, Laura Rosenthal (34) came to work at John Hancock Mutual Life Insurance with a black eye that she tried to explain away. But in late August of 1995, when she complained to her insurance exec husband Richard (40) that he'd burnt the ziti, he bludgeoned her to death, smashing her face beyond recognition with a softball-sized rock. He then ripped open her chest cavity, slicing her torso from throat to navel with a butcher knife, removed her heart and lungs, and impaled them on an 18-inch stake in their backyard.

After partially hiding the rest of her body under a blanket of mulch, Rosenthal gathered up his four-month-old daughter, Maria, in her car seat and drove to Marlboro, where police found him muttering about gun control and how he'd overcooked his pasta. He later pleaded not guilty by reason of insanity to charges of first-degree murder, claiming that his wife had been an alien. The jury didn't buy it; they convicted him of first-degree murder and gave him a life sentence without the possibility of parole.

Great Barrington: Seven years before the Columbine Massacre and two decades before Sandy Hook, a student named Wayne Lo perpetrated a mass shooting at Bard College at Simon's Rock. Lo was a gifted violinist, but also a homophobic racist, fascist, and Holocaust denier. Despite warnings and reports of Lo receiving guns at the dormitory and stockpiling ammunition, the administration never took the issue seriously enough to dismiss the student or repeatedly investigate.

On December 14, 1992, Lo traveled by taxi to Dave's Sporting Goods Store in Pittsfield and purchased an SKS semi-automatic rifle. Upon his return, he fired on Theresa Beavers in the school security area, fatally shot both Spanish language teacher Ñacuñán Sáez (37) and student Galen Gibson (18) and wounded three other students. Only when his rifle jammed did he drop his weapon and phone the police from the student union. He surrendered without protest. The ease with which 18-year-old Lo was able to obtain a rifle gave ammunition, so to speak, to gun control advocates. In February of 1994, Lo was found guilty of 17 charges against him and sentenced to two consecutive life sentences without possibility of parole. He is currently serving his sentence at MCI-Norfolk.

Holliston: In this quiet Boston suburb in the spring of 1992, computer exec. Kenneth Seguin (35) drugged his children while his wife Mary Ann (known as Polly) was out of the house they'd moved into just the week prior. He slashed his 7-year-old son Daniel's throat and his 5-year-old daughter Amy's wrists and arms and then hid their bodies under debris in Beaver Pond in Franklin. Later, he bludgeoned his 35-year-old wife while she slept and threw her into the Sudbury River, where her partially clad body washed up in Southborough.

Police found Seguin in a nearby wooded area with a slashed wrist, neck, and abdomen, claiming that two white intruders had given the children sleeping pills and whacked his wife with an ax while she slept. Then they'd stolen the pick-up truck, put both him and his wife inside, and dumped his wife at an undisclosed spot before abandoning him in Hopkinton State Park. The story was contradicted by Seguin's bloody handprint on the steering wheel of the family's pickup truck, along with a witness account of Seguin being seen at home the morning after the killings. He was convicted of murder and sentenced to serve life in prison for the murder of his wife, followed by two concurrent life sentences for the death of his children. His requests for parole have been repeatedly turned down.

Lawrence: In 1974, William R. "Willy" Horton and two accomplices robbed Joseph Fournier, a 17-year-old gas station attendant in Lawrence. Even though Fournier complied by handing over all the money in the cash register, Horton stabbed him 19 times and stuffed his corpse into a trash can, where he died of blood loss. Horton was convicted of murder and sentenced to life imprisonment without the possibility of parole.

On June 6th, 1986, Horton was released as part of a weekend furlough program from Northeastern Correctional Center, but he never returned. And on April 3, 1987, he went on a crime spree in Maryland that included twice raping a woman, assaulting her fiancé, and stealing his car. He was shot and captured and then sentenced in Maryland to two consecutive life terms plus 85 years.

Republican nominee George H.W. Bush used this case in his 1988 presidential campaign to push back against the prison reforms advocated by his more liberal Democratic opponent, Michael Dukakis. Opponents accused Bush of racial stereotyping because of his use of the nickname "Willy," which had never been used by Horton.

Leeds/Northampton: Kristen Heather Gilbert worked at the Northampton Veterans Affairs Medical Center (VAMC) from 1989-1996, where coworkers dubbed her the "Angel of Death" because of the high number of patients she resuscitated during her shifts. She was ultimately convicted of murdering four former soldiers by injecting epinephrine into their intravenous therapy bags, causing their hearts to pump out of control. She is actually believed to have murdered as many as 350 patients and caused as many as 300 emergencies during her seven-year tenure.

Nurses' suspicions prompted the hospital to launch investigations, during which Gilbert quit her job, attempted suicide, called bomb threats into the hospital as retaliation, and was institutionalized on seven separate occasions. She even confessed her involvement in the murders to her lover, who was also on staff, Persian Gulf War veteran James G. Perrault, with whom she was having an adulterous relationship. In the end, she was convicted of the murders of former soldiers Henry Hudon, Kenneth Cutting, Edward Skwira, and Stanley Jagodowski. Gilbert is currently serving four consecutive death sentences in Texas.

Needham: In 1934, the Millen-Faber Gang—comprised of Jewish immigrant brothers Murton and Irving Millen and Murton's high school friend, Abraham Faber—stole around $14,000 from the Needham Trust Company at gunpoint. During the robbery, they killed two police officers: Forbes McLeod and Francis Haddock. The murders were notable because they were the first committed in Massachusetts using a fully automatic weapon—a Thompson submachine gun they had stolen from state police. McLeod and Haddock were also the first police officers to be killed in the line of duty in Needham, Police arrested all three men, along with Murton Millen's wife, Norma. The men were convicted of murder, sentenced to death, and executed in 1935. Norma spent a year in prison after being found guilty as an accessory to robbery.

New Bedford: The New Bedford Highway Killer, who remains unidentified, terrorized the New Bedford area between March 1988 and April 1989, and was responsible for the deaths of at least nine women and the disappearances of at least two additional ones, plus numerous other assaults. Preying upon area sex workers and/or those with addictions, the killer left the bodies in nearby towns along Route 140. A road trip through Freetown, Dartmouth, and Westport will take you past these points of discovery.

Those murdered include Robbin Lynn Rhodes (29), found along Route 140 southbound in Freetown by a search dog; Rochelle Clifford Dopierala (28), found in a gravel pit in Dartmouth; Debra Medeiros (29), found in Freetown; Nancy Lee Paiva (36), last seen walking home from the "Whisper's Pub" and found nude in Dartmouth; Debra Greenlaw DeMello (35) also found nude in Dartmouth; Mary Rose Santos (26), last seen dancing at The Old Quarter Deck Lounge and found nude in Westport; Deborah McConnell (25); Sandra Botelho (24), found in the woods in Marion; and Dawn Mendes (25), found off Interstate 195. Police have considered several suspects for the crimes, including Anthony DeGrazia, a 26-year-old construction worker whom they arrested and charged. DeGrazia spent thirteen months in prison but was eventually released on bail, and he was found dead a month later; it was unclear whether it was suicide or homicide. A killer committed similar murders in Lisbon, Portugal; any connection remains unclear.

Also in New Bedford: Just before midnight on February 1, 2006, Jacob D. Robida, an 18-year-old neo-Nazi, visited a North End gay bar called Puzzles Lounge (now closed), armed with a hatchet, a machete, and a handgun, and began attacking patrons. Victims included regulars Alex Taylor and Robert Perry as well as Luis Rosado, a 23-year-old mentally challenged man. Robida escaped by running north on North Front Street and drove his Grand Am out of town. A three-day manhunt took authorities to Arkansas, West Virginia, and New Jersey. It ended with a gunfight in Arkansas in which Robida murdered police officer James W. Sell and ex-girlfriend Jennifer Bailey before shooting himself in the head.

North Attleboro: On June 17, 2013, a 15-year-old high school freshman who was jogging home from the gym found Odin Lloyd's dead body at the North Attleboro Industrial Park. He had been shot multiple times with a .45 caliber handgun. Lloyd (27) was a semi-professional football player who was murdered by Aaron Hernandez, the former tight end for the New England Patriots. The two had a disagreement two nights earlier outside the Rumor Nightclub in Boston (now permanently closed).

In 2015, Hernandez was found guilty of first-degree murder for the death of Lloyd and sentenced to life imprisonment without the possibility of parole at the Souza-Baranowski Correctional Center in Lancaster. But while he was on trial for Lloyd's murder, Hernandez was indicted for the 2012 South End drive-by shootings of Safiro Furtado and Daniel de Abreu, two immigrants from Cape Verde. The two had supposedly spilled liquor on Hernandez at the Cure Lounge (now closed) hours before they were gunned down in their car while stopped at a traffic light. A jury acquitted Hernandez of those charges in 2017.

Days after the acquittal, he committed suicide by hanging himself with a bedsheet tied around his jail cell window bars. He was posthumously diagnosed with what doctors called the worst case of chronic traumatic encephalopathy (CTE) they'd ever seen, and some wonder if repeated blows to his head might have ultimately prompted his murderous actions.

Plymouth: Englishman John Billington was one of the signers of the Mayflower Compact and an ancestor of both Richard Gere and U.S. President James Garfield. He arrived in Plymouth in 1620, having taken the trip aboard the Mayflower to escape creditors in England. Billington was a known troublemaker, and in September of 1630, after a heated argument over hunting rights, he fatally shot fellow colonist John Newcomen. He was convicted of murder and hanged, making him the first citizen of Plymouth to be convicted of murder and also the first to be hanged for any crime in New England.

Revere: Robert Donati (50), also known as Bobby D, was the personal driver for reputed underworld "capo de regime" lieutenant Vincent "The Animal" Ferrara," who was associated with the New England-based Patriarca crime family. In September of 1991, Donati went missing for four days and then was found, beaten, and stabbed in the trunk of his white 1980 Cadillac, several blocks from his home. His killer had also slit his throat, and the puddles of blood and brain tissue on his front porch were signs he had been hit several times with a blunt instrument.

While the murder remains unsolved, it's believed that Donati was one of the thieves involved in the Isabella Stewart Gardner Museum heist in 1990, and the hit was payback for his failure to remove prized works by Botticelli and Titian, as well as a dispute over payment. It could also have been mob payback because Donati occasionally acted as a police informant against the Patriarca family. Robbery was also a possibility because the victim's watch and ring were missing. as was his cash.

Salem: The Salem Witch trials took place mostly between the spring and fall of 1692 and began when a group of young girls who were having seizures in Salem Village (present-day Danvers) joined some adults in accusing several local women of witchcraft. After special courts heard cases, Bridget Bishop became the first "witch" to be hanged that June at Gallows Hill in Salem Town. Eighteen others followed—five in July, five in August, and eight in September—with more than 150 accused, at least seven of whom died in jail. After that, the hysteria began to die down, especially when one of the accused was Lady Mary Phips, the wife of Sir William Phips, the first governor of Massachusetts. It did not die down entirely, however: the trials continued under a new court until May of 1693. The General Court later annulled the guilty verdicts and granted indemnities to their families, but the damage was done, and Salem may forever be known for this miscarriage of justice.

South Truro: Christa Worthington was a 46-year-old single mother and fashion writer/author whose work appeared in Elle, Harper's Bazaar, Cosmopolitan, Women's Wear Daily, and the New York Times. On January 6, 2002, her body was found in her home on Cape Cod, where she had been raped and stabbed to death. Her unharmed two-year-old daughter Ava was by her side. In April of 2005, Christopher McCowen, a local garbage collector, was arrested for the crime. A jury convicted him of murder in 2006, and he was sentenced to life in prison without the possibility of parole. In 2008, a subsequent hearing alleged that racism tainted McCowen's trial and led to his conviction. Despite these claims of bias, the original conviction was upheld.

Springfield: Alfred Gaynor was, at least at one time, the person convicted of committing the most murders in Springfield history and is still considered one of the most prolific murderers statewide. He was convicted of slaying eight women from 1995 until 1998, though his actions also led to the death of a ninth person, a 22-month-old child. Most were crack and cocaine addicts whom Gaynor raped and choked and then posed in grotesque positions to shock those who discovered their bodies.

His first victim was Vera Hallums (45), a mother of four whom Gaynor tied with electrical cords, beat, and strangled on April 20, 1995. Next was Amy Smith (20), who was found dead in her apartment on July 11, 1996, approximately a week after being murdered. With her was her 22-month-old daughter Destiny, who died of starvation and dehydration. Authorities discovered the strangled corpse of Jill Ann Ermellini (34) in the cab of a truck on June 16, 1997. Robin M. Atkins (29) was left in a downtown alley in October of 1997, bound, gagged, and strangled. In November, both JoAnn C. Thomas (38) and Yvette Torres (33) were discovered dead in their respective residences, followed by two more victims the following February—Loretta Daniels (38), found in an alley, and Rosemary Downs (42), discovered in her home. Finally, Gaynor dumped the body of Joyce Dickerson-Peay (37) outside an empty restaurant in March of 1998.

Two years later, in the year 2000, he was convicted of four of the murders and was sentenced to life in prison without the possibility of parole. Then, in 2010, Gaynor pleaded guilty to four more deaths, but only to shorten the sentence of his nephew Paul Fickling, who had been implicated in the death of Amy Smith and her daughter.

Also in Springfield: On May 27, 2018, Springfield police stopped Stewart Rudolph Weldon at a red light because of a broken taillight. That's when a woman tied in the backseat claimed she'd been kidnapped, and that Weldon had beaten her with a hammer and raped her for over a month. After he was taken into custody, his mother, with whom he lived, complained to the police of a foul odor and excessive flies in her home. That smell turned out to be emanating from the decomposing bodies of three women: America Lyden (34) of Springfield, missing since December 1, 2017; Ernestine Ryans (47) from Ludlow, missing since March 18, 2018; and Kayla Jeanne Escalante (27), who had not been heard from since December but had yet to be reported missing. Weldon had kept their corpses in the basement, in a detached garage, and in a tool shed.

It was later determined Weldon was responsible for the sexual assaults of eight women in Springfield, and he was charged with three counts of first-degree murder, eight counts of strangulation, nine counts of aggravated rape, two counts of rape, five counts of aggravated kidnapping, and four counts of kidnapping. In September of 2021, Weldon changed his plea from not guilty to guilty and was sentenced to three life terms to run consecutively.

Taunton: On May 10, 2016, 28-year-old Arthur DaRosa wasn't having a good day. He'd been depressed following a breakup with his girlfriend and had been battling suicidal thoughts. For whatever reasons, and we'll never know what they were—he left his child's soccer practice and crashed his black Honda Accord into a red Ford Ranger pick-up truck parked near the field. Then he attempted to enter nearby residences, finally finding success at the home of Kathleen and Patricia Slavin. He entered the house and stabbed both women repeatedly. Patricia, 80, died from her wounds.

Next, DaRosa drove to the Silver City Galleria shopping mall (closed four years later on February 29, 2020, and demolished May 9, 2021), and crashed his car into the north entrance of Macy's. He got out and began physically assaulting shoppers inside the department store, including a pregnant woman. Next, he entered Bertucci's restaurant, where he stabbed unsuspecting diners, including server Sheena Savoy and patron George Heath, who tried to come to Ms. Savoy's assistance and died for his efforts. Off-duty Plymouth County sheriff deputy James Creed shot and killed DaRosa, bringing his murder spree to an end.

Truro: Antone Charles "Tony" Costa (25) was an unemployed carpenter /electrician and amateur taxidermist who harvested marijuana in Truro on Cape Cod. Between 1968 and 1969, he also used the forest clearing in or near where he grew his crops to hide the bodies of women he'd shot and dismembered. He became known as the "Cape Cod Cannibal" and the "Cape Cod Vampire" after the district attorney erroneously mentioned that there had been toothmarks on the victims' bodies. Susan Perry, who had been missing since September 1968, was found in February 1969 in the Old Truro Cemetery, cut into eight pieces. Parts of the bodies of Mary Ann Wysocki, Patricia Walsh, and Sydney Monzon were found a month later; Costa had shot them in the head with a .22 caliber pistol and then mutilated them using a knife, except for one that he hacked apart with an ax. Authorities found their bodies in shallow graves in a shrub-pine area off Cemetery Road.

Costa became acquainted with the women he later murdered when they checked into a Provincetown boarding house where he had been staying. The day after they checked out, they were never seen alive again. Costa procured Walsh's Volkswagen van, then prepaid parking for the vehicle in a private lot, which led to him becoming a suspect. A jury convicted him of the murders of Wysocki and Walsh, for which he was given two life sentences. Police believed these were not his only victims, but we may never know—at least not in the form of a confession. He committed suicide in 1974 at Walpole Correctional Institution.

Wakefield: On December 26, 2000, Michael McDermott (42), an employee with Internet consulting firm Edgewater Technology, Inc. since March, came armed to work with an AK-47, a 12-gauge pump-action shotgun, and a .32 caliber semi-automatic pistol. He opened fire at the corporate headquarters, and when he finished his five-to-eight-minute shooting spree, he'd fired 37 rounds of ammunition and murdered seven people. Two were killed in the reception area, the others in Human Resources and Accounting. Those murdered: Jennifer Bragg Capobianco (29), Janice Hagerty (46), Louis Javelle (58), Rose Manfredi (48), Paul Marceau (36),

Cheryl Troy (50), and Craig Wood (29). McDermott was arrested without resistance.

Money may have been a root cause of the shootings. McDermott had recently skipped out of his $840 East Weymouth apartment without paying owed rent, and his wages were subject to be garnished after the holidays due to roughly $5,000 in delinquent tax payments. He had complained about this the prior week. There were also rumors about prospective layoffs. During his trial, he made irrational comments that raised questions about his sanity, such as being a time traveler sent back to kill Hitler and his minions. These comments were consistent with his documented history of schizophrenia. More than two years after the shooting, McDermott was sentenced to life in prison at the Old Colony Correctional Center in Bridgewater without the possibility of parole.

Want more? There's lots!
  http://www.celebrateboston.com/crime.htm
  https://murderpedia.org/usa/massachusetts.htm
  https://murderpedia.org/usa-female/massachusetts.htm

Read Before You Leave: A Sampling of Massachusetts True Crime Books

(listed alphabetically by author)

Note: Some of these books may cover crimes not discussed elsewhere in this guide.

- Atkinson, Jay. *Legends of Winter Hill: Cops, Con Men, and Joe McCain, the Last Real Detective*. Three Rivers Press, 2006.
- Behn, Noel. *Big Stick-up at Brinks*. Grand Central Pub, 1978.
- Boser, Ulrich. *The Gardner Heist*. Harper Collins, 2009.
- Boyle, Maureen. *Shallow Graves*. University Press of New England, 2017.
- Burke, Timothy M. *The Paradiso Files*. Steerforth, 2008.
- Cooper, Becky. *We Keep the Dead Close*. Hachette UK, 2020.
- Cullen, Kevin, and Shelley Murphy. *Whitey Bulger: America's Most Wanted Gangster and the Manhunt That Brought Him to Justice*. W. W. Norton & Company, 2013.
- Daley, Christopher. *Murder & Mayhem in Boston*. Arcadia Publishing, 2015.
- Dresser, Thomas. *Mystery on the Vineyard: Politics, Passion, and Scandal on East Chop*. History Press Library Editions, 2008.
- Englade, Ken. *Murder in Boston*. Diversion Publishing Corp., 2014.
- Ethier, Eric. *True Crime: Massachusetts*. Stackpole Books, 2009.
- Farmer, Thomas J, and Martin T Foley. *A Murder in Wellesley*. UPNE,

2012.

- Faugno, Rachel. *Murder & Mayhem in Central Massachusetts*. Arcadia Publishing, 2016.
- Fleming, E.J. *Death of an Altar Boy*. Exposit, 2018.
- Flook, Maria. *Invisible Eden*. Crown, 2004.
- Ford, Beverly, and Stephanie Schorow. *The Boston Mob Guide*. History Press (SC), 2011.
- Frank, Gerold. *The Boston Strangler*. Open Road Media, 2016.
- Gibson, Gregory. *Gone Boy*. North Atlantic Books, 2011.
- Gorenstein, Nathan. *Tommy Gun Winter: Jewish Gangsters, a Preacher's Daughter, and the Trial That Shocked 1930s Boston*. ForeEdge, 2015.
- Hill, Frances. *A Delusion of Satan*. Tantor eBooks, 2014.
- Junger, Sebastian. *A Death in Belmont*. W. W. Norton & Company, 2006.
- Kurkjian, Stephen A. *Master Thieves: The Boston Gangsters Who Pulled off the World's Greatest Art Heist*. PublicAffairs, 2015.
- McPhee, Michele R. *A Date with Death*. Macmillan, 2010.
- ———. *Maximum Harm: The Tsarnaev Brothers, the FBI, and the Road to the Marathon Bombing*. University Press of New England, 2017.
- ———. *When Evil Rules*. Macmillan, 2009.
- Miller, Sarah. *Borden Murders: Lizzie Borden and the Trial of the Century*. S.L.: Yearling Books, 2019.
- Miller, Wayne. *Burn Boston Burn*. BookBaby, 2019.
- O'Donnell, Lawrence. *Deadly Force*. HarperCollins, 2018.
- Phelps, M. William. *Perfect Poison: A Female Serial Killer's Deadly Medicine*. Godalming: Pinnacle Books, 2003.
- Powers, Bill. *Murderous Rage: The Deadliest Mass Murder in Massachusetts History*. Powerscourt Press, 2022.
- Rodman, Liza. *Babysitter: My Summers with a Serial Killer*. Atria Books, 2022.
- Schechter, Harold. *Fatal*. Simon and Schuster, 2012.
- ———. *Fiend*. Simon and Schuster, 2012.
- Sharkey, Joe. *Deadly Greed*. Open Road Media, 2017.

- Sherman, Casey. *Helltown.* Sourcebooks, Inc., 2022.
- Sherman, Casey, and Dave Wedge. *Boston Strong.* ForeEdge from University Press of New England, 2015.
- Tejada, Susan. *In Search of Sacco and Vanzetti.* University Press of New England, 2012.
- Wallace, Robert. *Machine Guns & Typewriters.* Mindstir Media, 2023.
- Weeks, Kevin, and Phyllis Karas. *Brutal.* Harper Collins, 2009.
- Zalkind, Susan. *The Waltham Murders.* Little A, 2023.

Accommodations and Restaurants that are Crime/Justice-Related or Haunted

Crime/Justice-Related Accommodations

Boston

Hotel AKA Back Bay
154 Berkeley Street, Boston
617-266-7200
https://www.stayaka.com/hotel-aka-backbay
This Italian Renaissance revival hotel was once the headquarters of the Boston Police Department from 1920-1997. At the time of writing, its restaurant, the Precinct Kitchen & Bar, which paid tribute to the building's past, was evolving into a different venue. Stay tuned.

The Liberty Hotel
215 Charles Street, Boston
617-224-4000
https://libertyhotel.com
Built in 1851, the Charles Street Jail was once home to inmates such as Malcolm Little (Malcolm X) and Sacco & Vanzetti. Due to poor living conditions, the jail was declared unfit and closed for good on Memorial Day weekend, 1990. In 2001, Carpenter & Company entered into a lease agreement with the owner of Massachusetts General Hospital and converted the jail into a deluxe hotel. They painstakingly preserved the

atrium's grillwork and catwalks so the landmark building could retain its original character. Guests can take a 30-minute tour of the building and its history, capped off with a complimentary glass of champagne.

Fall River
Borden House Bed & Breakfast
230 Second Street, Fall River
https://lizzie-borden.com
(Phone number and email address available through an app on the website.)

The Borden House was once the home of the infamous Lizzie Borden, where her father and stepmother were ax-murdered. The Inn offers four rooms and two suites, each named after the people who once lived there. The Inn also runs tours of the house, and of the area, all listed in this guide. It is considered one of the country's most haunted houses and is operated by US Ghost Adventures.

Haunted Accommodations

While these hotels, inns, and Bed & Breakfasts aren't specifically crime-related, they are rumored to be haunted, and where there are souls at unrest, could murder be far behind?

Boston
Club Quarters Boston
161 Devonshire Street, Boston
617-357-6400 or 203-905-2100
https://clubquartershotels.com/boston/faneuil-hall
Ghost City Tours claims that poltergeists prowl the property, which is a hotspot for paranormal disturbances.

Omni Parker House Hotel
60 School Street, Boston

617-227-8600

https://www.omnihotels.com/hotels/boston-parker-house

In this building, which is over 160 years old, the ghost of former owner Harvey Parker roams the halls on the tenth floor. Rooms 303 and 1040 have been cited as particularly haunted.

Concord

Concord's Colonial Inn

48 Monument Square, Concord

978-369-9200 or 800-370-9200

colonial@concordscolonialinn.com

https://www.concordscolonialinn.com

During the Revolutionary War, this building was a doctor's home. Caretakers operated on injured soldiers in Room 24, and Room 27 was used as a morgue. The hotel claims apparitions of caretakers still walk the halls.

Deerfield

Deerfield Inn and Champney's Restaurant

81 Old Main Street, Deerfield

413-774-5587

frontdesk@deerfieldinn.com

https://www.deerfieldinn.com

On its website, the inn acknowledges that some guests have experienced a pinch on the bottom, a tug on the pillows, moving objects, and an unexplained knock on the door late at night.

Eastham

The Rugosa

4885 US-6 (aka 4885 State Highway), Eastham

508-905-9492

info@therugosa.com

https://www.therugosa.com

During this property's earlier iteration as the Penny House Inn, the "Goodnight Ghost" would touch guests while they slept, move around their personal items, and whisper to them. Whether the apparition stuck around when the property changed hands is unclear.

Nantucket

The Wauwinet Hotel

120 Wauwinet Road, Nantucket

508-228-0145

reservations@wauwinet.com

https://www.wauwinet.com

The property is believed to have been built on Native American burial grounds. Guests claim to experience lights with a mind of their own, unexplained footsteps, the sound of running water in the lobby, and a ghost with a floral scent.

The Nantucket Hotel

77 Easton Street, Nantucket

508-310-1734 or 866-807-6011

Reservations@thenantuckethotel.com

https://www.thenantuckethotel.com

Formerly called the Point Breeze Club and Hotel, rumored to be haunted. It is unclear if the male ghost who had been seen wearing period clothing came along when the title transferred.

Orleans

The Orleans Waterfront Inn & Restaurant

3 Old County Road, Orleans

508-255-2222

orleansinn@comcast.net

https://www.orleansinn.com

The building once housed a brothel where a prostitute named Hannah was murdered. She's still seen dancing naked through a fifth-floor window.

Salem

Hawthorne Hotel
18 Washington Square W, Salem
978-744-4080 or 800-SAY-STAY
info@hawthornehotel.com
https://www.hawthornehotel.com
Often ranked as one of the country's most haunted hotels, Rooms 325 and 612, along with the sixth floor itself, have been sites of paranormal activity.

Morning Glory Bed & Breakfast
22 Hardy Street, Salem
978-741-1703
bshea@morningglorybb.com
https://morningglorybb.com
Guests have seen the ghost of a young woman in period clothing, as well as the ghosts of children who once lived here.

Sudbury

Longfellow's Wayside Inn
72 Wayside Inn Road, Sudbury
978-443-1776
info@wayside.org
https://www.wayside.org
Room #9 is said to house the ghost of Jarusha Howe, a woman whose possibly unrequited love for a British sailor caused her to wait 44 years here for his return. He never came back, and she stayed on past her death.

Restaurants that are Crime/Justice-related

Boston

CLINK
215 Charles Street at the Liberty Hotel, Boston

617-224-4004
clink@libertyhotel.com
https://www.clinkboston.com

Alibi Bar & Lounge
215 Charles Street at the Liberty Hotel, Boston
857-241-1144
https://www.alibiboston.com
Restaurant, bar & lounge inside the former Charles Street Jail.

Concord

The Fife and Drum Restaurant
976 Barretts Mill Road, West Concord
978-371-7941
https://www.mass.gov/locations/fife-and-drum-restaurant
Located at Northeastern Correctional Center, this restaurant is open to the public and is used as a culinary arts program for the inmates housed at the facility. According to their website, you must bring a state-issued ID, but should not bring a purse, wallet, or cell phone. Meals are only $3.21 each. You must be at least 18 years of age. Inmates cannot receive cash so don't tip or reveal personal information.

Haunted Restaurants

Ashland

Stone's Public House
179 Main Street, Ashland
508-881-1778
stonestakeout@gmail.com
https://www.stonespublichouse.com
The spirit of 11-year-old Mary Smith, killed in 1863 by a train that passed the property, is said to haunt the restaurant.

Dracut

The Village Inn
544 Broadway Road, Dracut
978-459-4114
info@villageinndracut.com
https://villageinndracut.com

The ghost of a small boy has been seen in the lounge area, and the spirit of a girl wanders through a tunnel that runs between the restaurant and the barn buildings that are used for conventions.

Duxbury

The Sun Tavern
500 Congress Street, Duxbury
781-837-1027
https://www.suntavernrestaurant.com

The tavern is said to house the spirit of Lysander Walker, a hermit who committed suicide here.

East Otis

Knox Trail Inn
1898 East Otis Road, East Otis
413-269-4400
knoxtrailinn@gmail.com
https://www.theknoxtrailinn.com

Jake was a soldier from the Revolutionary War whose spirit has taken up residence here.

Salem

Rockafellas
231 Essex Street, Salem
978-745-2411
info@rockafellasofsalem.com
https://rockafellasofsalem.com

The building was once a jewelry store and a church. Jeweler Daniel Low died in the building in 1911 and may be the ghost in residence. Guests claim to have also seen the figure of a woman in a blue dress and have seen and heard ghosts both on the second floor and in the basement, where slaves may be buried.

Turner's Seafood at Lyceum Hall
    43 Church Street, Salem
    978-745-7665
    https://www.turners-seafood.com
The property was once an apple orchard that belonged to Bridget Bishop, the first to be convicted of witchcraft during the Salem Witch Trials. Employees say they have smelled the lingering scent of apples…and have seen the ghost of Bishop herself.

Springfield
    Theodore's and Smith's Billiards
    201 Worthington Street, Springfield
    413-736-6000
    mgmt@theodoresbbq.com
    https://theodoresbbq.com
Workers have reported the sound of balls rolling across the fourth and fifth floors (formerly a bowling alley), voices coming from nowhere, unexplained footsteps after closing, and more.

Champney's Restaurant is part of The Deerfield Inn, listed in the Accommodations section. Concord's Colonial Inn in Concord and Longfellow's Wayside Inn in Sudbury also have restaurants.

Crime Tours and Paranormal Tours

Boston

Beacon Hill Crime Tour: 2 hours, suggested for ages 16+. Reservations required. Pay what you wish at the end. This walking tour departs from the Park Street T Station on the eastern edge of Boston Common and ends at Cheers Bar at 84 Beacon Street.

Offered by Free Tours by Foot, 617-299-0764, boston@freetoursbyfoot. com, https://freetoursbyfoot.com/beacon-hill-crime-tour.

Beacon Hill True Crime Tour: 2 hours, Ages 12+, $35. The walking tour departs at 7:00 p.m. from the Massachusetts State House at 24 Beacon Street. Offered by TopDog Tours, 833-486-7364, support@topdogtou rs.com, https://topdogtours.com/tours/boston-tours/beacon-hill-true-crime-tour.

The Dark Side of Boston: 90 minutes, All Ages, Price $17 adults, $10 children 6-12, children under six free. The walking tour departs at 6:00 p.m. on select days from the corner of Hanover & Cross Streets in front of the statue of boxer Tony DeMarco across from the Greenway. 617-367-2345, info@bostonbyfoot.org, https://bostonbyfoot.org/tours/the-dark-side-of-boston

The Boston Crime Tour: 2+ hours, not recommended for very young children, $29.99 adult, $25.99 students/veterans. Walking tour departs from Old Northern Avenue Bridge (corner of Northern Avenue and Atlantic Avenue in the Seaport District). Bus tours are set to commence in 2025. info@crimetourboston.com, https://crimetourboston.com, No phone contact listed.

In Cold Blood True Crime Guided Tour: 2 hours, from $25, walking tour meets at 3:00 p.m. from the George Washington Statue in Boston Public Garden. https://wejunket.com/boston/103/in-cold-blood-boston-true-crime-experience. No phone contact listed, email through website or contact@wejunket.com.

Boston Boos & Brews Haunted Pub Crawl: from $30, Ages 21+, departs 5:30 p.m. from Boston Common Visitors Center at 139 Tremont Street. https://wejunket.com/boston/55/boston-boos-brews-haunted-pub-crawl. No phone contact listed, email through website.

Boston Ghosts Tour: 1 hour, from $25, walking tour departs 8:00 p.m. from 139 Tremont Street at the entrance to Boston Common. https://wejunket.com/boston/17/boston-ghosts-tour. No phone contact listed, email through website.

Haunted Pub Crawl: 2 hours, Ages 21+, from $29.99, walking tour departs at 9:00 p.m. from Samuel Adams Statue outside Faneuil Hall at 1 S. Market Street (corner of North and Congress Streets.). 855-999-9026, info@ghostcitytours.com, https://ghostcitytours.com/ghost-tours/boston-ghost-tours/haunted-pub-crawl.

The Death and Dying Ghost Tour: 90 minutes, Ages 16+, $34.99, Walking tour, departs at 9:00 p.m. from 24 Beacon Street in front of the Massachusetts State House gate. 855-999-9026, info@ghostcitytours.com, https://ghostcitytours.com/ghost-tours/boston-ghost-tours/death-dying-tour.

Ghosts and Gravestones Frightseeing Tour: 1.5 hours, Ages 13+ (no children under 6), from $44.48. The trolly and walking tour departs at 6:00 p.m. from the Marriott Long Wharf Hotel at 200 Atlantic Avenue, corner of State Street. Contact Historic Tours of America, Inc., Old Town Trolley Tours of Boston, 866-754-9136 (Old or 888-920-8687, https://w ww.ghostsandgravestones.com/boston#about.

Boston Detective Tours: 90 minutes, from $40, Departs from Boston Convention Exhibition Center at 425 Summer Street. Not offered daily; call to check for dates. Join Retired Boston Police Detective Joe Leeman on his gritty tour of Boston's criminal underworld by way of an old-fashioned Police Ride Along. 617-212-2502, https://bostondetectivetours.com.

Fall River

- Lizzie Borden House Tour: 1 hour, from $30, offered daily 10 a.m.- 4 p.m. (You can add on an extended tour through the basement for $6 more.)
- Lizzie Borden's Fall River Ghost Tour: 90 minutes from $25, walking tour, offered nightly 7 p.m.-9 p.m. (You can add on an extended tour of the first floor of the house for $6 more.)
- Lizzie's Ghost Hunt: 2 hours, from $40, offered nightly 10 p.m. - midnight. Oak Grove Cemetery Tombstone Tour offered nightly between 7 p.m. - 9 p.m., from $20 (Virtual tour $10).

More information for all tours at https://lizzie-borden.com/tours, part of US Ghost Adventures.

Nantucket

Nantucket Ghost Walk: Walking tours, offered seasonally, 80-90 minutes depending on route (town vs. cemetery). All ages, from $20-$25 adult, $10-15 for children, depending on age, cash only. Departs 8:00 p.m. from the corner of Centre and Main at the top of Main Street, in front of the steps of the Pacific National Bank. 774-325-8972. https://business.na ntucketchamber.org/events/details/the-original-nantucket-ghost-walk-town-route-06-09-2024-39061.

Salem

The following tours offered by Witch City Walking Tours:

- Mysteries and Murders of Salem: 2 hours, from $31, Ages 13+, Walking tour, departs 7:00 p.m. from Old Town Hall, 32 Derby Square.
- History & Hauntings of Salem: 2 hours, adults $31, children $21-$26, offered multiple times each day.
- Specters & Apparitions: A ghost-hunting tour of Salem, seasonal and only, offered only certain days of the week, $31, departs at 8:30 p.m., uses "professional ghost-hunting equipment."
- Spirits, Sinners & Scandals Adulteress Tour: 75 minutes, $36, Ages 18+, seasonal, departs 9:45 p.m., from 32 Derby Square.
- Spirits & Superstitions: Friday the 13th Tour, 90 minutes Ages 18+. Seasonal (only on Friday the 13th of any month that applies), $47.50 adults, $33.50 children ages 12-17, departs 7:00 p.m. Check for departure information.
- Murder Through a New Lens: Anniversary of Joseph White Murder (walking and photography tour), 2 hours, $31, all ages, Offered on limited weekends. Departs at 4:30 p.m. from 32 Derby Square.

Visit https://www.witchcitywalkingtours.com for more information on these tours, info@witchcitywalkingtours.com, 781-608-6986, info@witc hcitywalkingtours.com.

Tours offered by Salem Historical Tours:

- 1682 Salem Witchcraft Walk: 90 minutes, $25 adults, $18 children

6-12.
- Haunted Footsteps Ghost Tour: 90 minutes, $25 adults, $18 children 6-12.

All tours leave from 8 Central Street and run rain or shine, no refunds See https://www.salemhistoricaltours.com for more information, special events tours. Discounts offered for seniors 60+, students, and military, veterans, police, firefighters, teachers, EMTs, nurses, and Salem residents. 978-867-8174, thesalemhistoricaltours@gmail.com.

Several other companies compile dark tours of Salem, including:

- Viator: https://www.viator.com/Salem/d22414-ttd
- TripAdvisor: https://www.tripadvisor.com/Attraction_Products-g60954-Salem_Massachusetts.html
- Salem's own website at https://www.salem.org/things-to-do/tours.

All prices are per person. Tour offerings, prices, times, age restrictions, and meeting locations are subject to change.

Police/Crime/Prison/Courthouse Museums and Other Attractions

Boston

Isabella Stewart Gardner Museum
  25 Evans Way, Boston
  617-566-1401
  information@isgm.org
  See where one of the art world's biggest heists took place!

John Adams Courthouse
  1 Pemberton Square between the Massachusetts State House and Government Center, Boston
  617-557-1000
  The courthouse is open on weekdays from 8:30 a.m.- 4:30 p.m. Court sessions are open to the public. There are also one-hour group tours for students and small groups (25 or less), offered on a limited basis. For more information, visit https://www.mass.gov/info-details/visit-the-john-adams-courthouse.

John Joseph Moakley U.S. Courthouse
  One Courthouse Way, Suite 1-400, Boston
  Free, one-hour drop-in courthouse tours are available for all ages. Tours

are held Wednesdays at 2:00 p.m. Contact 617-748-9643 or 617-748-4185 with questions or visit https://discoveringjustice.org/programs/moakley-courthouse-tours.

Medford

Black Dahlia Memorial Plaque
Intersection of Salem Street (Mass Route 60) and Interstate 93, close to 192 Salem Street.

Elizabeth "Betty" Short, also known as "The Black Dahlia," was the victim of one of the nation's most infamous, unsolved crimes. Short lived at 115 Salem Street in Medford and attended Medford High School until June 1940, when she left to pursue her acting career in Hollywood. Her journey ended in a vacant Los Angeles lot on January 15, 1947, as a severed and mutilated corpse. This cold case will be discussed further in one of the West Coast editions of *Vacations Can Be Murder*.

Nantucket

The Old Gaol
15R Vestal Street, Nantucket
https://nha.org/visit/historic-sites/old-jail
Built in 1805, restored 2013-2014. Open seasonally from mid-June through August, Wednesday through Saturday, 11:00 a.m.-4:00 p.m. Cells on two floors allow you to put yourself in the shoes of those incarcerated on Nantucket in the 19th century.

Salem

Witch Dungeon Museum
16 Lynde Street, Salem, MA
978-741-3570
SalemWitchPirate@aol.com

https://www.witchdungeon.com/witchdungeon.html

This museum features a tour of the dungeon where those accused of witchcraft were held. Reenactment of the trial is also part of the exhibits.

Hours: April-November, daily; last performance starts at 5:00 p.m.

Admission: Adults, $13; children aged 4-13, $10; seniors over age 64, $12.

Salem Wax Museum and Salem Witch Village

   288 Derby Street, Salem

   978-740-2929

   Salemwaxmuseum1692@gmail.com

   https://salemwaxmuseum.com

Admission to the Wax Museum or Salem Witch Village from $10 each, but combination tickets are available. Closed January and February. Special tickets are required in October.

Plymouth

1749 Court House Museum

   1 Town Square, Plymouth

   508-830-4075

   plreference@hotmail.com

   https://seeplymouth.com/listing/1749-court-house-museum

Listed in the National Register of Historic Places, the 1749 Court House is a free museum filled with historical items from Plymouth's past. It is the oldest wooden Court House and the longest-used municipal building in America and is only steps away from historic Burial Hill Cemetery. Open daily mid-June through mid-October, 10:00 a.m. - 4:00 p.m.

Whitinsville

Massachusetts State Police Museum and Learning Center
  1 Memorial Square, Whitinsville
  508-839-0001
  info@mspmlc.org
  https://www.mspmlc.org
The Massachusetts State Police Museum and Learning Center celebrates the Massachusetts State Police's rich historical past through its interactive exhibits and Learning Center activities. Open Tuesdays and Saturdays 11:00 a.m. - 4:00 p.m.

State and Federal Prisons of Note in Massachusetts

Boston

Suffolk County Sheriff's Department
  Jail at Nashua Street
  200 Nashua Street, Boston
  Philip Haynes Markoff, the "Craigslist Killer" who murdered masseuse Julissa Brisman in 2009, committed suicide while incarcerated here in 2010.

The Charlestown State Prison

Now closed, this prison once held such notable prisoners as Malcolm X, Charles Ponzi, Sacco & Vanzetti (executed here by electric chair in 1927), and the Millen brothers and Abraham Faber of the Millen-Faber Gang (also put to death by electric chair in 1935). Bunker Hill Community College at 250 Rutherford Avenue now stands on the former prison site.

Bridgewater

Old Colony Correctional Center
1 Administration Road, Bridgewater
This medium-security men's prison shares its thirty-acre Bridgewater Correctional Complex with the Bridgewater State Hospital and the Massachusetts Treatment Center. Currently in custody in the Correctional Center are Paul Leahy, Richard Rosenthal, Christopher McCowen, Michael McDermott, and Stewart R. Weldon, among others. Albert DeSalvo (the Boston Strangler) escaped from the Bridgewater State Hospital, and Kenneth Francis Harrison, the Giggler, committed suicide by drug overdose there, right before he was to be transferred to the Concord State Prison.

Concord

MCI-Concord
965 Elm St, Concord
While this medium-security prison closed during the summer of 2024, it once held Malcolm Little (Malcolm X), defrocked priest John Geoghan (before he was moved to the Souza-Baranowski Correction Center), and hitman Joseph Barboza before he joined the Patriarca crime family. Barboza also led the biggest prison break in the jail's history but was caught less than a day later.

Lancaster/Shirley

Souza-Baranowski Correctional Center (SBCC)
100 Harvard Rd, Shirley
This maximum-security prison is located in Lancaster, though it receives mail through a post office box in Shirley. Directly north across the town border is the medium-security MCI-Shirley, where Kenneth Seguin is incarcerated (although they list him erroneously as Kenneth Sequin).

Current inmates include Alfred Gaynor and Phillip Chism; past inmates include Joseph Druce, who murdered defrocked priest and fellow prisoner John Geoghan, and both Keith Luke and Aaron Hernandez, who killed themselves here.

Norfolk

MCI-Norfolk

2 Clark Street, Norfolk

This medium security prison is where corrections officers Alfred Baranowski and James Souza were shot and killed by an inmate in an escape attempt. The maximum-security prison in Lancaster was named in their honor. Malcolm X was an inmate, and Wayne Lo is currently serving his sentence here.

Walpole

MCI-Cedar Junction (formerly MCI-Walpole)

MA-1A, South Walpole

This maximum-security prison was built to replace the Charlestown State Prison. It once held such infamous criminals as Antone (Tony) Costa, who committed suicide here in 1974, Wayne Lo (before being transferred to MCI-Norfolk), Albert DeSalvo (who was stabbed to death here in 1973), and John Salvi, who committed suicide here in 1996. Due to falling incarceration rates, the prison closed in June 2023.

Notable Crime-and-Justice-Related Burial Sites

Plot locations included where available, burial sites not always included in itineraries.

Roslindale

Oak Lawn Cemetery
427 Cummins Highway, Roslindale
Burial site of Odin Leonardo John Lloyd, murdered by football teammate Aaron Hernandez.

Salem

Saint Mary's Cemetery
226 North Street, Salem
Burial site for Marie Evelina "Evelyn" Corbin, Boston Strangler victim.

Salem Witch Trials Memorial
24 Liberty Street, just off Charter Street, Salem
Memorial for Bridget Bishop and others executed for allegedly being witches.

Springfield

Oak Grove Cemetery
  426 Bay Street, Springfield
  Burial site of Amy Smith, her daughter Destiny, JoAnn C. Thomas, Loretta Daniels, Rosemary Downs, and Robin Marie Ferrence Atkins, all murdered by Alfred Gaynor.

Saint Aloysius Cemetery
  1273 Berkshire Avenue, Springfield
  Burial site of Kayla Jeanne "Kay" Escalante, murdered by Stewart Rudolph Weldon.

Stoneham

Saint Patrick's Cemetery
  120 Elm Street, Stoneham
  Burial site of Janice Anne Miller Hagerty, killed at Edgewater Technology by Michael McDermott.

Taunton

Mayflower Hill Cemetery
  East Brittania Street, Taunton
  Burial Site of Jane Toppan (nee Honora Kelley), serial killer (Potters Field, Grave 984).

Saint Joseph Cemetery
  475 East Britannia Street, Taunton
  Burial site of both Arthur J. "AJ" DaRosa, murderer (Plot: St. Augustine, Lot 32-A) and one of his victims, Patricia Ann McGuire Slavin (St. Pius X, Lot 3).

Wakefield

Forest Glade Cemetery
  470 Lowell Street, Wakefield
  Burial site of Jennifer Bragg Poleman Capobianco, murdered by Michael McDermott at Edgewater Technology.

Lakeside Cemetery
  501 North Avenue, Wakefield
  Burial site for Mary Ann "Polly" Cox Seguin, son Daniel MacKay Seguin, daughter Amy Elizabeth Seguin, all murdered by Kenneth Seguin (Section 14, Lots 153-156).

Waltham

Calvary Cemetery and Mausoleum
  250 High Street, Waltham
  Burial site of Forbes Alexander McLeod, murdered by Murton Millen.

West Roxbury

Beth Abraham Cemetery
  350 Grove Street, West Roxbury
  Burial site of Abraham M. Faber, part of the Millen-Faber Gang.

The Gardens Cemetery
  670 Baker Street, West Roxbury
  Burial Site of Anna Elza Lejins Slesers, Boston Strangler victim (B, 185, 1).

Independent Pride of Boston Cemetery
  776 Baker Street, West Roxbury
  Burial site of Erik Hacker Weissman, Waltham triple homicide victim.

Puritan Cemetery (aka Puritan Mount Sinai Cemetery)

776 Baker Street, West Roxbury

Burial site of Murton Millen, murderer, and part of the Millen-Faber Gang (Section H, Side Right, Lot 12, Grave 4) and his brother Irving Millen (Section H, Side Right, Lot 12, Grave 3).

Saint Joseph Cemetery

990 Lagrange Street, West Roxbury

Burial Site of James Joseph "Whitey" Bulger Jr. (Saint Vincent 19, Lot 609).

Burial site of John Andrew "Jack" Kelly (Blackfriars Pub Massacre, Sect. FRF, Lot 82).

Woburn

Woodbrook Cemetery

100 Salem Street, Woburn

Burial site of Helen Elizabeth Blake, Boston Strangler victim (Lilac Path, Lot 105).

Wrentham

Wrentham Center Cemetery

Dedham Street (Route 1A), Wrentham

Burial site of Cheryl Anne Troy, murdered at Edgewater Technology by Michael McDermott.

Putting it All Together: Itineraries

Itinerary: True Crime Tour of Western Massachusetts

Moving from west to east, we begin in **Pittsfield**, specifically at Dave's Sporting Goods Store at 1164 North Street, where student Wayne Lo purchased an SKS semi-automatic rifle before taking a cab south to commence his shooting spree at Bard College at Simon's Rock, 84 Alford Road in **Great Barrington**, which killed two and wounded four. Drive east and dine amidst paranormal activity at the Knox Trail Inn at 1898 East Otis Road, **East Otis**. Continue northeast to **Leeds**, a village in **Northampton**, where Kristen Heather Gilbert murdered patients as part of her nursing work at the Northampton Veterans Affairs Medical Center (VAMC), 421 North Main Street. One of her victims, Edward S. Skwira, is buried at Saint Mary's Assumption Cemetery at 434 Haydenville Road in nearby **Haydenville**, Northampton (though some list the cemetery as part of Leeds. Check both on your GPS.)

Head south to **Springfield**, where Alfred Gaynor killed eight women, including Vera Hallums (apartment at 31 Leland Drive); Amy Smith and her daughter Destiny (apartment at 280 Dwight Street Extension); Jill Ann Ermellini, found dead in the cab in a truck at 406 Oak Street in Indian Orchard, an auto body yard; Robin M. Atkins, found bound, gagged, and strangled in a downtown alley next to 19 Spring Street; JoAnn C. Thomas, found in her home on the 800-block of Worthington Street; Yvette Torres, found in her 25 Healy Street apartment; Loretta Daniels, found in an

168

alley beside the Mason Square post office at 914 State Street; Rosemary Downs, found in her home on the 0-50 block of Lionel Benoit Road; and Joyce Dickerson-Peay, abandoned outside an empty restaurant on East Columbus Avenue. The Oak Grove Cemetery, at 426 Bay Street, is the burial site of Alfred Gaynor victims Amy Smith, her daughter Destiny, JoAnn C. Thomas, Loretta Daniels, Rosemary Downs, and Robin Atkins.

Also in Springfield, the home that Stewart Rudolph Weldon shared with his mother on the 1300 block of Page Boulevard is where police found the decomposing bodies of three women. One of these women, Kayla Jeanne "Kay" Escalante, is buried at Saint Aloysius Cemetery at 1273 Berkshire Avenue, **Indian Orchard** (a village within Springfield to the east of downtown).

Before leaving Springfield, dine with the ghosts rumored to reside at Theodore's and Smith's Billiards at 201 Worthington Street.

Drive northwest to make a quick stop at the Massachusetts Veterans Memorial Cemetery (1390 Main Street) in **Agawam**, where Henry R. Hudon, another of Kristen Heather Gilbert's victims, is buried. Then head east to **Whitinsville** (a neighborhood in Northbridge) to spend an interesting afternoon at the Massachusetts State Police Museum and Learning Center at 1 Memorial Square, before completing the tour with a drive-by of the Souza-Baranowski Correctional Center in Lancaster (100 Harvard Road). Current inmates include Alfred Gaynor and Phillip Chism, and past inmates included Joseph Druce, who murdered defrocked priest and fellow prisoner John Geoghan, and both Keith Luke and Aaron Hernandez, who killed themselves here.

(Omitted from this tour: cemetery stops at Holyoke and Lunenburg, and inns/restaurants in Deerfield, Dracut, and Sudbury.)

Itinerary: True Crime Tour Heading South to Boston

This itinerary is divided into four parts: the road south to Boston, Boston proper, some of the smaller neighborhoods within Boston, and then the Boston suburbs. Each requires no backtracking. You may wish to combine these tours or break them up with the suggested hotel stays.

The first part of the tour begins in **Lawrence,** where, in 1974, William "Willy" Horton murdered gas station attendant Joseph Fournier at a Marston Street Mobile station. Boston Strangler victim Mary Ann Brown's body was found in an apartment at 319 Park Street, and he murdered Joanne Marie Graff at the apartments at 54 Essex Street.

Next, drive southeast to **Andover**, where Fournier is buried at Sacred Heart Cemetery (80 Corbett Street). Also in Andover, Philip Chism's teacher and victim, Colleen Ritzer, is buried at the Spring Grove Cemetery at 124 Abbot Street.

Drive further southeast to **Danvers**, formerly Salem Village, where young girls accusing women of witchcraft ignited the hysteria that led to the Salem witch trials. This is also where Philip Chism attended Danvers High School at 60 Cabot Road, where he murdered Colleen Ritzer. Further southeast, you'll reach **Salem**, where they held the witch trials. You can visit the Salem Witch Trials Memorial at 24 Liberty Street. The Witch Dungeon

Museum is located at 16 Lynde Street, and the Salem Wax Museum and Salem Witch Village is at 288 Derby Street. Marie Evelina "Evelyn" Corbin was murdered by the Boston Strangler in her apartment at 224 Lafayette Street, and you can pay respects at her gravesite at Saint Mary's Cemetery, 226 North Street.

Hungry? Dine with the rumored ghosts at either Rockafellas at 231 Essex Street or Turner's Seafood at Lyceum Hall, located at 43 Church Street.

Considering all the witch and ghost tours offered by Witch City Walking Tours, Salem Historical Tours, and others—many after dark—you may want to spend the night. Both the Hawthorne Hotel at 18 Washington Square West, and the Morning Glory Bed & Breakfast at 22 Hardy Street, are said to be haunted.

Continue west to **Peabody**, where the burial sites of Albert DeSalvo, Sean Allen Collier (a Boston Marathon Bombing victim), and murderer John Salvi are buried at Puritan Lawn Memorial Park at 185 Lake Street. At the Maple Hill Cemetery (98 Canterbury Drive in Workman Circle off Sabino Farm Road), you can pay respects at the grave of DeSalvo victim Edes "Ida" Halpern Irga. To the southwest, in **Lynn**, the body of DeSalvo victim Helen Elizabeth Blake was found at 73 Newhall Street.

Take a side trip west to **Wakefield**, where Michael McDermott went on a shooting rampage at Edgewater Technology, its headquarters located at 200 Harvard Mill Square. Forest Glade Cemetery at 470 Lowell Street is the burial site of Jennifer Bragg Poleman Capobianco, one of his victims. Mary Ann "Polly" Cox Seguin, her son Daniel MacKay Seguin, and her daughter Amy Elizabeth Seguin, all murdered by Kenneth Seguin, are buried at Lakeside Cemetery, 501 North Avenue.

Drive southeast to **Revere,** where Robert Donati was found in the trunk of his white 1980 Cadillac on Savage Street, several blocks from his Mountain

Avenue home.

Drive southwest to finally arrive in Boston.

Touring True Crime Boston

You could easily spend two or three days exploring the true crime of Boston and its suburbs. Why not book a few nights at the Liberty Hotel (215 Charles Street), once the Charles Street Jail. You can dine at CLINK, their in-hotel restaurant, or visit their Alibi Bar and Lounge. Another option is the AKA Back Bay (154 Berkeley Street), which was once the city's police headquarters.

If you'd prefer to stay at a hotel that was also a crime site mentioned in this guide, you can choose from either the Westin Copley Place Hotel at 10 Huntington Avenue, where "Craigslist Killer' Phillip Haynes robbed escort Trisha Leffler, or the Boston Marriott Copley Place at 110 Huntington Avenue, where he murdered masseuse Julissa Brisman. Or, you can go in a more paranormal direction and book one of the Boston hotels thought to harbor ghosts: the Club Quarters Boston at 161 Devonshire Street or the Omni Parker House Hotel at 60 School Street.

Boston Strangler Albert DeSalvo killed his victims at the following apartment buildings: Anna Elza Slesers, 77 Gainsborough Street; Mary Mullen, 1435 Commonwealth Avenue; Nina Nioma Nichols, 1940 Commonwealth Avenue; Edes "Ida" Irga, 7 Grove Street; Jane Sullivan, 435 Columbia Road; Sophie L. Clark, 315 Huntington Avenue; Patricia Jane Bissette, 515 Park Drive; and Mary Anne Sullivan, 44-A Charles Street.

The Boston Marathon Bombs exploded around 210 yards apart at the finish line on Boylston Street near Copley Square. The first exploded at 671-673 Boylston Street outside Marathon Sports; the second at 755 Boylston Street. Each spot is commemorated by a memorial sculpture of granite, bronze, glass, and brick, completed in 2019.

Kenneth Francis Harrison, "The Giggler," lured Lucy Palmarin (6) into the cab he was driving and later tossed her into the Fort Point Channel, where she drowned. Her body was found wedged between some rubbish thrown into the Channel not far from the intersection of Dorchester Avenue and Broadway in South Boston. He bludgeoned and left Marine Corps veteran Joseph "Joe" Breen in a water-filled pit at a construction site outside the Novelty Bar (thought to have once been located at the corner of Washington and Kneeland Streets). His final victim was Kenneth "Kenny" Martin (9), whom he murdered in a tunnel under South Station, though he later confessed to throwing a 75-year-old woman off the Broadway Bridge in South Boston as well.

Aaron Hernandez and his victim, Odin Lloyd, had a disagreement two nights before Lloyd's murder outside Rumor Nightclub at 100 Warrenton Street at Stuart Street, now permanently closed. Years earlier, and hours before they were gunned down in their car while stopped at a traffic light, Hernandez had an altercation with two immigrants from Cape Verde, Safiro Furtado, and Daniel de Abreu, at the Cure Lounge at 246 Tremont Street in The Wilbur (also now closed).

Mobster James "Whitey" Bulger used the Lancaster Street Garage, a parking garage at 131 Lancaster Street (near North Station and the present-day TD Garden), as his "West End headquarters" when he led the Winter Hill Gang. Another organized crime-related spot is 105 Summer Street (at the time of writing, next to a now-closed GNC store). When Blackfriars Pub stood at that address, it was the site of a massacre that killed five men.

Master con artist Charles Ponzi set up the Security Exchange Company in the Niles Building at 27 School Street. The Brinks Robbery occurred in Boston's North End at 155 Prince (now 600 Commercial Street), the corner of Commercial and Prince Streets at what's still known as Brink's Garage. And one of the world's biggest art heists occurred at the Isabella Stewart Gardner Museum at 25 Evans Way.

If you want even more true crime in Boston, a wide selection of true crime and ghost tours are offered by Free Tours by Foot, Top Dog Tours, Junket, Ghost City Tours, and other companies listed.

For those more interested in the justice aspect of true crime, you can visit the John Adams Courthouse at 1 Pemberton Square between the Massachusetts State House and Government Center and the John Joseph Moakley U.S. Courthouse at One Courthouse Way. You can also walk past the Jail at Nashua Street at 200 Nashua Street, where Philip Haynes Markoff, the "Craigslist Killer," committed suicide. And Bunker Hill Community College at 250 Rutherford Avenue (at the intersection of Austin Street and New Rutherford Avenue) was once the site of the Charlestown State Prison, where the Millen-Faber Gang and Sacco & Vanzetti were put to death.

Itinerary: True Crime in Boston Neighborhoods

In the wake of school desegregation, numerous murders plagued the **Roxbury** section of Boston. Victims and the places their bodies were found include: Christine (Chris) Ricketts, discovered on the sidewalk on East Lenox and Reed Streets near Harrison Avenue alongside Andrea Foye; Daryal Ann Hargett, in her second-floor apartment at 20 Wellington Street; Darlene Rogers, found in Washington Park (located at the corner of Martin Luther King Jr. Blvd and Washington Street); Lois Hood Nesbitt, found at 9 Codman Park near Egleston Square; Sandra Boulware, found in a vacant lot less than 150 yards behind the Roxbury YMCA at 285 Martin Luther King Jr. Boulevard; and Bobbie Jean Graham, found in an alley behind 267 Commonwealth Avenue, a few doors down from her Back Bay apartment.

The cemeteries in **West Roxbury** mark the final resting places for a number of Massachusetts criminals and victims. Beth Abraham Cemetery (350 Grove Street) is the burial site of Abraham M. Faber, part of the Millen-Faber Gang, with Murton Millen buried at the Puritan Cemetery at 776 Baker Street. Anna Elza Lejins Slesers, one of the Boston Strangler victims, is buried at the Gardens Cemetery at 670 Baker Street. The Independent Pride of Boston Cemetery at 776 Baker Street is the burial site of Erik Hacker Weissman, one of the victims of the Waltham triple homicide. Finally, both crime boss James "Whitey" Bulger and Blackfriars Pub Massacre victim John "Jack" Kelly are buried at Saint Joseph Cemetery

176

at 990 Lagrange Street.

In the **Roslindale** section of Boston, you can visit the Oak Lawn Cemetery at 427 Cummins Highway to pay respects to Odin Leonardo John Lloyd, murdered by football teammate Aaron Hernandez. In the **Franklin Park** section, Caren Prater's body was found behind the Boston Parks Department office. And in **Dorchester**, Gwendolyn Yvette Stinson was found strangled in a ditch near her Park Street home, Desiree Denise Etheridge's body was left behind what was a Venetian blinds company on Fellow Street, and Valyric Holland was stabbed in her Dorchester residence on Hamilton Street. Also in Dorchester, the Cedar Grove Cemetery at 920 Adams Street is the final resting spot for Martin William Richard, another Boston Marathon Bombing victim. The Dorchester North Burying Ground at 585 Columbia Road at Stoughton Street, Upham, contains the grave of Jane Buckley Sullivan, Boston Strangler victim. Finally, you can visit the grave of Nina Frances Granger Nichols, another woman murdered by the Boston Strangler, at Evergreen Cemetery at 2060 Commonwealth Avenue in **Brighton**.

Itinerary: Touring True Crime in the Boston Suburbs

We start in **Cambridge,** where Boston Strangler victim Beverly Florence Samans was murdered at 4 University Road. It's also where Jane Toppan trained at Cambridge Hospital (the hospital grounds were situated on the south side of Mount Auburn Street, opposite Lowell and Channing Streets, likely the site of what's now the Mount Auburn Hospital). Her landlord, Israel Dunham, and his wife, Lovey, died at her hand in their home at what was likely 19 Wendell Street.

Travel northwest to **Medford** to view the Black Dahlia Memorial Plaque at the intersection of Salem Street (Mass Route 60) and Interstate 93, close to 192 Salem Street. Then head north to **Stoneham**, where Janice Ann Miller Hagerty, a victim of the Edgewater Technology shootings, is buried at Saint Patrick's Cemetery, 120 Elm Street.

Traveling west to **Woburn**, the burial site of Boston Strangler victim Helen Elizabeth Black is at Woodbrook Cemetery at 100 Salem Street. To the west and slightly south, you can view the former mansion of Charles Ponzi at 19 Slocum Road in **Lexington**. Then drive even further west to **Concord** to have lunch at The Fife and Drum Restaurant at 976 Barretts Mill Road, West Concord at the Northeastern Correctional Center, or stay and dine at the haunted Concord's Colonial Inn at 48 Monument Square. You can also drive by MCI-Concord at 965 Elm Street, once the prison that housed

Malcolm X and defrocked priest John Geoghan.

In **Waltham** to the southeast, 12 Harding Avenue is the site of the triple homicide which many believe was committed by Boston Marathon Bomber, Tamerlan Tsarnaev. At the Calvary Cemetery and Mausoleum (250 High Street), you can visit the burial site of Forbes Alexander McLeod, murdered by Murton Millen. To the southeast, you can drive down the 0-100 block of Franklin Avenue in **Watertown**, past the driveway where David Henneberry found Boston Marathon Bomber, Dzhokhar Tsarnaev, hiding in his boat.

Drive southeast to **Brookline,** where John Salvi shot up the reception area at Planned Parenthood at 1031 Beacon Street, and then continued his murder spree at Preterm Health Services, 1842 Beacon Street. At the Walnut Hills Cemetery at 96 Grove Street, you can pay respects to PFC Joseph "Joe" A. Breen, killed by Kenneth Francis Harrison.

To the southwest, in **Needham**, you can visit the Needham Bank at 1063 Great Plain Avenue (formerly the Needham Trust Company), the site of the bank robbery by the Millen-Faber Gang. One of the victims shot that day, Francis Oliver Haddock, is buried at Saint Mary's Cemetery at 1 Wellesley Avenue. Then drive west to the 0-50 block of Garvey Road in **Framingham,** where Richard Rosenthal impaled his wife's heart and lungs in their suburban backyard. Slightly southwest is the haunted Stone's Public House at 179 Main Street in **Ashland**, and then, to the south, in **Holliston**, Kenneth Seguin murdered his wife and children in their house, likely on the 0-50 block of Elm Street. Follow his route south to **Franklin** where he hid his children's bodies under debris in Beaver Pond (Beach is at 450 Beaver Street, open to residents only). Continue southeast to the Wrentham Center Cemetery on Dedham Street in **Wrentham**, the burial site for Cheryl Anne Troy, murdered at Edgewater Technology. The tour ends in North Attleboro (also spelled Attleborough), where a jogger found Odin Lloyd's dead body at the North Attleboro Industrial Park on John L.

Dietsch Boulevard after being shot by Aaron Hernandez.
This tour omits cemetery stops at Belmont and Gloucester.

Itinerary: True Crime Tour Heading South and to the Cape

(This tour can be a continuation of the previous tour by driving north from North Attleboro to Norfolk.)

We start in **Norfolk**, driving by MCI-Norfolk at 2 Clark Street, where Wayne Lo is currently serving time. Then southeast to **South Walpole**, where the now-shuttered MCI-Cedar Junction on MA-1A once held such infamous criminals as Antone (Tony) Costa. Wayne Lo, Albert DeSalvo, and John Salvi. Police apprehended the "Craigslist Killer," Philip Haynes Markoff, at a traffic stop on Interstate 95 in **Walpole**.

Travel northeast to **Braintree**, where the Slater-Morrill Shoe Company factory, located on Pearl Street, was robbed and two men killed, allegedly by Nicola Sacco and Bartolomeo Vanzetti. Walk the crime scene, a couple of blocks from Pearl Street between South Braintree Square and Ivory Street. The Slater & Morrill Factory (as it was then called) stood roughly where Burger King and Tennessee BBQ are now. The Parmenter-Berardelli Memorial to the two fallen men, located at the corner of French and Pearl Streets, includes a monument, photos, a storyboard, and a plaque located on a rock in front of a low stone wall. Also, Vincent Edward Solmonte, owner of the Blackfriar Pub and murdered in the massacre there, is buried at the Blue Hill Cemetery at 700 West Street.

To the east in **East Weymouth**, the summer cottage where "Merry Widow" Grayce Asquith was murdered is located at the Birches on Alpine Road near Whitman Pond. Michael McDermott also skipped out on paying the rent at his East Weymouth apartment months before shooting up Edgewater Technology. The address is believed to be the condo building at 263 Lake Street, where he lived with his wife, Monica.

North in **Hingham**, you can visit the grave of fashion writer Christa Worthington at the High Street Cemetery at 19 High Street (corner of Main/Rt 228). Continue south to **Brockton**, where neo-Nazi Keith Luke raped one woman and murdered her sister and a homeless man after breaking into his old apartment building on 103 Clinton Street. His van later crashed near the intersection of East Ashland and North Quincy Streets, and he was arrested after a shootout with police at the corner of North Quincy and Court Streets. At the Melrose Cemetery on 88 North Pearl Street, you can visit the burial sites of Frederick Albert Parmenter, murdered at the Slater-Morill Shoe Factory, and Debra Lanier Greenlaw DeMello, a New Bedford Highway Killer victim.

Continue south to **Bridgewater,** where the Burger King rest stop on Massachusetts Route 24 southbound is where Paul Leahy murdered Alexandra Zapp and then was shot by police lieutenant Stephen O'Reilly. Also in Bridgewater, the Old Colony Correctional Center at 1 Administration Road currently houses Paul Leahy, Richard Rosenthal, Christopher McCowen, Michael McDermott, and Stewart R. Weldon, among others.

Further south in **Taunton,** Arthur DaRosa smashed his Honda Accord into the Silver City Galleria shopping mall at 2 Galleria Mall Drive (off Route 24 and Route 140, now closed). He assaulted shoppers in Macy's and then fired at diners and staff at the Bertucci's restaurant, killing one before Plymouth County Sheriff Deputy James Creed shot him dead. Earlier, DaRosa had murdered Patricia Slavin at her home on the 200 block of Myricks Street. Both DaRosa and Slavin are buried at St. Joseph Cemetery at 475 East

Britannia Street. And the Mayflower Hill Cemetery, also on East Brittania Street, is the final resting place for murderer Jane Toppan (nee Honora Kelley). Toppan had been committed for life to the Taunton Insane Hospital (now called the Taunton State Hospital at 60 Hodges Avenue, which was mostly demolished and later rebuilt).

Continue south to **Fall River**, home to Lizzie Borden. You can stay at the Borden House at 230 Second Street, where her father and stepmother were murdered. It's said to be one of the most haunted homes in the country. Take a tour of the home or of the area through U.S. Ghost Adventures. Visit Oak Grove Cemetery at 765 Prospect Street, where Lizzie is buried, along with her father, birth mother, and stepmother.

To the southeast, in and around **New Bedford**, the yet uncaptured New Bedford Highway Killer left his victims at the following locations: **Freetown**: Robbin Lynn Rhodes, found along Route 140 southbound by a search dog; Deborah McConnell, discovered on Route 140 northbound; and Debra Medeiros, on the east side of Route 140 northbound. **Westport**: Mary Rose Santos, last seen dancing at The Old Quarter Deck Lounge (thought to have been located at 674 Pleasant Street in New Bedford, now gone), and found nude about 25 feet from Route 88 southbound. **Dartmouth**: Rochelle Clifford Dopierala, found in a gravel pit along Reed Road beneath a tree grove, about two miles from Interstate 195; Nancy Lee Paiva, last seen walking home from "Whisper's Pub" (120 County Street, New Bedford) and found nude off Interstate 195 westbound in Dartmouth, halfway between the Faunce Corner and Reed Road exits; Debra Greenlaw DeMello, found nude off the eastbound Reed Road ramp of Interstate 195, and Dawn Mendes, found on the westbound Reed Road ramp off Interstate 195. **Marion**: Sandra Botelho. found in the woods along the westbound side of Interstate 195. Rhodes and Paiva are both buried at the Pine Grove Cemetery (1100 Ashley Boulevard, New Bedford).

Also in New Bedford: Jacob D. Robida, an 18-year-old neo-Nazi, shot up a

North End gay bar called Puzzles Lounge at 426 North Front Street (now closed). He escaped by running north on North Front Street but eventually killed himself after a shootout with police in Arkansas. Robida is buried at Saint Mary's Cemetery at 1213 Kempton Street (US 6).

Drive northeast to **Plymouth** to stop for the night before heading to the Cape. This was the hometown of John Billington, the first colony resident to be convicted of murder. You can also visit the 1749 Court House Museum at 1 Town Square, the oldest wooden courthouse and the longest-used municipal building in America (open seasonally). Historic Burial Hill Cemetery is nearby.

Start the next day by driving south to **Bourne,** where the Cataumet Cemetery on County Road is the final resting place for Alden P. Davis, his wife Mary Louise "Mattie" Stebbins Davis, and their daughters, Anna Genevieve Davis Gordon, and Mary Eliza Davis Gibbs. All were poisoned by their private nurse, Jane Toppan. Head further south to **Cataumet**, where Davis and his wife had rented space to Toppan at their property on a street now called Mystery Lane; it's where Toppan murdered them. Continue east to **Centerville**, where Mary Anne Sullivan, Boston Strangler victim, is buried at Saint Francis Xavier Cemetery on Pine Street, a half mile off Strawberry Hill Road.

Should you wish to explore haunted hotels on **Nantucket**, take the ferry from Hyannis. The Steamship Authority runs a high-speed (one hour) and a traditional car ferry (just over two hours long) from the Hyannis Terminal at 141 School Street. Information is at https://www.steamshi pauthority.com. Prices vary, see https://www.steamshipauthority.com/ reservations/fares. Hy-Line Cruises runs a passenger-only ferry. For details, visit https://hylinecruises.com. Roundtrip rates start at $89 for adults and $54 for children ages 5-12. Advance reservations for cars are necessary, but you can also park your car on the Hyannis side, and just take the passenger ferry across (make sure in advance that parking will be available!). In Nantucket, the spirits await you at either the Wauwinet Hotel at 120 Wauwinet Road, or the Nantucket Hotel (formerly called the Point Breeze Club and Hotel) at 77 Easton Street. You can visit the Old Jail at 15R Vestal Streets, and if that doesn't satisfy your appetite for touring, ghost walking tours are offered as well.

Returning to the mainland, you may find paranormal activity northeast at the Orleans Inn and Restaurant at 3 Old County Road in **Orleans**, and even further east in **Eastham** at the Rugosa (formerly the Penny House Inn) at 4885 US-6 aka 4885 State Highway.

Northeast in **Truro**, Antone Charles "Tony" Costa killed Susan Perry, Mary Ann Wysocki, Patricia Walsh, and Sydney Monzon. Susan Perry's body was found on the grounds of Pine Grove Cemetery, off Old County Road. The mutilated bodies of the others were unearthed from shallow graves in a shrub-pine area off Cemetery Road. And in **South Truro**, Christa Worthington's corpse was discovered in her home on Depot Road, along with her daughter, who was left unharmed.

The final stop on the True Crime Cape Cod tour is **Provincetown**, where Tony Costa met two of his victims at a boarding house at 5 Standish Street (later called Victoria House, an inn that has since closed). Costa is buried at Saint Peter's Cemetery on Jerome Smith Road; the grave is unmarked, but is next to his mother's, marked "Bonaviri," adjacent to 40 Winslow Street. Also buried at this cemetery is one of his victims, Susan Ellsworth "Sue" Perry.

Unfortunately, the ferry connecting Provincetown with Plymouth does not permit cars.

   (Omitted from this tour: a cemetery in Fairhaven, and accommodations in Duxbury.)

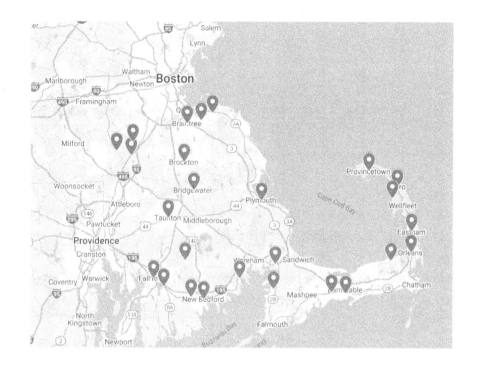

Massachusetts Victim Resources

This is a noncomprehensive summary of services available to victims of crime in Massachusetts. Information was taken directly from their websites. Visit/contact agencies for complete information and note that some programs offered by certain contractors focus on specific geographic areas. Inclusion does not equate to recommendation.

Victim Services

- U.S. Department of Justice, Office for Victims of Crime: Directory of Crime Victim Services (over 7000 resources): See https://ovc.ojp.gov/directory-crime-victim-services.
- National Center for Victims of Crime: Victim Connect Resource Center, 855-484-2846, see https://victimsofcrime.org.
- National Organization for Victim Assistance: 800-TRY-NOVA or 800-879-6682 or 703-535-6682, see https://trynova.org.
- Massachusetts Office for Victim Assistance: see https://www.mass.gov/orgs/massachusetts-office-for-victim-assistance.

Crime-centric List of Resources

Child Abuse

- National Center for Missing & Exploited Children: 800-843-5678, see https://www.missingkids.org/home.

Civil Legal Aid for Victims of Crime

- Civil Legal Aid for Victims of Crime: 844-878-6682, see https://mass clavc.org.

Civil Legal Help for People with Low Income

- Massachusetts Legal Assistance Corporation: 855-252-5342, see https://mlac.org/help .
- Community Legal Aid (Western Mass): 855-252-5342, https://comm unitylegal.org/what-we-do.
- Metrowest Legal Services: 800-696-1501, https://mwlegal.org.

Domestic Violence

- Domestic Shelters: see https://www.domesticshelters.org.
- Massachusetts Statewide Toll-Free Domestic Violence Hotline: Safe-Link - 24 hours/multilingual, 877-785-2020, see https://www.mass.g ov/info-details/domestic-violence-programs-for-survivors.
- Massachusetts Coalition Against Sexual Assault and Domestic Violence/Jane Doe, Inc.: 617-248-0922, see https://www.janedoe.org.
- SAFEPLAN Civil Court Advocacy: Provides assistance for obtaining restraining orders and harassment prevention orders, see https://w ww.mass.gov/info-details/victim-services-resources-and-training# safeplan-programs.

Drunk Driving Victims

- Mothers Against Drunk Driving: 877-MADD-HELP (877-623-3435). see https://madd.org/massachusetts.
- MOVA – Drunk Driving Trust Fund Programs: see https://www.mass. gov/doc/ddtf-program-listing-and-contact-information/download.

Elder Abuse

- Protecting Older Adults From Abuse: see https://www.mass.gov/pro tecting-older-adults-from-abuse
- Reporting Elder Abuse and Neglect: 24/7 Hotline at 800-922-2275, see https://www.mass.gov/info-details/report-abuse-of-adults-aged -60.
- Senior Care Elder Services: see https://seniorcareinc.org/protective-services.

Fraud

- Annual Credit Report Request Service from Annual Credit Report.com: see https://www.annualcreditreport.com/protectYourIdentity.actio n.
- National Consumers League Fraud Center (not limited to Massachusetts): see https://fraud.org.

Identity Theft

- Identity Theft Resource Center: 888-400-5530, see https://www.idth eftcenter.org.
- Federal Trade Commission - Identity Theft Resources: 877-438-4338, see https://consumer.ftc.gov/identity-theft-and-online-security.

Online Criminal Case Status, Inmate Status, and Sex Offender Registry

- Public Access to Court Electronic Records: see https://pacer.uscourts. gov (charge involved).
- Massachusetts Court Records: see https://massachusettscourtrecord s.us/criminal-court-records/inmate.
- National Sex Offender Public Registry: see https://www.nsopw.gov.

- Massachusetts Sex Offender Registry Board: 978-740-6400 or Toll Free 800-936-3426, see https://www.mass.gov/orgs/sex-offender-registry-board.

Sexual Assault

- Statewide Resources for Sexual Rights Offenders: see https://www.mass.gov/info-details/statewide-resources-for-sexual-assault-survivors
- Amherst Police Department Sexual Assault Resources: see https://www.amherstma.gov/998/Sexual-Assault-Resources
- Domestic Violence & Sexual Assault Resources: see https://www.mass.gov/info-details/domestic-violence-sexual-assault-resources

Survivors of Homicide

- Victim Compensation and Assistance Division; Provides financial assistance to eligible victims of violent crime, including uninsured medical and dental care, mental health counseling, funeral and burial costs, and income lost due to the inability to work. 617-727-2200 x2160 or 617-586-1340, see www.mass.gov/massachusetts-victims-of-violent-crime-compensation.
- Massachusetts Office for Victim Assistance (MOVA): Provides social and emotional support, housing advocacy, financial assistance, and education and employment assistance. Call 844-878-MOVA (6682), MOVA@mass.gov, see https://www.mass.gov/orgs/massachusetts-office-for-victim-assistance or https://www.mass.gov/askmova.
- Survivors of Homicide Victims Network (SHVN): 617-825-1917. Offers a community of solidarity, healing opportunities, and ongoing communications regarding community events and resources. SHVN meets via Zoom on the first Thursday of each month, see https://ldbpeaceinstitute.org/survivors-of-homicide-victims-network.
- Center for Homicide Bereavement: Offers crisis intervention and

ongoing bereavement counseling for all ages and for families and bereavement support groups, see https://www.mass.gov/info-details/list-of-homicide-bereavement-services-by-massachusetts-county.
- Eliot's Survivor Services: available in Boston, Holyoke, Wakefield, and Worcester. see https://www.eliotchs.org/cyf/survivor-services.

Victim Advocacy

- Victim Rights Law Center: see https://victimrights.org.
- Finding Legal Help: 866-627-7577, see https://www.mass.gov/info-details/finding-legal-help.

Victim Compensation

- Massachusetts Victim Compensation Program for federal and state violent crimes: see https://www.mass.gov/massachusetts-victims-of-violent-crime-compensation.

Victim Notification System

- The U.S. Department of Justice's Victim Notification System (VNS) is an automated system that provides victims of federal cases with information about scheduled court dates and the outcome of significant court events, as well as the offender's custody or release status. 866-365-4968 (1-866-DOJ-4YOU), see www.notify.usdoj.gov.

Victim Rights and Services Complaints

- The Office of the Victims' Rights Ombudsman was established to receive and investigate complaints filed by crime victims against DOJ employees and has implemented procedures to promote compliance with crime victims' rights and obligations. The Department of Justice will investigate the allegations in the complaint to determine whether rights were violated by an employee. See https://www.justice.gov/usao/office-victims-rights-ombuds.

Victim Witness Assistance Program

- Victim and Witness Services: The Victim/Witness Assistance Unit provides advocacy and information about the court process to victims and witnesses of crime, as well as information about victim rights and referrals to community resources, in accordance with the Massachusetts Victim Bill of Rights. See https://www.northwesternda.org/victimwitness-assistance.

Programs subject to change or end without notice.

Chapter 4: Vacations Can Be Murder in New Hampshire

New Hampshire Crime Statistics

New Hampshire may appear serene, but it's seen its fair share of crime. ABC-TV affiliate WMUR9 reported that in 2022, the murder rate increased significantly from each of the two years prior, numbering 28 instead of 16, yet down from the record 33 homicides in 2019. The rate of 27 murders stayed steady in 2023. The state's average number of annual murders is 19, according to the Attorney General's office, and Senior Assistant Attorney General Ben Agati assured residents the state is still one of the safest in the nation.

Crimestats.dos.nh.gov reported that in 2022, New Hampshire experienced 1,804 violent crimes, consisting of 28 murders, 580 sex crimes, 225 armed robberies, and 971 aggravated assaults. Property crimes numbered 20,398. (Note: Even though these are 2022 figures, the data remains fluid; the numbers changed each time I researched this site.)

According to Safewise.com, the safest cities in the state for 2024 included Danville, Strafford, Hopkinton, Rye, and Enfield, with the most dangerous, according to travelsafe.abroad.com, listed as Manchester (violent crime rate 4.42 per 1,000 residents), Conway, Littleton, Laconia, and Rochester (all of which have crime rates of less than 3 per 1,000 residents).

World Population Review reports that in 2020, New Hampshire had the second-lowest crime rate in the United States, with only Maine reporting fewer crimes.

Summary of serial killings, mass shootings, mob hits, and other crimes

(listed alphabetically by location)

For those traveling throughout New Hampshire, here is just a sampling of true crime that occurred in the state. Should you wish to visit these cities, exact addresses, where available, are listed in the "Itineraries" section at the end of the chapter:

Allenstown: Terry Peder Rasmussen, also known as the "Chameleon Killer," was a serial murderer with multiple identities who, unusually, developed close relationships with his victims before killing them. Rasmussen was born in Colorado, but after extended stays in California and Arizona, he ended up in New Hampshire as "Bob Evans" in the late 1970s.

In 1978, while still in California, he dated Marlyse Elizabeth Honeychurch and her two daughters, Marie Elizabeth Vaughn and Sarah Lynn McWaters. They were last seen alive after enjoying Thanksgiving dinner with her family.

By 1981, he was dating and living with Denise Beaudin in Manchester, NH. Then, she and her six-month-old daughter Lisa (aka Dawn) were also never seen again.

The bodies of four of Rasmussen's victims—Honeychurch, Vaughn, McWaters, and an unidentified child believed to be Rasmussen's biological daughter—were discovered in oil barrels in Bear Brook State Park in Allenstown on two separate occasions in 1985 and 2000 but not identified until years later. It's believed Rasmussen relocated them to New Hampshire before killing Beaudin, whose body was never recovered. Her daughter Lisa remained unharmed; Rasmussen kidnapped her and kept her for five years before abandoning her in a California RV park in 1986.

In 2017, when authorities connected Rasmussen to the Allenstown murders with the help of DNA evidence, he was already deceased, having died in prison in 2010 while serving fifteen years to life for the murder of his partner, Eunsoon Jun, whom he "married" in an unofficial backyard ceremony using the name Larry Vanner.

Bedford: John Walter Bardgett, who alternately called himself the "Nurse of Mercy" and the "Nurse of Death," was 25 when he was charged with killing at least two elderly patients at the Harborside-Northwood Nursing home. He admitted to administering morphine intravenously when he was only authorized to inject them under the skin. Though he pleaded not guilty to murder, witnesses reportedly overheard him bragging about killing Clara Hamm (92), on September 9th, 2001, and Dorothy Koch (91) just hours later on September 10th. Both women died within an hour of receiving the drugs, though defense attorneys argued that both women were terminal, with one in hospice, and the morphine didn't cause their deaths. The body of a third possible victim, Helen Peyant (71), could not be investigated due to cremation.

Bardgett was acquitted of murder, negligent homicide, and manslaughter, but was found guilty of administering morphine without a doctor's orders. He plea-bargained his sentence down to two consecutive 12-month prison terms, with all time suspended, and was forced to give up his nursing license. The jury was deadlocked on four smaller charges, and he may be retried in the future.

Colebrook: Carl C. Drega was an authority-hating carpenter with homes in both Columbia and Bow, who had a history of zoning disputes with the town. It's unclear whether he snapped or planned it in advance, but on August 19, 1997, he went on a shooting spree and settled old scores. He started his rampage in Colebrook, when two state troopers noticed rust on the back of his red pickup truck and pulled him over into the parking lot of a supermarket. Drega didn't take it well. First, he fired at Trooper Scott Phillips with an AR-15 assault rifle, finishing him off with four shots from a pistol at point-blank range. Then, he shot and killed the second trooper, Leslie Lord. Appropriating their police cruiser, Drega drove to Bridge Street, where he murdered Vickie Bunnell, a lawyer and part-time judge, but formerly a selectman who had wrangled with him over zoning. When Dennis Joos, editor of the News and Sentinel, tackled him, Drega shot and killed him as well.

From there, Drega headed to his Columbia home, an arsenal containing all the ingredients for a larger bombing and shooting spree, and he burnt it to the ground. Then he drove to Vermont, wounding a New Hampshire fish and game officer on the way, before pulling off onto a road near Dennis Pond in Brunswick, Vermont (though some sources place this final confrontation 11 miles away in Bloomfield, Vermont). A gunfight with twenty officers ensued, culminating in Drega's death. Authorities uncovered a "hit list" of other targeted victims in his truck, indicating the fatalities might have been greater had the impasse not ended as it did.

Concord: On October 19, 1991, unemployed truck driver James Colbert (39) strangled his estranged wife Mary Jayne (30) in bed and smothered his three daughters, Patricia (10 weeks), Emily (2.5), and Elise (1.5) while they slept. His wife had feared such violence, having obtained a restraining order against him earlier, citing sexual assault and threats of violence. Two weeks prior to the attacks, Colbert had relocated to Chester.

Following the murders, Colbert drove to Boston and attempted to jump off the Tobin Bridge before being talked down by police and taken to Mass General for psychiatric evaluation. Colbert confessed to the murders and pleaded insanity, insisting that a past sexual assault by an uncle clouded his ability to deal with the stress of being recently fired and his wife filing for divorce. He received a life sentence without the possibility of parole, unsuccessfully attempted suicide again while in jail, and twenty-one years later, died in prison, reportedly of cancer.

Derry: Anyone who's seen the movie *To Die For* with Nicole Kidman is familiar with the story of Pamela Ann (Wojas) Smart. She worked as a media coordinator for the Winnacunnet High School in Hampton, where she seduced 15-year-old student William "Billy" Flynn, reportedly threatening to break things off if he didn't murder her 24-year-old husband, Gregory (also referred to in the research material as Greggory or Gregg). Her motive: his death would save her from a messy divorce, and his $140,000 life insurance policy didn't hurt, either. Flynn recruited three friends to assist in the murder, which occurred May 1, 1990, at the couple's condo and was meant to look like a burglary gone wrong. Smart later admitted to the affair but claimed no knowledge of the murder plans. Secretly taped evidence from student Cecilia Pierce that contradicted Smart's testimony helped convict her, and she is currently serving a life sentence in Bedford Hills, NY. Her four accomplices have since been paroled or released.

Dover: When Howard Long moved from Massachusetts to New Hampshire in the early 1930s, he'd already committed two separate assaults on pre-teens, followed by stays in reformatories and hospitals for the criminally insane. Once in New Hampshire, and working as a filling station owner, Long committed two abductions, assaults, and murders: one of nine-year-old Armand Nadeau of Dover in 1936, and the other, in 1937, of ten-year-old Mark Neville Jensen of Leonia. In both cases, the boys' skulls had been crushed. After the police uncovered evidence linking him to the second killing, Long ultimately confessed to both murders. He was executed by hanging on July 14, 1939, at the New Hampshire State Prison in Concord. Capital punishment was abolished in New Hampshire in 2019; Long remains the last person executed in the state.

Epping: Sheila LaBarre is a convicted murderer who preyed upon developmentally disabled young men like Kenneth Countie (24) and Michael DeLoge (38), luring them to her home with the promise of sex and a place to stay, and then torturing and killing them and burning their remains. She rationalized this by claiming they were pedophiles, and she was an avenging angel sent by God. Police investigated LaBarre after receiving a report from Elaine Sommer, a Walmart employee. Sommer had recently noticed LaBarre pushing Countie in a wheelchair through the store, with the man looking cut up, bruised, and seemingly having trouble walking. That, coupled with a bizarre phone call they received from LaBarre days later that included a recording of Countie confessing to pedophilia, prompted police to check in.

When they arrived at the 115-acre farm Sheila had inherited from local chiropractor, Dr. Wilfred LaBarre, whose name she'd appropriated without the benefit of marriage, and who had died suddenly, leaving her all his possessions—they discovered piles of burning material, including potential evidence such as a human bone. LaBarre was arrested on April 2, 2006, and on June 20, 2008, despite pleas of insanity and childhood trauma caused by molestation, incest, and physical abuse, she was convicted on two counts of murder. LaBarre was sentenced to life in prison without the possibility of parole and is serving her time at the New Hampshire Correctional Facility for Women in Concord.

Gilmanton was the 1861 birthplace of Herman Webster Mudgett, better known as one of the country's first serial killers, H.H. Holmes. The professed killer of over 130 people, he also attended Phillips Exeter preparatory school in Exeter, graduating at the age of sixteen. (For more, see the Vermont chapter in this book, and the edition of *Vacations Can Be Murder* covering Illinois.)

Hampton: On May 14, 2011, Julianne McCrery checked into the Stone Gable Inn in Hampton with her son, Camden Hughes. She dosed the six-year-old boy with NyQuil and, once asleep, turned him over onto a pile of pillows and smothered him to death. Then, she drove the body up to South Berwick, ME, and left it in a secluded, wooded area. After a nationwide search for his identity, the boy's body was discovered, and witnesses remembered seeing Julianne's car in the area. McCrery said she had initially traveled to Maine from their home in Texas because it was the only place she could purchase castor beans. She claimed she planned to commit suicide by poisoning herself with the ricin-laced beans and killed her son only because she was the only person capable of raising him. Others alleged she considered the boy an inconvenience and, after the murder, hoped to proceed with her life without him. McCrery is currently serving a 45-year sentence at the New Hampshire Prison for Women in Goffstown.

Hampton Falls (now considered South Seabrook): Eliphaz Dow was characterized by the Selectmen of Hampton Falls as "an idle and disorderly person that neglects his calling, mispends (sic) his time, and takes no care to provide for his support."[1] On December 12th, 1754, at the home of his brother, Noah, Dow accidentally encountered his enemy, Peter Clough, who had previously accused him of killing his cow. Though Clough was a larger man, Dow accepted his invitation to fight. They went outside, upon the urging of Noah, where Dow clobbered Clough with his brother's hoe, killing him instantly.

Though he'd characterized the murder as self-defense, since Clough had often threatened his life, Dow was tried and convicted of murder in Portsmouth, where he became the first male to be hanged in New Hampshire on May 8th, 1755. There is a dispute as to the location of the gallows, which were either at the intersection of South Street and Sagamore Avenue or at Ward's Corner. He was buried in an unmarked grave.

Etna: Dartmouth College was rocked when two of their professors, Half Zantop (62) and Susanne Zantop (55), both originally from Germany, were stabbed to death in their home on January 27, 2001. Two high school students, James J. Parker (16), and Robert W. Tulloch (17), had arrived at their door posing as research surveyors but in truth, had intended to get the couple's PIN numbers, rob them to fund a move to Australia, and then murder them. They absconded with only $340 in cash but left behind incriminating evidence: distinctive knife sheaths and a bloody footprint. A guest arriving for dinner discovered the bodies. After a three-week investigation, the two teens were arrested and charged with first-degree murder. Parker's sentence was reduced to 25 to life for testifying against Tulloch, who received the mandatory sentence of life imprisonment without parole. Both were held at the New Hampshire State Prison for Men in Concord, but Parker was granted parole in 2024, having earned advanced degrees in prison, participating in artistic and sports activities, and developing inmate education guides.

Lake Ossipee: In 1916, six months after taking out a $20,000 joint life insurance policy with his third wife, Florence, stockbroker Frederick L. Small was en route to Boston when their two-story cottage on the south shore of Ossipee Lake burst into flames. Florence's body was found floating in the flooded basement; the floor on the main level had been compromised by the fire. Evidence of a timed arson device killed Small's alibi, and it was clear he'd taken no chances: the wife whose body he'd assumed would be lost in the flames appeared to have been chloroformed and shot, her skull crushed, and her neck strangled. A jury convicted Small of murder, and he was executed by hanging on January 15, 1918.

Manchester: In November 1914, Canadian-born Oscar J. Comery poisoned his 25-year-old wife Bertha, substituting her quinine with strychnine, though his motive remains unclear. He had a successful career in the burgeoning field of auto repair (though some references list him as a chauffeur), but had been philandering with several women, including one named Eunice Campbell. The death was originally considered caused by indigestion following a large meal, but minds changed once her clergyman went to the police and shared the deathbed discussion he'd had with Bertha, where she discussed her life's misgivings.

At that point, authorities exhumed Bertha's body from the Pine Grove Cemetery and found evidence of strychnine poisoning. At the time of his conviction, Oscar Comery was dating a woman he'd been seeing since she was twelve, a fact that contributed to the jury handing down a guilty verdict, The judge sentenced him to a punishment more severe than life in prison, in February of 1916, he was executed by hanging at New Hampshire State Prison, one of only three people in New Hampshire to receive that sentence in the 20th century.

Mont Vernon: On October 4, 2009, Steven Spader (17) and Christopher Gribble (19), the two founding members of the Disciples of Destruction, along with three recruits seeking to pass their initiation, randomly invaded the home of 42-year-old nurse, Kimberly Cates and her eleven-year-old daughter, Jaimie. Spader murdered Kimberly by slashing her thirty-six times with a machete. He later bragged about this to his fellow inmates while awaiting trial. He also left Jaimie severely maimed, cutting off portions of her left foot, splitting open her head, puncturing her lung, and breaking her jaw.

After the boys fled, Jaimie managed to stagger to the phone and call the police. Spader and Gribble buried their weapons, presumably hoping to use them again, but were identified, apprehended, and ultimately convicted of first-degree murder, conspiracy to commit murder, and attempted murder. This was due, in part, to the testimony of the three recruits, who turned against Spader in exchange for a plea agreement. They were sentenced to life plus seventy-six years. Spader declined to appeal or seek a lesser sentence, asserting it showed weakness, and it's reported that rather than seeking rehabilitation in prison, he attempted to recruit others to help him escape.

Multiple Locations around New Hampshire: In the 1980s, a number of women's bodies were found with multiple stab wounds in remote locations throughout New Hampshire. Locals feared that a serial killer was on the loose. These women have collectively been called victims of the Connecticut River Valley Killer, and a majority were seen hitchhiking before they disappeared. While there have been suspects, there has never been an arrest.

The New Hampshire victims included Cathy Millican (26), whose body was found in October 1979 in **New London**; Mary Critchley, a student whose remains were uncovered in July 1981 in **Unity**; Bernice Courtemanche (17), last seen in **Claremont** and discovered drowned on April 1986 near **Newport**, her body found by a fisherman near Sugar River; Courtemanche's personal nurse, Ellen Fried (26), who was last seen at Leo's Market in **Claremont** and discovered eighteen months later in **Kelleyville**; and Eva Morse (27), last seen near Route 12 in Claremont and whose body was found in April of 1986 in **West Unity**, 500 feet from where Critchley's body had been discovered five years before. Two other victims were found in Vermont.

Northwood: Known as the "Northwood Murderer," Franklin B. Evans was born in Strafford and lived an itinerant lifestyle before settling in Northwood at the home of his sister and her husband, Sylvester Day. In his previous travels, Evans had posed as a botanical physician and an Adventist preacher, but he was working as a laborer for local farmers when he was entranced by his fourteen-year-old niece, Georgianna Lovering. In 1872, despite an earlier unsuccessful attempt at seduction, Evans managed to lure Lovering to a forest to birdwatch. She was never seen alive again. Her strangled, raped, and mutilated corpse was found in a swamp, with other body parts hidden under a rock half a mile away.

Evans helped investigators find the remains, claiming a man from Kingston, named Webster, had killed Lovering, and Evans had helped him hide the body. When police eventually discounted that story, Evans confessed to Lovering's death, and later, to the 1850 abduction, rape, and murder of a five-year-old girl in Derry. Authorities believe he was guilty of additional attacks and murders in Maine and Massachusetts. He was convicted and hanged on February 18, 1874.

Pembroke: Joseph LaPage was a French-Canadian woodcutter living in New Hampshire who, in 1875, brutally raped and murdered a 17-year-old girl, Josie Langmaid, after assaulting her in the woods between their home and her school, Pembroke Academy. Her remains were discovered half a mile away in Suncook, her head removed and found about 400 yards from her mutilated body. Aspects of the murder resembled that of a schoolteacher named Marietta Ball, killed the previous year in St. Albans, VT. One of the tenants in Ball's boarding house recognized the similarities and tipped off the police. LaPage was arrested in Suncook, where he lived with his wife and children. He was convicted and hanged in Concord in March of 1878.

Portsmouth: Ruth Blay was a 31-year-old teacher from South Hampton.

On December 30, 1768, she became the last woman executed in the state of New Hampshire. Blay had given birth to a baby she later claimed was stillborn. She'd wrapped the infant girl's body in a blue quilt and hidden it under the floorboards of Benjamin Clough's barn, a makeshift schoolhouse in South Hampton, next to the house where she was staying. Schoolchildren found the body. Blay was convicted, not of murder but of concealing the birth of an illegitimate child. The execution took place at what's now South Cemetery in Portsmouth, and she was buried there in an unmarked grave. Much controversy surrounded the case, and the story of Ruth Blay became a rallying cry for those championing against injustice in the local community. The quilt is currently on display at the Portsmouth Historical Society.

Also in Portsmouth: The finding of a dead infant floating in a well in August of 1739 drew attention to two single women who had recently been pregnant (or so townspeople believed). Both Sarah Simpson (27) and Penelope Kenny (20) were accused of infanticide. Both women claimed their children had been stillborn: Simpson said she'd buried hers; Kenny claimed she'd tossed hers into the river. At the time, women engaging in sex before marriage, and giving birth to "bastard" children, were crimes dealt with harshly. Hiding evidence of stillbirths was a matter of survival. Nevertheless, both women were convicted, most likely imprisoned on Prison Lane, and hanged on December 27, 1739—the first convicts ever executed in the state of New Hampshire. The mother of the child discovered floating in the well was never found.

Smuttynose Island (Isles of Shoals): Louis Wagner, a fisherman, had once been a lodger at the home of John and Matthew Hontvet and Ivan Christensen on Smuttynose Island. It's believed he sailed back to the house in early March of 1873, in order to rob the home while the men were away, and the women were alone. Karen Christensen, asleep in the kitchen, awoke upon the intruder's entry. She was later found cut and battered, having been attacked with a chair. Maren Hontvet heard her sister's screams and pulled her into a bedroom, where both women, along with Karen's sister-in-law Anethe Christensen, were trapped. They tried to escape through a downstairs window, and the intruder killed Anethe with an ax just after she reportedly screamed the name "Louis." Only Maren escaped, and in pursuing her, the killer left a size-11 bloody footprint in the snow.

As the story goes, with $16 of stolen funds instead of the $500 he'd been hoping for, Wagner sailed back to Portsmouth and interacted with tenants at the Johnson Boarding House, where he was staying. He then traveled to Boston, where he was apprehended based based on Maren's account, and sent back back to Portsmouth. Though he proclaimed his innocence until the day he died, he was tried and convicted in Maine, where he was executed by hanging on June 25, 1875. The ax he supposedly used to kill Anethe is on display at the Portsmouth Athenaeum, but his guilt has been challenged, and many consider this an unsolved crime. The house where the murders took place burned down in 1885.

Want more New Hampshire crime? Check out Murderpedia at https://murderp edia.org/usa/new-hampshire.htm.

Read Before You Leave: A Sampling of New Hampshire True Crime Books

(listed alphabetically by author)

Note: Some of these books may cover crimes not discussed elsewhere in this guide.

- Benson, Michael. *The Burn Farm*. Pinnacle Books, 2012.
- Carey, Richard Adams. *In the Evil Day*. University Press of New England, 2015.
- Ferland, Dr. David. *Historic Crimes & Justice in Portsmouth, New Hampshire*. Arcadia Publishing, 2014.
- Flynn, Kevin. *Wicked Intentions*. Macmillan, 2009.
- Flynn, Kevin, and Rebecca Lavoie. *Notes on a Killing: Love, Lies, and Murder in a Small New Hampshire Town*. Berkley Books, 2013.
- ———. *Our Little Secret*. Penguin, 2010.
- Ginsburg, Philip E. *The Shadow of Death*. Open Road Media, 2018.
- Lehr, Dick, and Mitchell Zuckoff. *Judgment Ridge*. HarperCollins, 2009.
- Mallett, Renee. *The "Peyton Place" Murder*. WildBlue Press, 2021.
- ———. *Wicked New Hampshire*. Arcadia Publishing, 2020.
- Marvin, Carolyn. *Hanging Ruth Blay: An Eighteenth-Century New Hampshire Tragedy*. History Press Library Editions, 2010.
- Mayo, Matthew P. *Myths and Mysteries of New Hampshire: True Stories of the Unsolved and Unexplained*. Globe Pequot, 2014.

- McCrery, Julianne. *Goodnight, Sleep Tight! How to Fall Asleep and Go Back to Sleep When You Wake Up.* Trafford, 2009. (Note: not true crime, but written by a murderer.)
- O'Connor, Marianne. *Haunted Hikes of New Hampshire.* Peter E. Randall Publisher, 2019.
- Petrie, Janice. *Perfection to a Fault: A Small Murder in Ossipee, New Hampshire, 1916.*
- Seatales Publishing Company, 2000.
- Rutledge, Lyman V. *Moonlight Murder at Smuttynose.* Star King Press, 1958.
- Sawicki, Stephen. *Teach Me to Kill.* Self-published, 2019.
- Stanway, Eric. *Stone-Cold Murder.* Self-published, 2013.

Accommodations and Restaurants that are Crime/Justice-Related or Haunted

While there are no prisons converted into hotels in the state, here is a list of hotels that are haunted. Where ghosts congregate, there are probably unsettled souls, possibly due to violent deaths.

Haunted Accommodations

Bretton Woods

Omni Mount Washington Resort
310 Mount Washington Hotel Road, Bretton Woods
603-278-1000 or 800-843-6664
https://www.omnihotels.com/hotels/bretton-woods-mount-washington

Carolyn, the wife of former owner Joseph Stickney, can still be seen grieving, years after her death. Room 314 is said to be especially spirit-ridden.

Durham

Three Chimneys Inn and ffrost Sawyer Tavern
17 Newmarket Road, Durham
603-868-7800 or 888-399-9777
info@threechimneysinn.com
https://www.threechimneysinn.com

Dates back to 1649. The original owner's daughter drowned in the creek close to the property, and her spirit never left.

Gilford

Kimballs Castle Innkeeper's Cottage

The castle, which is closed, is at 59 Lockes Hill Road, Gilford, NH. Get details about booking accommodations from Patrick at:

https://www.airbnb.com/rooms/37801841?source_impression_id=p 3_1708820251_ROinRN8Th1SfQhum

Hart's Location

The Notchland Inn

2 Morey Road (off Route 302), Hart's Location

603-374-6131 or 800-866-6131

innkeepers@Notchland.com

https://notchland.com

Nancy Barton, who died in a snowstorm here, is said to write messages to guests on their steamy bathroom mirrors.

Jackson

Christmas Farm Inn and Spa

3 Blitzen Way, Jackson

603-383-4313

guestservices@christmasfarminn.com

https://christmasfarminn.com

The building dates back to 1778, and at one time, the red house on the property was used as the Jackson Jail. Guests say they've heard voices, the sound of children running, and have seen white floating apparitions.

Littleton

The Beal House Inn and Restaurant

2 West Main Street, Littleton

(603) 444-2661

info@thebealhouse.com

https://www.thebealhouseinn.com

The inn dates back to 1833. Look for objects moving and doors slamming, seemingly on their own.

Meredith

The Nutmeg Inn

80 Pease Road, Meredith

603-677-7245

innkeeper@nutmeginn-nh.com

https://www.nutmeginn-nh.com

Dating back to 1763, reportedly one of the stops on the Underground Railroad. Come say hi to Charlie, a friendly and feisty apparition who helps with building repairs.

Portsmouth

The Hotel Portsmouth

40 Court Street, Portsmouth

603-433-1200

stay@thehotelportsmouth.com

https://www.larkhotels.com/hotels/the-hotel-portsmouth

The hotel has gone through many iterations in the past 135+ years, including its use as a halfway house for released mental patients. If you're looking for apparitions, check out Suite 204. Don't be surprised to find elevators moving on their own, or a ghost sliding into bed beside you.

Tilton

Tilton Inn and Onions Pub & Restaurant

255 Main Street, Tilton

603-286-7774

tiltoninn@metrocast.net

https://www.thetiltoninn.com

The inn dates back to 1875 and was the site of three major fires over its lifetime, one that killed a pre-teen named Laura, who still lingers at the property. It's considered one of the most haunted hotels in the state.

Crime and Justice-Related Restaurants

Concord
Margarita's
1 Bicentennial Square, Concord
603-224-2821
https://www.margs.com/concord
From 1890-1975, the building served as a prison. The restaurant has a few tables tucked away in the old jail cells, and is also rumored to be haunted.

Newport
The Old Courthouse Restaurant
30 Main St, Newport
603-863-8360
theoldcourt@aol.com
http://eatatthecourthouse.com
The restaurant is fairly new (2004), but it's housed in the former Superior Court for Sullivan County, built in 1826.

Haunted Restaurants

Gilford
Ellacoya Barn and Grille
2667 Lakeshore Road, Gilford
603-293-8700
ellacoyabg@metrocast.net
https://www.ellacoyabandg.com
Beware of flying glasses!

Kingston

The Kingston 1686 House
127 Main Street, Kingston
603-642-3637
https://www.facebook.com/TheKingston1686HouseRestaurant
Once a residential home, psychics report multiple spirits dwell here.

Windham

The Windham Restaurant
59 Range Road, Windham
603-870-9270
windhamrestaurant@hotmail.com
https://www.windhamrestaurant.com
Rumored to be haunted by at least three ghosts, including Jacob, who fell down the front staircase after suffering a fatal heart attack; a little boy named William, who died inside after being hit by a horse-drawn carriage; and an unknown little girl.

For more choices, please note that some of the hotels listed in the Haunted Accommodations section, specifically the OMNI Mount Washington Resort in Bretton Woods, the Three Chimneys Inn in Durham, the Beal House Inn in Littleton, and the Tilton Inn in Tilton, also have restaurants.

Crime Tours and Paranormal Tours

North Conway

A Walk with Spirits Ghost Tour (Seasonal, Halloween, no other information available.)

Leaves from Main Street, North Conway. https://www.halloweennewe ngland.com/locations/a-walk-with-spirits-ghost-tour

Portsmouth

- Shadows and Stones Cemetery Tour:1 hour, all ages (may have been discontinued).
- Legends, Ghosts, and Graves Tour: 2 hours, all ages.

The above tours offered by New England Curiosities. Most tours are priced at $24 adults, $16 children, 16 and under, 603-343-7977, roxiezwicker@g mail.com

https://newenglandcuriosities.com/legendary-tours/historic-portsmo uth-legends-and-ghost-walk/

Self-Guided Haunted Walking Tour of Portsmouth:40-60 minutes, from $7.75, available through a smartphone app. Starts at Ceres Bakery, 51 Penhollow Street, and ends at the Portsmouth Brewery at 56 Market Street. Offered by WalkinTours, 855-957-1272, https://www.viator.com/to

urs/Portsmouth/Self-Guided-Haunted-Walking-Tour-in-Portsmouth/
d24529-222222P18

Deadwicks Spectral Stroll: (Seasonal, Halloween) 1 hour, $21, departs
from Deadwick's Ethereal Emporium at 19 Sheafe St, Portsmouth, 603-
319-6946 https://www.halloweennewengland.com/events/spectral-stro
ll-haunted-history-deadwicks-nh

*All prices are per person. Tour offerings, prices, times, age restrictions, and
meeting locations are subject to change.*

Police/Crime/Prison/Courthouse
Museums and Other Attractions

New Hampshire has no police, crime, or courthouse museums, though there had been a police motorcycle museum in Meredith that closed. There are memorial markers for crime victims listed under the Burial Sites section.

Gilmanton

Birthplace of H.H. Holmes

500 Province Road, Gilmanton

While a more complete version of Holmes' story will be covered in a different edition that covers Illinois, New Hampshire is notable as the place of his birth as Herman Webster Mudgett, born on May 16th, 1861. The tall, white-paneled house, which stands in the middle of town, was built in 1825 and is still a private home, so it is closed to the public. Please respect the privacy of the current residents. Across the street is Gilmanton Academy, where Holmes attended school. It is now home to the town's offices and the local historical society museum.

State and Federal Prisons of Note in New Hampshire

Concord

New Hampshire State Prison for Men
   281 North State Street, Concord
   The state's oldest prison facility, housing maximum-, medium-, and minimum- security prisoners. Best-known inmates have included Howard Long, who was executed here, as well as James J. Parker and Robert W. Tulloch, who murdered Half and Susanne Zantop. Parker has since been paroled.

New Hampshire State Prison for Women
   42 Perimeter Road, Concord
   Opened in 2018 to replace the old Goffstown facility, this prison houses maximum-, medium-, and minimum-security prisoners. Pamela Smart was imprisoned here until she was moved to the Bedford Hills (NY) Correctional Facility for Women in 1993. Sheila LaBarre and Julianne McCrery are also reportedly incarcerated here.

Notable Crime-and-Justice-Related Burial Sites

Plot locations included where available, burial sites not always included in itineraries.

Allenstown

Saint John the Baptist Cemetery
129 River Road, Allenstown
Burial site of Maryse Elizabeth Honeychurch, Marie Elizabeth Vaughn, and Sarah Lynn McWaters, all killed by Terry Rasmussen. Also, the burial site for murderer Joseph LaPage.

Center Osipee

Grant Hill Cemetery
12 Main Street, Center Osipee
Burial site of Florence Aileen Curry Small, victim of husband Frederick Small.

Charlestown

Pine Crest Cemetery
Old Claremont Road, Charlestown
Burial Site of Eva Marie Morse, thought to be a victim of the yet-to-be-apprehended Connecticut River Valley Killer.

Claremont

Mountain View Cemetery
Located between Main Street and North Street in Claremont
Burial site of Bernice Courtemanche (Section Z, Lot 19A), thought to be a victim of the yet-to-be-apprehended Connecticut River Valley Killer.

Colebrook

Memorial to the Victims of Carl Drega
6 Bridge Street, Colebrook
In the small park outside the News and Sentinel offices, a black stone rectangle bears the portraits of all four of Carl Drega's victims, including editor Dennis Joos and Vickie Bunnell.

Saint Brendan's Catholic Cemetery
5 South Main Street, Colebrook
Burial site of Carl Drega victim, Scott Edward Phillips.

Concord

(Calvary and Blossom Hill are a pair of adjacent cemeteries at the same address.)

Calvary Cemetery
207 North State Street, Concord

Burial site for Oscar Joseph Comery, murderer. (single grave, Row 5, next to wall).

Blossom Hill Cemetery
  207 North State Street, Concord
  Burial site of the four victims of James Colbert: Mary Jayne Jenovese Colbert, Patricia Joyce Colbert, Elise Corinne Colbert, and Emily Rebecca Colbert, all in Section N.

Derry

Forest Hill Cemetery
  Cemetery Road (off East Derry Road), Derry
  Burial site of Gregory (Gregg) Smart (Sec. 30 Rutter Ave, Plot 51A So Half, Grave 3).

Dover

Saint Charles Cemetery
  Old Rochester Road, Dover
  Burial site of Armand Nadeau, victim of Howard Long.

Groveton

Northumberland Cemetery
  328 Lancaster Road, Groveton
  Burial site of murderer Carl Drega (Plot E-5).

Manchester

Pine Grove Cemetery
  765 Brown Avenue, Manchester
  Burial site of Dorothy Rosamond Crawford Koch, allegedly killed by

John Walter Bardgett (Plot 873 One West (Section 83 master map).
Burial site of murderer, Howard Long (Plot 3662).
Burial site of Bertha Catherine Schaller Comery, victim of husband, Oscar Comery.

Mont Vernon

Greenlawn Cemetery
1-7 Cemetery Road, Mont Vernon
Burial site of Kimberly L. Piasecki Cates, victim of Steven Spader and Christopher Gribble.

Northwood

Harvey Lake Cemetery
First New Hampshire Turnpike (Route 4), Northwood
Burial site of Sylvester Day and his wife, relatives, and caretakers of Georgianna Lovering.

Portsmouth

South Cemetery (a collection of five small cemeteries including Proprietors Burying Ground, Elmwood, Harmony Grove, Sagamore, and Cotton Cemeteries).
Corner of Sagamore and South, Portsmouth
Harmony Grove: Burial site of both Karen and Anethe Christensen, the two victims of the Smuttynose murders. To find the site, walk alongside the short rock road that delineates the cemetery at Sagamore Avenue until you find the tombstone of James M. Pickering. From there, take the grassy path to the left for a few hundred feet. The graves face the path on the left.

Proprietors Burying Ground: Burial site of Ruth Blay. The highest point on South Street, now South Cemetery, was the site of her hanging.

Calvary Cemetery
  990 Middle Road, Portsmouth
  Burial site of Mark Neville Jensen, victim of Howard Long (Section B, Lot 20, Grave 5).

Suncook

The memorial marker for Josie Langmaid, victim of Joseph LaPage, is on Academy Road, directly across from the driveway entrance to the Three Rivers School at 243 Academy Road.

Putting it All Together: Itineraries

Itinerary: True Crime Tour of Southwestern and South-Central New Hampshire

This tour falls 37 miles short of completing a circle, starting north and heading west, then southeast before swinging back to the northwest.

We start in **New London**, where the body of one of the Connecticut River Valley Killer's victims, Cathy Millican, was found at the Chandler Brook Wetland Preserve. Drive southwest to **Newport,** where Bernice Courtemanche's body was found by a fisherman in the woods, just off Cat Hole Hill Road, and where Ellen Fried's body was found near the banks of the Sugar River in the village of **Kelleyville**. While in Newport, check out the New Courthouse Restaurant at 30 Main Street. It's housed in the former Superior Courthouse for Sullivan County, built in 1826.

Head west to **Claremont**, where two more of the Connecticut River Valley Killer's victims were last seen alive: hitchhiker Bernice Courtemanche and her personal nurse, Ellen Ruth Fried. Fried shopped at Leo's Market at 130 Main Street, and later, her abandoned car was found on Jarvis Hill Road near a payphone she'd used. Courtemanche is buried at the Mountain View Cemetery, located between Main and North Streets. Drive south and pass through **Unity**, where Mary Critchley's remains were found in July 1981, in the woods off Unity Stage Road. Eva Morse's remains were discovered in **West Unity**, just five hundred feet away. Both are assumed to be victims of that same unidentified killer.

Next, head west to **North Charlestown**, where Eva Morse was last seen hitchhiking along Route 12. You can visit her grave to the south at the Pine Crest Cemetery on Old Claremont Road in **Charlestown**, where she was laid to rest. Next, drive southeast to **Mont Vernon**, where Steven Spader and Christopher Gribble, along with three initiates of the Disciples of Destruction, randomly invaded the 0-50 block of Trow Road, home of 42-year-old nurse Kimberly Cates and her eleven-year-old daughter Jaimie, murdering Cates and leaving Jaimie maimed. Cates is buried at Greenlawn Cemetery at 1-7 Cemetery Road.

Travel northeast to **Bedford** to view the exterior of Harborside-Northwood Nursing home at 30 Colby Court, where John Walter Bardgett interned and was accused of murdering three elderly patients. Further northeast in **Manchester**, the apartment at 925 Hayward Street is where Terry Rasmussen, passing himself off as "Bob Evans," lived with Denise Beaudin and her daughter Lisa in the early 1980s. Manchester is also where Oscar J. Comery poisoned his 25-year-old wife Bertha at their home at 128 Armory Street (though employment records from the Amoskeag Manufacturing Co. list her home as 761 Belmont). Her body was exhumed from the Pine Grove Cemetery at 765 Brown Avenue when authorities suspected poisoning post-burial. This is also the burial site of Dorothy Rosamond Crawford Koch, one of John Walter Bardgett's victims, as well as murderer Howard Long.

Continue north to **Bow**, where you can drive past 85 Bow Bog Road. the house and adjoining land owned by Carl Drega that led to so many zoning disputes, it inspired his vendetta against government officials that culminated in a mass shooting incident. In **Suncook** to the east, Joseph LaPage lived with his wife and children and was arrested for the murder of Josie Langmaid, who was buried in a graveyard in what's now Pinewood Road. The town placed a memorial obelisk across the street from the Three

Rivers School at 243 Academy Road, where her body was discovered. Once there, you'll find directions to the spot where her head was found.

Travel northeast to **Allenstown**, where four bodies (the Allenstown Four) were hidden for years in oil barrels in Bear Brook State Park. Three of the victims were Marlyse Elizabeth Honeychurch and her two daughters, Marie Elizabeth Vaughn and Sarah Lynn McWaters, murdered by Terry Rasmussen. Their gravesites are at Saint John the Baptist Cemetery at 129 River Road, where you can also visit the burial site of murderer Joseph LaPage. Drive northwest to **Pembroke**, where LaPage murdered Josie Langmaid after assaulting her somewhere in the woods at or near Gile's Swamp, located between their home on Buck Street and her school, Pembroke Academy.

The tour ends to the northwest in the capital city of **Concord**, home of two state prisons: one for men at 281 North State Street, where James J. Parker, Robert W. Tulloch, and Howard Long were imprisoned, and another for women at 42 Perimeter Road, where Pamela Smart, Sheila LaBarre, and Julianne McCrery have been jailed. On the 0-50 block of Merrimack Street, James Colbert murdered his wife and three daughters, and they're all buried at the Blossom Hill Cemetery at 207 North State Street. The adjacent Calvary Cemetery (same address) is the final resting place of murderer Oscar Joseph Comery. Lighten your visit with a stop at Margarita's at 1 Bicentennial Square, where some of the tables are set in the old jail cells of the former prison, which closed in 1975. It's also said to be haunted.

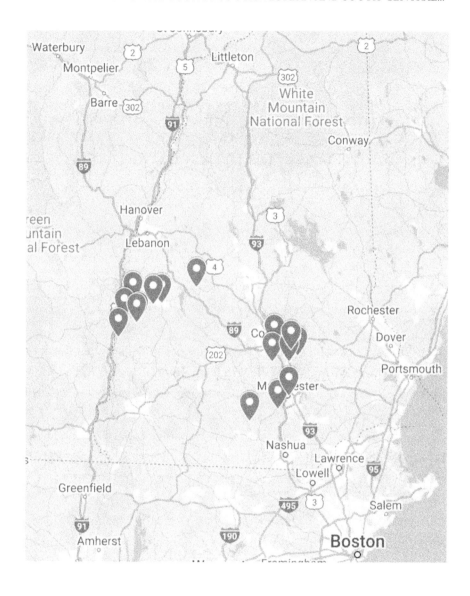

Itinerary: True Crime Tour of Southeastern and Central New Hampshire

(This is not a continuation of the tour above. To combine the two, you would need to drive 35 miles south to start the tour that follows.)

Begin your tour of southeastern New Hampshire in Rockingham County. In **Windham**, stop for lunch at the Windham Restaurant at 59 Range Road, which is said to be haunted. Then continue north to **Derry,** where Pamela Smart's husband, Gregory (Gregg), was murdered at the Summerhill Condominiums on Misty Morning Drive by William "Billy" Flynn, at the behest of Pamela Smart, who had seduced him. Smart is buried at Forest Hill Cemetery on Cemetery Road.

Drive northeast to **Kingston** and grab a bite with apparitions at the Kingston 1686 House at 127 Main Street, and then head north to **Epping**, where Sheila LaBarre inherited a 115-acre farm on the 0-100 area of Red Oak Hill Lane and tortured, then murdered, developmentally disabled young men she insisted were pedophiles. The Wal-Mart at 35 Fresh River Road is where witnesses saw her pushing one of her victims in a wheelchair.

Travel southeast to **South Seabrook** (once called **Hampton Falls),** where Eliphaz Dow murdered his enemy Peter Klough with a hoe outside the home of Dow's brother Noah, located at what's now Lower Collins Street.

According to the local historical society, the exact house no longer stands.

Continue northeast to **Hampton** and the Winnacunnet High School at 1 Alumni Drive, where Pamela Smart worked and met Billy Flynn. Hampton is also where Julianne McCrery murdered her son Camden Hughes at the Stone Gable Inn at 869 Lafayette Rd. (If you want to follow her path, drive north to Dennett Road in **South Berwick, ME**. She left the body in a secluded area of woods, 32 feet from the road.)

Head further northeast to **Portsmouth,** where you can spend the night at the haunted Hotel Portsmouth at 40 Court Street and enjoy the haunted ghost tours offered by New England Curiosities and WalkinTours. They'll likely mention Eliphaz Dow, who was the first male to be hanged in the state. There is a dispute as to the location of the gallows, which were either at the intersection of South Street and Sagamore Avenue or at Ward's Corner. He was buried in an unmarked grave.

Burial sites you *can* visit include those of Karen and Anethe Christensen at South Cemetery (a collection of five small cemeteries at the corner of Sagamore and South). These were the two victims of the Smuttynose murders. Ruth Blay is buried in an unmarked grave at Proprietors Burying Ground, part of South Cemetery. The highest point on South Street (now part of South Cemetery) was the site of her hanging. Benjamin Clough's barn, where she buried her stillborn infant—the reason she was hanged—is gone, but the quilt that's assumed to have been found with the baby is on display at the Portsmouth Historical Society at 10 Middle Street. And at Calvary Cemetery at 990 Middle Road, you can pay your respects to Mark Neville Jensen, victim of Howard Long.

Also in Portsmouth: While there's no information on the location of the well where the dead baby was found floating, the incident ultimately led to the hanging of Sarah Simpson and Penelope Kenny for different infanticides. Before their executions, both women were most likely imprisoned on Prison Lane (currently the site of the Music Hall at 28

Chestnut Street) and were hanged from a large tree on the corner of Middle Road and South Street. From Portsmouth, if you are visiting in season, there are one-hour crossings you can take for the six-mile boat trip to Smuttynose Island, part of the **Isles of Shoals**, where fisherman Louis Wagner reportedly murdered Karen and Anethe Christensen.

Technically, the Isles of Shoals belong to Maine, but the tours leave from New Hampshire, run by the Isles of Shoals Steamship Company (https://islesofshoals.com/) and Portsmouth Harbor Cruises (https://po rtsmouthharbor.com/). According to Atlas Obscura, visitors are allowed to walk the privately owned island during daylight hours when following the rules posted at the cove. There is a walking trail available during the summer season.

Wagner eventually sailed back home and spoke with tenants at the Johnson Boarding House at 25 Water Street (now Marcy Street), where he was staying. You can see the ax, the supposed murder weapon, at the Portsmouth Athenaeum at 9 Market Square.

From Portsmouth, paranormal fans may wish to take a side trip northeast into Strafford County to **Durham** to spend the night and/or dine at the rumored-to-be-haunted Three Chimneys Inn at 17 Newmarket Road. If not, head northwest to **Northwood**, where Franklin B. Evans, aka the "Northwood Murderer," lived at the home of Sylvester Day, the brother of Evans' first wife, on Bennett Bridge Road on the edge of Bow Lake. (The house stands on the right-hand side of the road just before an old stone bridge.) Evans murdered Day's niece (though some accounts place her as his sister-in-law), Georgianna Lovering. The Days are buried at Harvey Lake Cemetery on First New Hampshire Turnpike (Route 4).

Head north into Belknap County. The first stop is **Laconia**, where Howard Long picked up ten-year-old Mark Neville Jensen at the corner of Union Avenue and Main Street before murdering the boy. Further northwest in **Gilmanton**, you can view the exterior of the birthplace of serial killer H.H. Holmes at 500 Province Road. Across the street is Gilmanton Academy, where he attended school; it's now home to the town's offices and local historical society museum.

Further northwest is **Gilford** (changed from the original Guilford), where Mark Neville Jensen's body, with crushed skull, was found in a wooded area. You can dine with spirits at the Ellacoya Barn & Grille at 2667 Lakeshore Road or stay at the Kimballs Castle Innkeeper's Cottage. The castle, which is closed, is at 59 Lockes Hill Road. Get details for directions to the cottage from Patrick at:

https://www.airbnb.com/rooms/37801841?source_impression_id=p 3_1708820251_ROinRN8Th1SfQhum.

Further northwest, you'll find the haunted Nutmeg Inn at 80 Pease Road in **Meredith**. Then, head south via New Hampton to **Tilton,** where the Tilton Inn and its pub and restaurant at 255 Main Street are also reported to be home to a ghost or two.

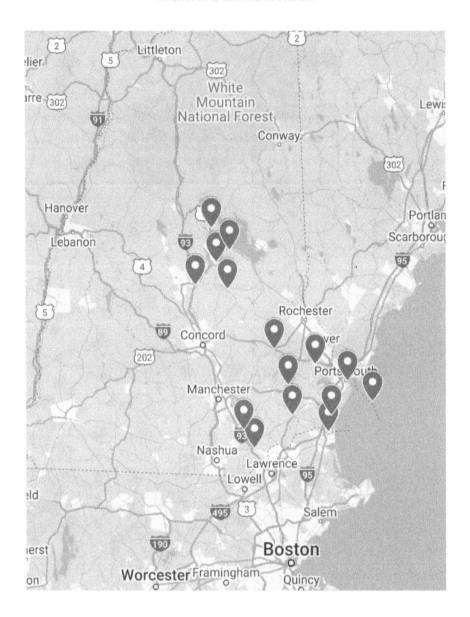

Itinerary: True Crime Tour of North and Central New Hampshire

This tour starts north, moves south, and then curves back north, creating a near circle. We start in Coos County in **Colebrook**, where Carl Drega's 1997 shooting spree started in the parking lot of LaPerle's IGA supermarket at what's now 64 Trooper Leslie G. Lord Memorial Highway. It continued on to 1 Bridge Street, where he shot Vickie Bunnell and Dennis Joos. You can see the small black stone rectangular memorial to the victims at 6 Bridge Street, in a small park outside the News and Sentinel, where Joos worked as editor. One of his victims, Scott Edwards Phillips, is buried at Saint Brendan's Catholic Cemetery at 5 South Main Street. Drega was ultimately killed in a shootout with police after he abandoned his vehicle near Dennis Pond in Brunswick, Vermont, and tried to ambush police, shooting from a nearby hill.

Before that final shootout, Drega had traveled home to 385 US Route 3 in **Columbia** and burnt it down, leaving the booby-trapped barn with its arsenal of explosive materials untouched.

To see his burial site, travel south to the Northumberland Cemetery at 328 Lancaster Road in **Groveton**.

To the southwest in Grafton County, the Beal House Inn in **Littleton** is rumored to be haunted. So is the Omni Mount Washington Resort in **Bretton Woods** (especially Room 314), though it will require a half-hour side trip east.

Continue southwest to **Etna**, where Dartmouth College professors Half and Susanne Zantop were stabbed by two high school students in their home on the 100 block of Trescott Road. Driving east to **Lake Ossipee** in Carroll County, you can drive by the south shore of the lake to 60 Pine Shore Road, the site of the house Frederick L. Small boobytrapped to kill his wife, Florence. That house burnt to the ground, and Mrs. Small is buried at Grant Hill Cemetery at 12 Main Street in **Center Ossipee**.

If you're traveling around Halloween, drive north to **North Conway** to take part in the Walk with Spirits Ghost Tour, offered by Halloween New England. Otherwise, end your tour by continuing northwest to **Jackson** to commune with ghosts at either the Christmas Farm Inn and Spa at 3 Blitzen Way, or the Notchland Inn in **Hart's Location** on 3 Morely Road off Route 302.

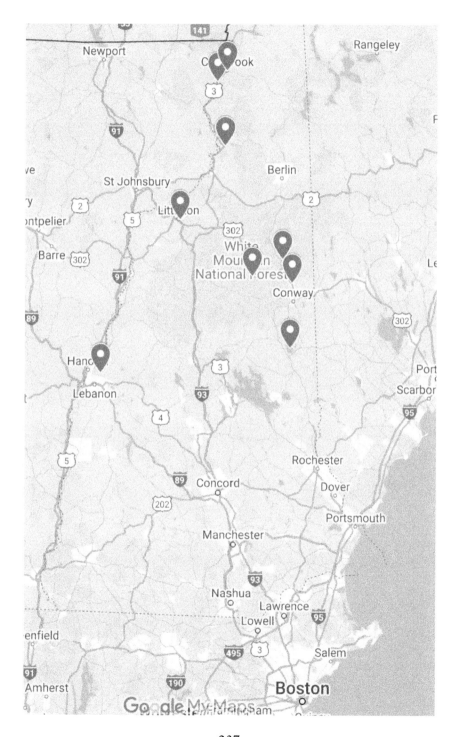

New Hampshire Victim Resources

This is a noncomprehensive summary of services available to victims of crime in New Hampshire. Information was taken directly from their websites. Visit/contact agencies for complete information and note that some programs offered by certain contractors focus on specific geographic areas. Some resource categories and content may overlap. Inclusion does not equate to recommendation.

Victim Services

- Office for Victims of Crime: see https://ovc.ojp.gov/states/new-hampshire
- New Hampshire Coalition against Domestic and Sexual Violence/-Granite State Services: see https://www.nhcadsv.org/support-services---programs.html
- VICTIMS, INC. (The Joan Ellis Victim Assistance Network): see http://www.victimsinc.org/services-1.

Crime-centric List of Resources

Child Abuse

- Court Appointed Special Advocates (CASA) of New Hampshire is a nonprofit that recruits, trains, and supports community volunteers to serve as advocates for children throughout the state who have

experienced abuse or neglect, 800-626-4600. see https://casanh.org/
- Granite State Children's Alliance—New Hampshire's Network of Child Advocacy Centers: Community partnerships dedicated to pursuing the truth in child abuse cases and coordinating social services for child victims of crime. see https://cac-nh.org/.
- Vinelink: Repository of services for abused children, see: https://vinelink.vineapps.com/search/providers;siteRefId=NHSWVINE;serviceCategory=CHILD_SERV;stateServed=NH
- New Hampshire Department of Health and Human Services (DHHS): 800-894-5533 or 603-271-6562, see https://www.dhhs.nh.gov/programs-services/child-protection-juvenile-justice.

Civil Legal Help for People with Low Income

- NH Legal Assistance (NHLA): NHLA's mission is to fulfill America's promise of equal justice by providing civil legal services to New Hampshire's poor, including education and empowerment, advice, representation, and advocacy for systemic change. 800-562-3174, see https://www.nhla.org.
- Legal Assistance—various resources from the New Hampshire Judicial Branch: see https://www.courts.nh.gov/self-help/getting-started/legal-assistance.

Domestic Violence

- Domestic Shelters: List of resources and more, see https://www.domesticshelters.org/help.
- National Domestic Abuse Hotline: 800-799-7233 or text START to 88788, see https://www.thehotline.org/?utm_source=youtube&utm_medium=organic&utm_campaign=domestic_violence.
- Vine lists numerous services, see https://vinelink.vineapps.com/search/providers;siteRefId=NHSWVINE;serviceCategory=VICTIM_ASST;stateServed=NH.

- Haven: Serves women, men, children, and all people of marginalized genders and identities affected by domestic and sexual violence. Services Rockingham and Strafford Counties. 603-994-SAFE (7233), see https://havennh.org.
- New Hampshire Coalition Against Domestic and Sexual Violence: 603-224-8893, see https://www.nhcadsv.org.
- NH Domestic and Sexual Violence Helpline Center provides free and confidential support services to anyone impacted by domestic violence, sexual assault, stalking, human trafficking, or child abuse. 866-644-3574, see https://www.thehotline.org.

Drunk Driving Victims

- Mothers Against Drunk Driving: 877-MADD-HELP (877-623-3435) see https://madd.org/new-hampshire.

Elder Abuse

- Report Adult Abuse or Neglect by contacting APS Central Intake: 603-271-7014 or 800-949-0470 (in-state only). See https://www.dhhs.nh.gov/report-concern/adult-abuse.
- New Hampshire Coalition Against Domestic and Sexual Violence: also helps elder abuse victims, 603-224-8893, see https://www.nhcadsv.org/elder-abuse.html.

Fraud

- New Hampshire Banking Department: see https://www.banking.nh.gov/consumer-assistance/avoiding-scams-and-fraud.
- New Hampshire Attorney General's Consumer Protection Hotline: 888-468-4454 or email the New Hampshire Attorney General at doj-cpb@doj.nh.gov.
- Annual Credit Report Request Service from Annual Credit Report.com:

see https://www.annualcreditreport.com/protectYourIdentity.actio
n.

- National Consumers League Fraud Center (not limited to New Hampshire): see https://fraud.org.

Identity Theft

- Identity Theft Resource Center: see https://www.idtheftcenter.org.
- New Hampshire Department of Justice: see https://www.doj.nh.gov/
citizens/consumer-protection-antitrust-bureau/identity-theft.

Online Criminal Case Status, Inmate Status, and Sex Offender Registry

- New Hampshire Judicial Branch Case Access Portal: see https://odyp
a.nhecourt.us/portal.
- More Information on accessing court cases: see https://www.nhd.usc
ourts.gov/access-case-files.
- Public Access to Court Electronic Documents (PACER): Information at
https://www.nhd.uscourts.gov/access-case-files. Get a PACER login
and password online by registering at https://pacer.psc.uscourts.gov/
pscof/registration.jsf or by calling 800-676-6856.
- For Inmate status, check the New Hampshire Department of Corrections site at https://business.nh.gov/inmate_locator.
- NH Sex Offender Registry Search: see https://business.nh.gov/NSO
R/.

Sexual Assault

- National Sexual Assault Hotline: 800-656-4673, see https://rainn.org.
- Bridges: domestic and sexual violence support, dedicated to helping
victims and survivors of domestic and sexual violence. Helpline: 603-
883-3044, https://www.bridgesnh.org.

- National Human Trafficking Hotline: 888-373-7888 or text 233733 or email help@humantraffickinghotline.org: see https://humantraffickinghotline.org/en. Search for local NH services at https://humantraffickinghotline.org/en/find-local-services.
- uSafeUS: Free smartphone app that places key resources directly into the hands of NH college students who have experienced sexual assault, as well as their friends, family, and others who can help. uSafeUS also offers interactive safety features and information on how to support friends and other loved ones in the aftermath of an assault, see https://www.usafeus.org.
- NH Adult Sexual Assault Survivors Booklet: see https://www.doj.nh.gov/sites/g/files/ehbemt721/files/inline-documents/sonh/sexual-assault-survivors-booklet.pdf.
- The Reality of Sexual Assault in New Hampshire: Includes resources. See https://www.doj.nh.gov/sites/g/files/ehbemt721/files/inline-documents/sonh/reality-of-sexual-assault-in-nh.pdf.
- New Hampshire Sexual Assault Survivors' Rights: see https://www.doj.nh.gov/sites/g/files/ehbemt721/files/inline-documents/sonh/new-hampshire-sexual-assault-survivors-rights.pdf.

Survivors of Homicide

- Survivors of Homicide Guide: An 80-page comprehensive guide to what to do and where to go for help, see https://mm.nh.gov/files/uploads/doj/remote-docs/homicide-survivor-guide.pdf.

Victim Advocacy

- New Hampshire Coalition Against Domestic & Sexual Violence/Granite State Services & Programs: see https://www.nhcadsv.org/support-services---programs.html.

Victim Compensation

- The New Hampshire Victims' Compensation Program helps innocent victims of violent crime with expenses directly related to crime injuries. See https://www.doj.nh.gov/bureaus/victims-compensation-progra m.

Victim Notification System

- Victim Services Unit: 603-271-7351 or 888-NH NOTICE (888-646-6842); email victim.services@doc.nh.gov, see https://www.correctio ns.nh.gov/victim-services/about-victim-services.
- Victim Notification System (VNS): An automated system that keeps registered victims informed of a defendant's status from arrest to release. (866) 365-4968, see https://www.notify.usdoj.gov.
- Victim Information and Notification Everyday (VINE): A free service that provides information about offenders and criminal cases. Call 800-542-9904, or use the VINELink mobile app. See https://vinelink. vineapps.com/search/NH/Person.

Victim Rights and Services Complaints

- Victims's Rights are discussed at https://www.courts.nh.gov/student s/guide-new-hampshire-courts/victims-rights.
- Victim Services: Contact the New Hampshire Department of Corrections' Victim Services by calling (603) 271-7351, toll-free at 1-888-NH NOTICE (888-646-6842), or by emailing victim.services@doc.nh.gov. See victim.services@doc.nh.gov.

Victim/Witness Assistance Program

- New Hampshire Department of Justice lists several programs that provide orientation, information, and support throughout the judicial process within the Superior Courts and in some District Courts, see https://www.doj.nh.gov/bureaus/office-victimwitness-assistance/vi

ctimwitness-assistance-programs.

Programs subject to change or end without notice.

Chapter 5: Vacations Can Be Murder in Rhode Island

Rhode Island Crime Statistics

If you want to travel somewhere safe, Rhode Island might be a great choice. In 2023, Wisevoter.com ranked it the fifth safest state in the country. According to Safewise.com, you had a 2 in 1,000 chance of being the victim of a violent crime and a 13.1 in 1,000 chance of having something happen to your property.

Neighborhoodscout.com breaks these numbers down: in 2023, Rhode Island experienced 1,885 violent crimes (16 murders, 416 rapes, 269 robberies, and 1,184 assaults) and 14,058 property crimes. That's a better bet than, say, New Mexico, which Forbes ranked as the most dangerous state in 2023, where the violent crime rate was 7.8 per 1,000 and the property crime rate was 29.84.

Safewise.com lists Rhode Island's safest cities as Bristol, South Kingstown, Cumberland, North Kingstown, and East Providence. Meanwhile, Travelsafe-abroad.com warns that the state's most dangerous cities are Woonsocket, Pawtucket, Providence, Central Falls, and Newport.

Summary of serial killings, mass shootings, mob hits, and other crimes
(listed alphabetically by location)

For those traveling throughout Rhode Island, here is just a sampling of true crime that occurred in the state. What's most notable about these summaries is the number of killers who have preyed upon small children and vulnerable women. Should you wish to visit these cities, exact addresses, where available, are listed in the "Itineraries" section at the end of the chapter:

Barrington: James Mitchell DeBardeleben II was a kidnapper, rapist, torturer, counterfeiter, and suspected serial killer, a guy FBI profiler Roy Hazelwood described as "the best documented sexual sadist since the Marquis de Sade."[1] He spent much of his time in shopping malls passing counterfeit bills, earning him the nickname, the "Mall Passer."

Once he was arrested in 1983, the Secret Service searched his storage locker for his counterfeiting equipment and found something far darker. Audiotapes and photographs of sex slayings, a "death kit" for quick murders on the run, even a bloody pair of women's underwear—evidence that linked him to as many as eighteen-years-worth of serious sexual crimes and murders in multiple states, including Louisiana, Michigan, Delaware, New York, and North Carolina.

His main crime in Rhode Island (for which he was later charged but not tried) was the murder of Edna Therrel MacDonald, a real estate agent who met a "Mr. Peter Morgan" on the evening of April 29. 1971, allegedly to show a home on Heritage Road in Barrington. During their meeting, evidence suggests that after a struggle, McDonald was bound and gagged, suffered a blow to her head, and had been strangled with one leg of her stockings. (This was not the last time he murdered a real estate agent; Jean Mcphaul met a similar fate in Bossier City, Louisiana. She was left hanging from the rafters in the attic of a For Sale home.)

In 1988, DeBardeleben was convicted and sentenced to 375 years in prison. In 2011, while serving that sentence, he died of pneumonia at the Federal Medical Center in North Carolina.

Also in Barrington, Christopher Hightower (42) was a commodities broker who also taught Sunday school at the local congregational church and counseled troubled teens. On September 20, 1991, he paid a visit to former pal and client, patent attorney Ernest Brendel. Hightower shot him with a high-powered crossbow, strangled his drugged and sleeping wife Alice

250

with her own scarf, and then kidnapped and buried their eight-year-old daughter Emily alive. And he still wasn't done.

Next, he drove down to the Connecticut home of Brendel's sister, Christine Scriabine, and tried to scam her out of a fortune. He claimed Brendel owed the mob money and that his family, along with Hightower's own sons and wife Susan, had been kidnapped and would not be returned until the money was repaid. He described himself as the intermediary, negotiating a $300,000 ransom for their release. Hightower told Christine not to call the authorities, but the first thing she did when he left was call the FBI.

What came out was, not only was Hightower not an intermediary, but he was also a murderer and a fraudster. He had mismanaged Brendel's funds, prompting Brendel to file a complaint that could have cost Hightower his license. Not only that, but he was in debt, and his estranged wife had filed a restraining order against him because he'd told her he'd paid $6,000 to a hitman to eliminate her.

Hightower was arrested the next Monday, September 23, 1991, brazenly driving Brendel's bloodstained Toyota. The victims' bodies were found weeks afterward in a shallow grave, less than a half mile from their home. In 1993, Hightower was convicted of three murders and sentenced to life in prison without the possibility of parole. That prison stay began at the high-security unit of the Adult Correctional Institution in Cranston, but a month in, he was attacked, and later moved to a prison in Illinois.

Burrillville: On November 9, 1985, Janine Callahan (24) left her home in Natick, Massachusetts, to walk to her job at Zayle's. A month later, her body was found at the end of a Burrillville street under a discarded Christmas tree, naked except for a pair of gym socks. Police were unable to determine the cause of death due to the amount of trauma to the body. They believed the killer lived nearby. The case is still under investigation.

Cranston: Amasa Sprague was the owner of the A&W Sprague Textile firm and a member of an influential Rhode Island family. But December

31st, 1843, turned out to be less than the beginning of a happy new year because when Sprague left his 28-room mansion, he was murdered. His attacker beat him, shot his wrist, and left his bludgeoned body face down on the street.

One person with a motive for the murder was John Gordon, who worked for the victim. Sprague had induced the city council to remove the liquor license of an establishment run by Gordon's brother, Nicholas. Despite the evidence being circumstantial, Gordon was tried at the Old State House, convicted, and hanged in the state prison yard on February 14, 1845, an execution that turned controversial in the ensuing years.

Rhode Island abolished the death penalty in 1852, and even though it has been reintroduced and shot down since, Gordon was the last person executed in Rhode Island. When the Rhode Island General Assembly considered reintroducing it in the 1990s, this case was brought up as an example against doing so.

In 2011, a play called "The Murder Trial of John Gordon," penned by playwright Ken Dooley, triggered State Representative Peter Martin to introduce a resolution granting Gordon a posthumous pardon due to allegations of anti-Roman Catholic and anti-Irish immigrant bias that may have played into his conviction and execution. Governor Lincoln Chafee officially pardoned Gordon that year. Historians speculate that the actual killer was Sprague's brother William II, a politician who was frustrated when Sprague refused to expand their business.

Cumberland: Stanley "Stosh" Stowik Sr., an 80-year-old lifelong Cumberland resident, retired town employee, and U.S. Navy Korean war veteran, was killed in his home on Oct. 10, 2015. The case remains unsolved, but police have listed his next-door neighbor at the time, convicted felon William Donnelly, as a person of interest.

They had good reason: shortly after the murder, Donnelly was charged with a neighborhood break-in, including theft of a gun, but the case was dismissed due to lack of evidence. Donnelly has a history of murder dating back to his 1982 conviction for the death of Hyung U. Kim, his supervisor at a surgical supply company in Providence. He was due to serve 18 years, but was released in 1988 due to his defense attorneys not being advised of a pertinent psychiatric report concerning his mental competency.

In 1993, Donnelly was found guilty of embezzlement from his workplace, a Smithfield gas station, and after Stowik's murder, he was arrested for making a $250 fraudulent credit card purchase of a chainsaw at Lowes in Massachusetts. The credit card did not belong to Stowik.

Lincoln: On August 10, 2011, a Lincoln Woods park ranger approached a car parked in a driveway just outside the park entrance because it had sat for hours with its windshield wipers running. He called in nearby State Police, who noticed blood on the bumper and forced open the trunk to discover the body of Ronny Almonte (25) of both Providence and Pawtucket. Almonte had been murdered "execution style": repeatedly shot in the face, his hands bound behind his back. His family believed he was targeted by an acquaintance who blamed him for stolen drug money. The case remains unsolved.

Newport: Newport is the land of the wealthy, so it's no surprise that scandal lurks within its city limits. True crime-wise, it's perhaps best known as the site of the case against Danish-born British lawyer and socialite Claus von Bülow. A former assistant to J. Paul Getty, von Bülow was convicted and later cleared of twice trying to kill his wife, Sunny, by injecting her with insulin to aggravate her hypoglycemia (low blood sugar). It's been reported that Mrs. Von Bülow was heiress to a $75 million fortune, though some sources cite a higher net worth. She went into a coma in December 1979 after the first attempt, and recovered, but the second coma, which began in December of 1980, left her in a vegetative state until her death 28 years later. Von Bülow was initially convicted and sentenced to thirty years in prison after the 1982 trial but appealed. The conviction was overturned after a second trial in 1985 where he was defended by Alan Dershowitz. The case was one of the first major criminal trials to be televised in the United States, and the story was later made into a movie called *Reversal of Fortune*, starring Glenn Close and Jeremy Irons.

Billionaire tobacco heiress Doris Duke was in the spotlight on October 7, 1966, when her Dodge Polara lurched forward and killed her interior designer, Eduardo Tirella, outside her Newport mansion. Some sources report that the car crushed Tirella against the iron gates, then dragged his body across the road before pinning him underneath when it struck a tree. Other accounts indicate that he was hit inside the gates, dragged by the car across Bellevue Avenue, and then crushed against a tree. The police wrote it up as an "unfortunate accident," and Duke paid $75,000 to the family. A 13-year-old paperboy named Robert Walker witnessed the accident but didn't come forward; he'd been warned by his father to keep quiet, fearing retribution. Years later, after the deaths of Duke in 1993 and of Walker's father in 2000, Walker, now 68, approached author Peter Lance, who wrote up the incident as *Homicide at Rough Point* and encouraged police to reopen the case and investigate it as a murder. In 2021, a five-month reinvestigation controversially yielded no additional legal action. Duke's mansion is now the Rough Point Museum and is open for tours.

You may have heard the saying, "The butler did it," but apparently, sometimes, it's the maid. In 1984, at "Bois Dore," the 36-room French mansion owned by heiress Carolyn Mary Skelly Burford, maid Barbara Polk walked off with $2.2 million in jewelry from an unlocked bedroom bureau. She and her accomplice, Mary Coite, kicked in the back door while Burford was out to dinner (though some accounts have her entertaining friends at home). Polk's husband, William, notified the police after Barbara threw him out of the house for daring to question the origin of the loot.

Road rage! On August 30, 1990, Adam Emery (27) and his wife Elena were picking up food at a seafood stand in Warwick, two miles from the Rocky Point Amusement Park, when a car sideswiped theirs. Emery became enraged and chased after what he believed was the offending vehicle. He caught up to a Ford LTD in Cranston and fatally stabbed the driver, Jason Bass (20), with a military knife. Paint chips later confirmed that Bass's car was not involved in the original incident. Emery was convicted in 1993 of second-degree murder and faced 20 years to life in prison.

After he was released on bail, pending formal sentencing. Emery immediately went to Kelly's Sporting Goods in Cranston and bought sweats, athletic socks, and 80 pounds of strap-on weights. He and Elena ate lunch at a Burger King and then later, abandoned their green Toyota, lights on, engine running, on the Claiborne Pell Newport Bridge overlooking Narragansett Bay. Elena's purse and Emery's cut-up credit cards and license were found in the back seat. Some believed the couple had jumped to their deaths; others think they set it up to look that way.

In 1994, a skull was recovered on Narragansett Bay that was identified as that of Elena Emery. No trace of Adam Emery has been found. He was declared legally dead in 2004, though in 2010, the FBI placed him on their Most Wanted List due to multiple unconfirmed sightings. They believe he may be in Italy or Florida.

North Providence: In 2000, Kimberly Sue Morse was a 32-year-old exotic dancer who came home to her one-bedroom basement apartment early on a mid-January morning and was attacked from behind as soon as she stepped into her kitchen. Her assailant cut her throat and stabbed her repeatedly, leaving her to bleed to death on her kitchen floor. The next afternoon, a smoke detector guided neighbors and firefighters to her apartment, where Morse's body was discovered in the bathtub, draped in gasoline-doused towels, and set aflame. Police found possessions missing, suggesting theft as at least a partial motive, though others suspected the murderer was the boyfriend with whom she had recently broken up. Despite a $20,000 reward, the case remains unsolved.

Providence: On April 16, 2005, Esteban Carpio stabbed eighty-four-year-old Madeline Gatta in front of her home in an attempted robbery. Witnesses were able to share the license number of his rented red van, and police apprehended him the same afternoon at his girlfriend's apartment. At police headquarters, the arresting detectives escorted Carpio to a conference room and removed his handcuffs. During questioning, the suspect requested a glass of water. When Det. Timothy McGann departed to retrieve it, Carpio locked the door, grabbed Det. Sgt. James L. Allen's .40–caliber Baretta semi-automatic pistol, and after a struggle, shot him twice in the chest.

By the time the other detectives broke down the door with a battering ram, Allen was dead, and as reported by a witness, Carpio escaped from the Providence Public Safety Complex by shooting out and then descending from a third-story window. After an extensive manhunt, police caught him, thanks to a vigilant taxi driver who'd heard the police reports and alerted them to a suspicious-sounding dispatch request, asking for a cab to drive to either Boston or New York.

Once recaptured, Carpio claimed he was hearing voices and blamed the devil for his actions. At trial, where Carpio allegedly wore a mask to prevent him from spitting at police officers, experts claimed he suffered from schizophrenia and paranoid psychosis. Nevertheless, the jury found him guilty. For the discharge of a firearm while committing a crime of violence, Carpio received a sentence of life imprisonment and is currently incarcerated in the maximum-security prison in Cranston. He also received a consecutive term of twenty years for the felony assault of Mrs. Gatta with a dangerous weapon.

Also in Providence: William "Billy" Sarmento is an example of a boy who fell through the cracks of mental health care. In his youth, he acted bizarrely, running away from home and living in sewers and abandoned houses. He committed arson and suffered from violent mood swings, displaying a penchant for firearms and the devil. Even though his father, Ed, had been treated for bipolar syndrome and schizophrenia, his parents didn't seek out help to stop him from running away.

By the age of 18, Sarmento had already spent time in mental institutions. When he knifed a fellow teenager over an argument about a bike, he was sent to the Adult Correctional Institute, where he engaged in activities that screamed "mental illness," such as "banging his head against the walls of his cell, stuffing toilet paper down his throat, cutting his arms, rocking in the corner of his cell, and urinating on himself...he also read the Bible incessantly." [2]

Despite recurring arrests, he continued to display violent tendencies, among them, threatening to shoot his girlfriend and abusing animals. But he didn't sink to murder until November 4th, 1987, when, during a bike ride with Frankie Barnes, he stabbed the nine-year-old boy and tossed his body into Cranston's Tongue Pond. The body remained there for six weeks until a letter guided the police to the place of his murder. Then, on December 14th of the same year, 6-year-old Jason Wolf met the same fate, lured out on a walk with Sarmento, who hit him with a wooden board and left his body in Mashapaug Pond. A letter blaming another man led police to Sarmento, who claimed Satan had commanded his actions. A jury found him not guilty by reason of insanity, and he was committed to the State Institute for Mental Health in Cranston, which in 1994, merged with Zambarano Memorial Hospital to become the Eleanor Slater Hospital.

Mob violence has punctuated decades of Providence history, especially in the Federal Hill section. In 1932, Arthur "Daddy" Black, an entrepreneur who worked an illegal numbers pool, was assassinated at his office by a group of Black killers under the direction of Italian mobsters. But life became significantly more violent starting in 1954 when crime boss Raymond Patriarca consolidated his rule after his predecessor, Philip Buccola, fled to Sicily. For example, in August of 1955, a mob hit on George "Tiger" Balleto at Bella Napoli Café riddled his back with bullets. On April 20, 1968, attackers ambushed and killed Rudolph Marfeo and Anthony Melei inside Pannone's Meat Market. In 1975, mobsters murdered Dickie Callei at the Acorn Social Club in a gangland-style killing. The killers weren't taking any chances, either. With three skull fractures, stab wounds in the face, chest, and abdomen, and bullet wounds that had pierced his heart and lungs, they dumped his corpse into a pre-dug grave in the woods.

And there's more. In 1978, mobster Nicky Pari lured a suspected police informant named Joseph "Joe Onions" Scanlon into a Federal Hill building (now gone), struck him in the face, and fired a bullet through his head. It wasn't until 2009 that investigators recovered the body from behind an apartment building in East Providence. In 1982, Raymond "Slick" Vecchio violently met his end at Vincent Restaurant, reportedly diagonally across the street from the business address of Raymond Patriarca. The suspected killer was a strongman named Kevin Hanrahan, who himself was shot outside the Arch Restaurant in 1992. And on May 7, 1994, mobster Barry Kourmpates, part of the Golden Nugget crew, disappeared. Authorities found his body the next day at Beavertail State Park, where his attackers had set his body on fire after shooting him in the back. Apparently, he had been robbing protected businesses and not kicking something back to the bosses.

Providence has also seen its share of gang violence. The largest number of victims from any local shooting resulted from an incident on May 14th, 2021, in Washington Park, when four young male members of the "Get Money Family" gang, driving a Dodge Ram, parked in front of a house owned by David Carides (26), an alleged Lakeside Street Gang member. Five or six people stood on the porch or nearby. The men in the car unleashed more than forty rounds from semi-automatic pistols. At least two of the people on the porch reciprocated fire. Before the gunfight was over, nine people were wounded either by bullets or glass shards. A gang member named Ricardo Cosme Tejada (21) was eventually sentenced to 14 years at the Adult Correctional Institution for multiple felony charges stemming from his role in the shooting.

South Kingstown (Peace Dale section): Perhaps the most frightening thing about Michael Woodmansee's story is that he might be living among us. He resided in Peace Dale with his father, a police reservist. On May 18, 1975, when Woodmansee was sixteen, he murdered his neighbor, five-year-old Jason Foreman. The boy was last seen running toward the volunteer fire station, not more than 30 yards from Woodmansee's home. The crime went unsolved until Woodmansee attempted to intoxicate, then strangle, paperboy Dale Sherman (14) on April 15, 1982. The boy escaped and reported the incident to his father, who, in turn, confronted and punched Woodmansee and then contacted the police.

At the station house, one of the officers suspected Woodmansee might know something about Foreman's murder and asked questions accordingly. Woodmansee ended up confessing, and when police searched his home, they not only discovered an incriminating journal, but they also found Foreman's skull and bones, picked clean. In 1983, Woodmansee confessed to second-degree murder in a plea bargain agreement that kept the gorier details of the incident from the jury. He was sentenced to 40 years, but because of a law in Rhode Island that rewards good convict behavior, he got out in 28. In September 2011, due to public uproar over his early release, his legal counsel agreed to have him voluntarily committed to the Eleanor Slater Hospital in Cranston. Whether or not he is still there is unknown, due to privacy laws.

Warren: James A. Soares Jr. (24) and his girlfriend Nicole Pacheco often dined al fresco in their backyard, directly over the cesspool of the home. Now we know why. When his father James (60) and his mother Marian (53) failed to show up for their reunion in July 2008, their family filed a missing person's report. James Jr. gave the police a bevy of excuses for why his parents weren't at home, questionable since Marian's credit cards and cell phone remained in the house. James' stories kept changing, until finally, after ten days of inquiries, he admitted he'd stuffed his parents' bodies into the cesspool. Police unearthed them using a backhoe. James Jr, who had a history of stealing from his parents to fund his drug problem, had apparently indulged in a spending spree after the murders, purchasing video game players, a computer, and a television. On April 28, 2010, he pleaded guilty to first-degree murder, among other charges, and received two life sentences plus extra time behind bars. He will be up for parole after the year 2050.

Warwick: At the time of his arrest and conviction, Craig Chandler Price was the youngest serial killer in U.S. history. Having already been arrested for petty theft, by age 16, he'd committed four murders in his Buttonwoods neighborhood, including the July 27, 1987, stabbing murder of Rebecca Spencer (27) and the September 1, 1989 murder of Joan Heaton (39), her daughter Jennifer (10), and her seven-year-old youngest daughter, Melissa. He stabbed each victim at least 30 times, in some cases, double that, with such force that the handles broke off the knives.

Price was arrested a month before his 16th birthday and was tried and convicted as a minor. Yet he made it clear that once he was released and his criminal records sealed at age 21, he would strike again. This sparked outrage with Citizens Opposed to the Release of Craig Price, among others, who lobbied successfully for perpetrators of serious crimes like murder to be tried as adults. Unfortunately, this could not apply to Price retroactively.

It turned out to be a moot point. Due to the extensive crimes that he committed while at the Rhode Island Training School, including contempt, extortion, and assault, Price received an additional sentence of 10-25 years at the Adult Correctional Institution in Cranston. His release date had been set for May 2020, but after being transferred in 2004 to various prisons in Florida due to his violent tendencies, he was sentenced to another 25 years in 2019 for stabbing a fellow inmate at the Suwannee Correctional Institution in Live Oak.

Woonsocket: Jeffrey S. Mailhot was an ordinary man who'd never received a traffic ticket in his life, much less a criminal record. That's what made it even more shocking when he turned out to be the "Rhode Island Ripper" who, in 2003 and 2004, strangled and dismembered prostitutes in his bathroom using a bow saw, a technique he'd learned from watching *The Sopranos*. He then bagged their remains and distributed them throughout various dumpsters in his and neighboring communities. That's how Audrey L. Harris (33) met her end in February 2003, Christine C. Dumont (42) in April 2004, and Stacie K. Goulet (24) in July of that year. Only Jocelin Martel (27), whom Mailhot picked up outside the Thundermist Health Center, managed to escape. Her description led police to Mailhot's arrest. Once he confessed, police were able to locate only Goulet's remains at a Johnston landfill. Mailhot was arrested on July 17, 2004, and later sentenced to three life terms at the Rhode Island Maximum Security Prison in Cranston. He will be eligible for parole in 2047, at age 77.

Also in Woonsocket: On October 24, 2004, 24-year-old Katherine Bunnell, her boyfriend, Gilbert Delestre, and Delestre's cousin, came home from a night of drinking, only to find a mess that her nephew, toddler Thomas "TJ" Wright (3), had left, having spilled milk and yogurt in her apartment's living room. According to the 15-year-old babysitter's eyewitness account, Bunnell lost her temper. She dragged Wright from his bed, pulled him downstairs, beat him repeatedly, slammed his head against the floor, and threw him across the room. The boy, who had been left in Bunnell's care when his mother, Karen Wright (Bunnell's sister), went to prison for marijuana possession, suffered a broken leg, brain damage, and blunt force injuries that proved fatal.

Bunnell and Delestre blamed each other for the boy's death; in 2008 and 2009 individual trials, both were found guilty of second-degree murder and sentenced to life in prison plus ten years. Bunnell must serve more than twenty-three years in prison before becoming eligible for parole. Delestre, who had been held at the Wyatt Detention Center in Central Falls, passed away at Rhode Island Hospital on August 25, 2019. The case became part of a civil lawsuit indicting Rhode Island's foster care system.

More crime in Woonsocket: On March 17, 1994, detectives found the dead body of alleged prostitute and drug user Megeann Paul in her room on the third floor of a rooming house, with a knife lodged in her abdomen and another thrown into the sink. The positioning of the stab wounds indicated a struggle, and her face was covered with a sheet as if the killer, who likely knew her before the attack, didn't want to look her in the eye, postmortem. Though Paul "entertained" countless people in her home, the DNA found under her fingernails has yet to match up with possible suspects.

The case remains unsolved, but it was not the first time this rooming house had a connection to a crime. Justin Troy Frabotta (23), a suspect in the July 15, 2011, shooting of Neil James Coppinger (24), was arrested and charged with assault and intent to commit murder. Frabotta lived at this same address.

Want more? As printed on their website, the Pawtucket Police Cold Case Unit, in partnership with the Rhode Island Department of Corrections and law enforcement agencies statewide, has created a cold case playing card deck. These cards highlight 52 unsolved violent homicides and missing persons cases that occurred throughout the state. Check out the cards at https://coldcaseri.com.

Read Before You Leave: A Sampling of Rhode Island True Crime Books

(listed alphabetically by author)

Note: Some of these books may cover crimes not discussed elsewhere in this guide.

- Barylick, John. *Killer Show*. ForeEdge, 2015.
- Caranci, Paul F. *The Hanging and Redemption of John Gordon: The True Story of Rhode Island's Last Execution*. Arcadia Publishing, 2013.
- Caranci, Paul. *Scoundrels*. Stillwater River Publications, 2016.
- Carroll, Leah. *Down City*. Grand Central Publishing, 2018.
- Crane, Elaine Forman. *Killed Strangely*. Cornell University Press, 2014.
- Crane, Elaine Forman. *The Poison Plot*. Cornell University Press, 2018.
- Davis, Donald A. *Death of an Angel*. St. Martin's Paperbacks, 2011.
- Dershowitz, Alan M. *Reversal of Fortune*. Random House, 2013.
- Hightower, Susan, Kensington Publishing Corporation Staff, and Mary Ryzuk. *Shattered Innocence*. Pinnacle Books, 2000.
- James, Scott. *Trial by Fire*. Thomas Dunne Books, 2020.
- Lance, Peter. *Homicide at Rough Point*. Tenacity Media Books, 2020.
- Lang, Denise. *A Call for Justice*. Avon, 2000.
- Oliveira, Bobby. *Rogues of Rhode Island*. Omni Publishing Company, 2024.
- Ouimette, Gerard Thomas. *What Price Providence?* Ouimette, 2012.
- Pezza, Kelly Sullivan. *Murder & Mayhem in Washington County, Rhode*

Island. Arcadia Publishing, 2015.

- Pezza, Kelly Sullivan. *Murder at Rocky Point Park*. Arcadia Publishing, 2014.
- Pingitore, Raymond, and Paul Lonardo. *Thrill Killers*. Berkley, Reprint edition, 2008.
- Phelps, M. William, *The Unforgettable Fire: Notorious Rhode Island, Massachusetts, and Connecticut*. Notorious USA, 2014.
- Raven, Rory. *Wicked Conduct*. Arcadia Publishing, 2018.
- Reilly-McGreen, M. E. *Witches, Wenches & Wild Women of Rhode Island*. Arcadia Publishing, 2013.
- Rosencrance, Linda, and Edward Lee. *Ripper*. Pinnacle Books, 2010.
- Smith, Keith. *Men in My Town*. Book Surge Publishing, 2009.
- Stanford, Larry. *Wicked Newport*. Arcadia Publishing, 2008.
- Stanton, Mike. *The Prince of Providence*. Wheeler Publishing, Incorporated, 2004.
- Worcester, Wayne, Randall Richard, and Tim White. *The Last Good Heist*. Rowman & Littlefield, 2016.

Accommodations and Restaurants that are Crime/Justice-Related or Haunted

Crime/Justice-Related Accommodations

Newport

Jailhouse Inn

13 Marlborough Street, Newport

401-847-4638

reservations@jailhouse.com

https://www.jailhouse.com

Dating back to 1772, The Jailhouse Inn was originally built as a prison to service the whole colony of Rhode Island. It was also the site of many prison escapes. It remained the headquarters of the Newport Police Department until 1986, when developers converted it into the Jailhouse Inn. It's also rumored to be haunted.

And speaking of haunted hotels, the following accommodations are said to be visited by spirits. Where souls are not at rest, could murder be the reason?

Haunted Accommodations

Block Island (East Shoreham)

Hygeia House (vacation rentals)

582 Beach Avenue, New Shoreham

401-856-9920

https://www.thehygeiahouse.com

In its past lives, the 12-bedroom Hygeia House served as a hospital, morgue, dancehall, and more. Guests have encountered a female spirit in the Uncle Carder Room.

Charlestown

General Stanton Inn

4115 Old Post Road, Charlestown

401-364-8888

innkeeper@thegeneralstantoninn.com

https://www.thegeneralstantoninn.com

Dating back to 1655, when it was a schoolhouse in its former life. The Washington Room is said to be haunted by a male ghost who gets guests' attention by tapping them on the shoulder. He also throws things when he is ignored.

Middletown

The Newport Beach Hotel & Suites

One Wave Avenue Middletown

401-846-0310 or 833-454-5982

frontdesk@newportbeachhotelandsuites.com

https://www.newportbeachhotelandsuites.com

Haunted by a dark-skinned male who hangs out at the bar and a little girl who runs and laughs in the hallways. Others kill time in the kitchen, the annex, and the maintenance shop.

Newport

Castle Hill Inn

590 Ocean Avenue, Newport

401-849-3800 or 888-466-1355

info@castlehillinn.com

https://www.castlehillinn.com

Dating back to 1875, a female ghost has been seen strolling through the hotel. She occasionally smashes hotel china.

Hotel Viking

One Bellevue Avenue, Newport

844-806-4895

stay@hotelviking.com

https://www.hotelviking.com

Ghosts party in an old ballroom that's no longer in use.

Outlook Inn (formerly the Pilgrim House Inn)

123 Spring Street, Newport

401-845-9400

Theoutlookinn@vacationnetwork.com

https://www.theoutlookinn.com

Late-night partying spirits laugh, play music, and stare from windows down at the street.

Providence

Graduate Providence (formerly Providence Biltmore)

11 Dorrance Street, Providence

401-421-0700

info@graduateprovidence.com

https://graduatehotels.com/providence

Financed by satanist Johan Lessie Weisskopf, the building was named the most haunted place in Rhode Island in the year 2000, thanks to murders dating back to the Prohibition era. In 2008, six guests supposedly just vanished and have yet to be found.

Warwick

La Quinta Inn & Suites Warwick Providence Airport (formerly the Fairfield Inn)

36 Jefferson Blvd, Warwick

401-941-6600

https://www.wyndhamhotels.com/hotels/warwick-rhode-island?brand_id=LQ

Rooms 316 and 506 are thought to be especially haunted.

Crime and Justice-Related Restaurants

Cranston

Chapel Grill Restaurant

3000 Chapel View Boulevard, Cranston

401-944-4900

tracey@circerestaurantbar.com

https://www.chapelgrilleri.com

The Chapel Grill's Cathedral Bar was once the place of spiritual healing as part of the rehabilitative Sockanosset School for Boys, aka the Sockanosset Boys Training School. Most of the buildings have been redeveloped into a mix of retail and residential units.

Haunted Restaurants

Chepachet (Gloucester)

Tavern on Main

1157 Putnam Pike, Chepachet

401-710-9788

https://tavernonmainri.com

With five ghosts in residence, the Tavern on Main claims to be one of the most haunted restaurants in Rhode Island. Some date back to the Dorr Rebellion of 1842. In October, the owner hosts paranormal investigation dinners.

Newport

The White Horse Tavern

26 Marlborough Street, Newport

401-849-3600

jarred@whitehorsenewport.com (general manager Jarred LaPlante)

https://whitehorsenewport.com

America's oldest tavern, thought to be one of the ten most haunted bars in the country. The building is haunted by the ghost of an old man who rented a room in the 18th century and a girl who often cries.

North Kingstown

Carriage Inn

1065 Tower Hill Road, North Kingstown

401-294-0466

admin@carriageinndining.com

https://carriageinndining.com

Dating back to 1760, it was formerly an inn and tavern. The ghosts consist of men, women, and children; some look as if they've worked in a brothel.

Portsmouth

Valley Inn Restaurant

2221 West Main Road, Portsmouth

401-847-9871

joevalleyinn@cox.net

https://www.facebook.com/valleyinnrestaurantri

Haunted by Rebecca Cornell, who allegedly died in her bed during a fire, but who may have been murdered. Her son Thomas was hanged for her death, supposedly based on the word of a ghost. His daughter, in utero at the time of his execution, ended up being the great-great-great-great-grandmother of Lizzie Borden.

Crime Tours and Paranormal Tours

Providence

Crime and Cuisine on Federal Hill: 3-3.5 hours, from $75, No age limits listed, meets at 2:00 p.m. Saturdays and Sundays at Garibaldi Park, 99 Atwells Avenue, at the base of the La Pigna gateway arch. Offered through the Providence Tour Company, 401-408-6608, hello@pvdtourco.com, https://www.pvdtourco.com/crime-and-cuisine-tour.

Haunted History Walking Tour of Providence: up to 105 minutes, from $30, no age limits listed, meets at Prospect Terrace, 60 Congdon Street. Offered by Providence Ghost Tour, bookable through Viator at
https://www.viator.com/tours/Providence/Providence-Ghost-Tour/d22849-438652P1.

Providence Ghosts, Phantoms, and Poltergeists Walking Tour (aka Providence: Doomed Artists Haunted Walking Tour): 1 hour, adults from $25, children from $16, meets at the benches near the Rhode Island Holocaust Memorial in Memorial Park, 5 Main Street. Offered through US Ghost Adventures, https://www.getyourguide.com/providence-l32591/providence-doomed-artists-haunted-walking-tour-t432436.

Newport

Newport Olde Town Ghost Walk: up to 90 minutes, from $12-$20, all ages, departs most nights, May through Halloween, at 8:00 p.m. from next to the Mainsail Restaurant and Skiff Bar on the second floor of the Newport Marriott, info@ghostsofnewport.com. https://www.ghostsofnewport.com.

Newport Ghosts Seaside Hauntings and Hags Tour: 1 hour, adults from $25, Children from $16, meets 8:00 p.m. at the center of Washington Square in Eisenhower Park. Offered through US Ghost Adventures, https://usghostadventures.com/newport-ghost-tour.

Westerly

Downtown Westerly Ghost Tour: 105 minutes, from $30, recommended for ages 11+, meets at 8:00 p.m. in front of Westerly Town Hall, offered through Seaside Shadows Haunted History Tours, info@seasideshadows.com, https://www.seasideshadows.com/westerly-ri.

All prices are per person. Tour offerings, prices, times, age restrictions, and meeting locations are subject to change.

Police/Crime/Prison/Courthouse Museums and Other Attractions

Providence

Gun Totem
South Main Street, Providence
Located across from Providence's Federal Courthouse, view the 3,500-pound obelisk constructed with more than 1,000 reclaimed guns by artist Boris Baily.

Providence Place Mall
One Providence Place, Providence
The mall stands on the site of the original Rhode Island State Prison, which opened in 1838 and closed in 1877.

Newport

Gravelly Point
Washington Street, Newport
A Wyndham Inn and a yachting club stand on the site where, in 1723, 26 pirates were hanged in Rhode Island's largest mass execution. A plaque commemorating the event can be seen in adjacent Mary Ferrazzoli Park.

Rough Point Museum
  680 Bellevue Avenue, Newport
  401-849-7300
  visit@newportrestoration.org
  http://bit.ly/3WvhVCM
  Doris Duke's former mansion was the site of the "unfortunate accident" that occurred when Duke's car ran over her interior designer and killed him. The case was reopened after a witness surfaced decades afterward.

North Scituate

Rhode Island State Police Museum
  311 Danielson Pike, North Scituate
  rispmuseum@gmail.com
  https://rispmuseum.org
  Founded in 2006, the museum shares the history of the Rhode Island State Police and preserves its artifacts, documents, and photographs for posterity.

South Kingstown

Old Washington County Jail
  2636 Kingstown Road, South Kingstown
  401-783-1328
  erica@southcountyhistorycenter.org
  https://southcountyhistorycenter.org/about-the-old-washington-cou
nty-jail
  One of the oldest surviving jails in Rhode Island, dating back to 1792. Also, the headquarters of the South County History Center.

State and Federal Prisons of Note in Rhode Island

Cranston

Rhode Island Department of Corrections:

- High Security Center, a supermax facility at 54 Power Road, Cranston
- Maximum security facility at 1375 Pontiac Avenue, Cranston
- John J. Moran Medium security facility at 51 West Road, Cranston
- Minimum security facility at 16 Howard Avenue, Cranston
- Gloria McDonald Women's facility at 20 Fleming Road, Cranston

I've included these listings to be consistent with other chapters, but there's not much to see here because other than Jeffrey Mailhot and Esteban Carpio, many of Rhode Island's most notorious inmates are serving terms out of state. This includes Craig Price (sent to Florida in 2004), Christopher Hightower (sent to Illinois in 1993), and mobster Antonio Cucinotta, who gunned down two men at the Hockey Fans Social Club in Cranston because he felt disrespected (sent to an undisclosed location).

Also in Cranston:
Eleanor Slater Hospital
111 Howard Avenue, Cranston

Psychiatric hospital, likely home to William "Billy" Sarmento and Michael Woodmansee, if the latter is still there; his commitment was voluntary.

Notable Crime-and-Justice-Related Burial Sites

Plot locations included where available, burial sites not always included in itineraries.

Note: Most Rhode Island cemeteries have alternate names, starting with "Rhode Island Historical Cemetery," followed by the city and the cemetery number.

The addresses here are accurate for either name.

Cranston

Pocasset Cemetery

417 Dyer Avenue, Cranston

Burial site of Amasa Sprague, initially believed to have been murdered by John Gordon (Section 38-M-2, Oak Path).

Saint Ann Cemetery

72 Church Street, Cranston

Burial site of Sgt. James Lloyd "Jimmy" Allen, murdered by Esteban Carpio (Section 52, Lot 17, Grave 2).

Burial sites of mobsters Rudolph G. Marfeo (Section 2, Lot 105, Grave 2) and Anthony Melei (Section 28, Lot 826, Grave 1), were both killed during the same incident at Pannone's Market.

Burial site of mobster Joseph "Joe Onions" Scanlon (no plot listed).

Burial site of mobster Raymond "Slick" Vecchio (Section 41, Lot 532,

Grave 3).
   Burial site of Kevin Thomas Hanrahan (Section 44, Lot 144, Grave 1).

Cumberland

Resurrection Cemetery
   259 West Wrentham Road, Cumberland
   Burial site for Stanley "Stosh" Stowik Sr., cold case

East Greenwich

Glenwood Cemetery
   316 Cedar Avenue, East Greenwich
   Burial site of Rebecca Spencer, murdered by Craig Chandler Price.

East Providence

Springvale Cemetery
   Pawtucket Avenue, East Providence
   Burial site of Frankie Lee Barnes Jr., murdered by William "Billy" Sarmento.

Gates of Heaven Cemetery
   550 Wampanoag Trail, East Providence
   Burial site of Raymond Loreda Salvatore Patriarca, crime boss.

Exeter

Rhode Island Veterans Memorial Cemetery
   301 South County Trail, Exeter
   Burial sites of Joan Marie Bouchard Heaton, her daughters Jennifer Marie Heaton and Melissa Joan Heaton, all murdered by Craig Chandler Price (Section A-4, Row 1, Site 4).

Jamestown

Cedar Cemetery
Cedar Lane, Jamestown
Burial site of Arthur "Daddy" Black, illegal numbers runner and "Lottery King."

Portsmouth

Saint Mary's Episcopal Churchyard
324 East Main Road, Portsmouth
Burial site of Sunny von Bülow, originally thought to have been murdered by her husband, Claus von Bülow.

Providence

North Burial Ground
5 Branch Avenue, Providence
Burial site for John Gordon, executed for the murder of Amasa Sprague, pardoned posthumously.
Burial site for Jason K. Bass, murdered by Adam Embry (East of Main, Single Grave #371).

Swan Point Cemetery
585 Blackstone Blvd, Providence
Burial site for author H.P. Lovecraft (Group 281, Lot 5, Space 10).

South Kingstown

Riverside Cemetery
169 High Street, South Kingstown
Burial site of Jason Douglas Foreman, murdered by Michael Wood-mansee.

Warwick

All Saints Cemetery
  389 Greenwich Avenue
  Burial site of Jason R.A. Wolf, murdered by William "Billy" Sarmento.

West Warwick

Station Fire Memorial Park
  211 Cowesett Avenue, West Warwick
  This was the site of the Station Nightclub, which, on February 3rd, 2003, burned down due to pyrotechnics set off during the "Great White" rock concert. A memorial now stands in its place to honor the 100 patrons who perished that night. Nearly 300 others were injured. It was the second-worst nightclub fire disaster in U.S. history, up until that point.

Putting it All Together: Itineraries

Itinerary: Rhode Island True Crime Tour

Despite being such a small state, a true crime tour of Rhode Island could take two or three days, considering the crime-related and/or haunted hotels and late-night ghost tours available.

The tour starts in **Westerly**, where the downtown evening ghost tour given by Seaside Shadows Haunted History Tours lasts almost two hours. Drive east to **Charlestown** to stay at the haunted General Stanton Inn at 4115 Old Post Road. Next, head northeast to the Peace Dale section of **South Kingstown**, where five-year-old Jason Foreman was last seen running toward the volunteer fire station at the bottom of Hill Street, not more than 30 yards from killer Michael Woodmansee's home on the 0-100 block of Schaeffer Street. You can pay your respects to Jason Foreman at the Riverside Cemetery at 169 High Street. You can also visit the Old Washington County Jail at 2636 Kingstown Road.

Head northeast to **North Kingstown** to catch sight of a ghost or two over lunch at the Carriage Inn at 1065 Tower Hill Road before continuing northwest. At the Rhode Island Veterans Memorial Cemetery at 301 South County Trail in **Exeter**, you can visit the burial sites of Joan Marie Bouchard Heaton and her daughters, Jennifer Marie Heaton and Melissa Joan Heaton, all murdered by Craig Chandler Price. Then drive north to **East Greenwich**, where Price's other victim, Rebecca Spencer, is buried at the Glenwood Cemetery at 316 Cedar Avenue.

To the north, in **West Warwick**, you can visit Station Fire Memorial Park at 211 Cowesett Avenue, which pays tribute to the victims of the disastrous nightclub fire of 2003. To the east, in the Buttonwoods neighborhood of **Warwick**, Craig Chandler Price murdered Rebecca Spencer in her home on the 0-100 block of Inez Avenue and Joan Heaton and her daughters in their home on the 0-100 block of Metropolitan Drive. Jason Wolf, murdered by William "Billy" Sarmento, is buried at the All Saints Cemetery at 389 Greenwich Avenue. The La Quinta Inn & Suites Warwick Providence Airport at 36 Jefferson Blvd is said to harbor ghosts.

Drive north to **Cranston,** where, in 1844, Amasa Sprague was murdered near his mansion at 1351 Cranston Street, now home to the Cranston Historical Society and the Governor Sprague Mansion Museum. John Gordon was tried for the crime at the Old State House (now the headquarters for the Rhode Island Historical Preservation & Heritage Commission at 150 Benefit Street) and was hanged where the Providence Place Mall now stands at One Providence Place. Sprague is buried at the Pocasset Cemetery at 417 Dyer Avenue.

Also in Cranston, William "Billy" Sarmento tossed the body of Frankie Barnes into Tongue Pond, located next to Lowes at 247 Garfield Avenue, and in a road rage incident, Adam Emery stabbed Jason Bass on a road near Park Avenue. After his trial, Emery and his wife bought sporting goods at Kelly's Sporting Goods at 125 Sockanosset Crossroad (a Wines & More Store at the time of publication) before driving to Newport and abandoning their car.

Cranston houses the majority of prisons that are part of the Rhode Island Department of Corrections (54 Power Road, 1375 Pontiac Avenue, 51 West Road, 16 Howard Avenue, and 20 Fleming Road), one of which is home to Jeffrey Mailhot. It's also the location of the Eleanor Slater Hospital, home to William "Billy" Sarmento and possibly Michael Woodmansee. And the Saint Ann Cemetery at 72 Church Street is the final resting place for Sgt. James Allen, murdered by Esteban Carpio, as well as New England mobsters Rudolph Marfeo, Anthony Melei, Joseph "Joe Onions" Scanlon, Raymond "Slick" Vecchio, and Kevin Hanrahan.

Before leaving, enjoy a meal at the Chapel Grill Restaurant at 3000 Chapel View Boulevard, once part of the Sockanosset School for Boys, a reform school that later turned more vocational.

Drive northwest to **Johnston,** where the only remains of Jeffrey Mailhot's victims, that of Stacie K. Goulet, were recovered at the Central Landfill at 65 Shun Pike. To the west in **North Scituate**, you can visit the Rhode Island State Police Museum at 311A Danielson Pike. Next, drive northwest to **Chepachet** to grab lunch at the haunted Tavern on Main at 1157 Putnam Pike. Then north to **Burrillville**, where Janine Callahan's body was found under a discarded Christmas tree at the end of what's now known as Cherry Farm Road.

To the northeast, in **Woonsocket,** Jeffrey S. Mailhot murdered prostitutes at his apartment at 221 Cato Street. It's also where Katherine Bunnell and her boyfriend, Gilbert Delestre, murdered her nephew Thomas "T.J." Wright (3) at the Walnut Hill apartments at 2229 Diamond Hill Road. The rooming house at 233 North Main Street is where alleged prostitute Megeann Paul met her demise.

Drive southeast to **Cumberland**, where 80-year-old cold case murder victim Stanley "Stosh" Stowik Sr. was killed at his home on the 0-50 block of Indiana Avenue. He's buried at the Resurrection Cemetery at 259 West Wrentham Road. To the southwest in **Lincoln**, Ronny Almonte's body was found inside the trunk of a car parked in a driveway about 200 yards outside the Twin River Road entrance to Lincoln Woods Park. Further southwest in **North Providence**, Kimberly Sue Morse had been an exotic dancer at the Foxy Lady Gentlemen's Club at 318 Chalkstone Avenue and had lived at the Brick Manor Condominiums, flanked by Cynthia Drive and Garibaldi Streets, when she was murdered in her one-bedroom basement apartment.

To the southeast in **Providence**, Esteban Carpio stabbed eighty-year-old Madeline Gatta in front of her home on the 0-100 block of Swift Street. Once apprehended, he shot Det. Sgt. James L. Allen, with the detective's own gun, then escaped through the third-floor window of the Providence Public Safety Complex at 325 Washington Street. William "Billy" Sarmento, who grew up on Valley Street, tossed the body of 6-year-old Jason Wolf into Mashapaug Pond (bordered by Adelaide Avenue at its northeast edge, the Huntington Business Park on its northwest edge, and Ocean State Job Lot off Reservoir Avenue to the south).

Arthur "Daddy" Black, an entrepreneur who worked an illegal numbers pool, was assassinated at his office at 160 Cranston. Several mobsters also met their end in Providence at establishments that have since closed, been demolished, or have changed their names. The list includes George "Tiger" Balleto at Bella Napoli Café at 93 Atwells Avenue; Rudolph Marfeo and Anthony Melei, both gunned down inside Pannone's Meat Market at 282 Pocasset Avenue in the Silver Lake neighborhood; Dickie Callei, who was killed at the Acorn Social Club at 141 Acorn Street; and Raymond "Slick" Vecchio, who was shot at Vincent Restaurant on Atwells Avenue, diagonally across from 168 Atwells, reportedly the business address of Raymond Patriarca. Vecchio's suspected killer, Kevin Hanrahan, was shot outside of the Arch Restaurant on Atwells Avenue. And a gunfight between two rival gangs in 2021 occurred on Carolina Avenue.

Before leaving Providence, be sure to visit the Gun Totem on South Main Street, across from the courthouse, as well as the Providence Place Mall at One Providence Place, originally the site of the Rhode Island State Prison, where John Gordon was hanged for the murder of Amasa Sprague. Gordon's body is buried at the North Burial Ground at 5 Branch Avenue. Jason Bass, stabbed to death by Adam Embry, is interred at the same cemetery. Horror fans will want to visit author H.P. Lovecraft's tombstone at the Swan Point Cemetery at 585 Blackstone Boulevard. Don't leave town without taking one or more of the mobster and ghost tours offered by several companies in Providence, and since some end late in the evening, consider staying overnight at the Graduate Providence Hotel at 11 Dorrance Street, said to be haunted.

Drive east to **East Providence**, where the body of Joseph "Joe Onions" Scanlon was unearthed behind the Lisboa apartment complex on Bollocks Point Avenue. At the Springvale Cemetery on Pawtucket Avenue, you can visit the burial site of Frankie Lee Barnes Jr., murdered by William "Billy" Sarmento, while the Gates of Heaven Cemetery at 550 Wampanoag Trail, is the final resting place of crime boss Raymond Loreda Salvatore Patriarca.

To the southeast in **Barrington**, James Mitchell DeBardeleben II murdered real estate agent Edna Therrel MacDonald, leaving her dead body in a home on Heritage Road. And Jones Circle was once the home of commodities broker Christopher Hightower's in-laws. It's where Hightower and his family had been staying prior to his killing former friend and client, Ernest Brendel, and his family at their home on the 0-100 block of Middle Highway. Hightower buried their bodies in a shallow grave near St. Andrew's School at 63 Federal Road.

Then, drive southeast to **Warren**, where James A. Soares Jr. murdered his parents and stuffed their bodies into the cesspool of their backyard on the 0-50 block of Baltimore Avenue. Due south, in **Portsmouth**, you can visit the grave of Sunny von Bülow at Saint Mary's Episcopal Churchyard at 324 East Main Road and have a bite to eat at the ghostly Valley Inn Restaurant at 2221 West Main Road. Further south in **Middletown**, you may want to stay overnight at the haunted Newport Beach Hotel & Suites at One Wave Avenue.

To the southeast, in **Newport**, Doris Duke was driving the car that crushed her interior designer to death outside her Rough Point mansion, now the

Rough Point Museum at 680 Bellevue Avenue. At "Bois Doré," the 36-room French mansion at 115 Narragansett Avenue, Carolyn Skelly Burford's maid robbed her blind. Adam Emery and his wife Elena jumped from the Claiborne Pell Newport Bridge overlooking Narragansett Bay. Suicide or sham? No one is certain.

There's lots of reported paranormal activity in Newport. You can grab a bite with ghosts at The White Horse Tavern at 26 Marlborough Street before visiting Gravelly Point at Mary Ferrazzoli Park, where you can visit the plaque commemorating the mass hanging of 26 pirates. Perhaps you'll meet one or two during one of the ghost tours offered in town. Then you can spend the night at the Jailhouse Inn, a former jail at 13 Marlborough Street, or at one of the three haunted hotels in town: the Castle Hill Inn at 590 Ocean Avenue, the Hotel Viking at One Bellevue Avenue, or the Outlook Inn (formerly the Pilgrim House Inn) at 123 Spring Street. The tour ends after driving west to **Jamestown**, where mobster Barry Kourmpates was found in Beavertail State Park on Beavertail Road, having been shot in the back before being set aflame. You can also visit the grave of Arthur "Daddy" Black at Cedar Cemetery on Cedar Lane.

Rhode Island Victim Resources

This is a noncomprehensive summary of services available to victims of crime in Rhode Island. Information was taken directly from their websites. Visit or contact agencies for complete information and note that some programs offered by certain contractors focus on specific geographic areas. Some resource categories and content may overlap. Inclusion does not equate to recommendation.

Victim Services

- Rhode Island Victim Services and Information about Voice: an online system that streamlines service delivery and allows state agencies to better serve victims of crime in Rhode Island, see https://riag.ri.gov/about-our-office/divisions-and-units/criminal-division/victim-services.
- RI Victims of Crime Helpline: 800-494-8100, see www.helplineri.com. Live chat is available at www.ricadv.org (click on box that says "24 HR HELPLINE" at the top right of the screen, or visit www.bvacri.org and click on the bottom of the home page that says "Live Chat" on the right side of the screen.
- Family Service of Rhode Island: FSRI responds alongside police to provide assistance to victims at crime scenes, including crisis intervention, stabilization, language support, and service referral, see https://www.familyserviceri.org/programs/victim-service-programs.

- Rhode Island Victims' Resource Guide: see https://www.rifreeclinic.o rg/wp-content/uploads/2022/10/RI-Attorney-General-Victims-of-Crime-Resource-Guide.pdf.

Crime-centric List of Resources

Child Abuse

- RI DCYF: The Department of Children, Youth and Families is the state child welfare, children's mental health, and juvenile corrections services agency. They also assist families with children who are at risk of being abused, neglected, wayward, or delinquent. The Child Abuse Hotline is manned 24/7 and can be contacted at 800-RI-CHILD (1-800-742-4453), or see https://dcyf.ri.gov.

Civil Legal Help for People with Low Income

- Rhode Island Legal Services provides high-quality legal assistance and representation to low-income individuals and eligible client groups, 800-662-5034 or 401-274-2652, see https://www.helprilaw.org.

Domestic Violence

- RI Coalition Against Domestic Violence: 24-hour helpline at 800-494-8100, see https://ricadv.org/help-for-victims-in-criminal-cases.
- Domestic Shelters: List of resources and more, see https://www.dom esticshelters.org/help.
- National Domestic Abuse Hotline: 800-799-7233 or text START to 88788, see https://www.thehotline.org/?utm_source=youtube&utm _medium=organic&utm_campaign=domestic_violence,
- Elizabeth Buffum Chase Center: serves individuals and families affected by domestic violence and sexual assault, 401-738-1700, contact Stephanie Joyal at stephaniej@ebchouse.org, or see https://w

ww.ebccenter.org.

Drunk Driving Victims

- Mothers Against Drink Driving: 877-MADD-HELP (877-623-3435), see https://madd.org/rhode-island.

Elder Abuse

- Rhode Island Office of Healthy Aging: 401-462-3000 or 833-918-6603, see www.oha.ri.gov.
- Elder Abuse Resources in Rhode Island: see https://riag.ri.gov/elder-abuse

Fraud

- Rhode Island Attorney General's Office: helps protects consumers against scams, 401-274-4400, prompt 6, email consumers@riag.ri.gov, see https://riag.ri.gov.
- Rhode Island Department of Human Services (DHS): investigates fraudulent activity affecting customer benefits, 855-697-4347, see https://dhs.ri.gov/resources.
- Annual Credit Report Request Service from Annual Credit Report.com: see https://www.annualcreditreport.com/protectYourIdentity.action.
- National Consumers League Fraud Center (not limited to Rhode Island): see https://fraud.org.

Identity Theft

- Identity Theft Resource Center: see https://www.idtheftcenter.org.
- Attorney General's Office: see https://riag.ri.gov/what-we-do/civil-division/public-protection/consumer-protection/id-theft.

Online Criminal Case Status, Inmate Status, and Sex Offender Registry

- Public Access to Court Electronic Documents (PACER): Information at https://pacer.uscourts.gov/. Get a PACER login and password online by registering at https://pacer.psc.uscourts.gov/pscof/registration.jsf or by calling 800-676-6856.
- Rhode Island Department of Corrections, Incarceration Search: see https://doc.ri.gov/family-visitors/incarceration-search.
- Rhode Island Sex Office Registry: see https://www.sheriffalerts.com/cap_main.php?office=56404.

Sexual Assault

- National Sexual Assault Hotline: 800-656-4673, see https://rainn.org.
- Day One: Day One's mission is to reduce the prevalence of sexual abuse and violence and to advocate for those affected by it, 401-421-4100, info@dayoneri.org, see www.dayoneri.org.
- Sojourner House: Comprehensive domestic violence and sexual assault agency, 401-765-3232, see www.sojournerri.org.
- National Human Trafficking Hotline: 888-373-7888 or text 233733 or email help@humantraffickinghotline.org, see https://humantraffickinghotline.org/en.
- Sexual Assault Victims Bill of Rights and Resources for Victim Support: see https://riag.ecms.ri.gov/savbor.

Survivors of Homicide

- Survivors of Homicide: Offers one-on-one counseling, support groups, support throughout the judicial process, personal advocacy in working with law enforcement and other community agencies, and planning and business meetings to further our advocacy and educational goals, Based in Connecticut but available to survivors everywhere, see https://www.survivorsofhomicide.com/about-us,

Victim Advocacy

- Blackstone Valley Advocacy Center: Provides comprehensive services to victims of domestic violence, sexual violence, and prevention education to the community at large. 800-494-8100, see https://www .bvacri.org/residential.

Victim Compensation

- Office of Victims of Crime (OVC): Information on VOCA-Funded Victim Assistance Program, and VOCA-Funded Victim Compensation Program, see: https://ovc.ojp.gov/states/rhode-island.
- Crime Victim Compensation Program (CVCP): A program that provides up to $25,000 in reimbursement to victims of violent crime. This can be used for expenses such as medical, dental, and counseling, funeral expenses, relocation, and more. To be eligible, victims must file a police report within 15 days of the crime and file a claim with CVCP within 3 years, see https://treasury.ri.gov.
- Project Victim Services: Provides financial assistance for expenses that are not already covered by insurance, worker's compensation, and other sources, see https://childadvocate.ri.gov/project-victim-services.

Victim Notification System

- RI VINE: Computer-assisted telephone services providing offender custody information and notification of offender custody status. Registration is necessary to receive their services, see https://doc.r i.gov/victims/victim-information-and-notification-everyday-vine.

Victim Rights and Services Complaints

- Department of Justice: Victims can file a complaint if they feel a Department of Justice employee has failed to provide them with their rights as a victim. Complaint forms are available in English and Spanish. See https://riag.ri.gov/about-our-office/divisions-and-units/civil-division/public-protection/civil-community-rights-0.
- Office of the Victims' Rights Ombudsman (National): Victims can file a complaint with the Office of the Victims' Rights Ombudsman, who will then forward the complaint to the relevant office, see https://www.justice.gov/usao/crime-victims-rights-ombudsman-victims-rights.

Victim/Witness Assistance Program

- Rhode Island State Police Victims' Assistance Program: A program that provides a trained Victims' Assistance Provider to help victims and witnesses immediately after an incident. The provider can help identify the most appropriate follow-up and referrals, see https://risp.ri.gov/community-programs/victims-assistance-program.

Programs subject to change or end without notice.

Chapter 6: Vacations Can Be Murder in Vermont

Vermont Crime Statistics

OnlyinYourState.com ranks Vermont as one of the safest states in the nation. NeighborhoodScout.com reports that in 2023, there were only 1,362 violent crimes committed in the state, or about 2.10 per every 1,000 residents (16 murders, 198 rapes, 94 robberies, and 1,054 cases of assault). That is one-third the average rate of murder when compared with the U.S. as a whole, an 18% lower rate of robbery, and close to 40% less than the U.S. rate of assault. However, by the end of 2023, there was a 185% rise in firearm homicides, so time will tell if the state's ranking holds in 2024. There were also 11,615 property crimes or 17,94 per every 1,000 residents. The chances of becoming a victim of a property crime in Vermont are one out of 56.

Using 2023 figures, OnlyinYourState.com lists certain Vermont cities as more dangerous than others, including St. Albans, Brattleboro, Winooski, Burlington, and Barre (highest violent crime rate, 554 per 100,000 residents). Safewise.com reports the 2024 safest cities in Vermont as Barre Town, Swanton, Stowe, Middlebury, and Shelburne.

Summary of serial killings, mass shootings, mob hits, and other crimes
(listed alphabetically by location)

Should you wish to visit these cities, exact addresses, where available, are listed in the "Itineraries" section at the end of the chapter.

Vermont may be low on the list of states with the most serial killings, but they make up for it in the number of unsolved disappearances and cold cases that exist in the state:

Andover: On November 4, 1914, in the hamlet of Simonsville, former Representative Henry Wiggins and his wife Georgia were found murdered in the barn and woodshed adjoining their home. George Warner, their son-in-law, blamed the couple for his estrangement from his wife and shot them both. He was eventually convicted of the crime and became the first person to be executed in Vermont's electric chair. All three are buried in the Simonsville Cemetery.

Barre: Lucina Courser Broadwell (29) was murdered in Barre on May 4, 1919. The mother of three was found clothed only in shoes, stockings, and kid gloves, with the rest of her clothing found under her body or nearby. Her hands were tied behind her back with one of her undergarments and tied around her neck, a shirtwaist secured by a man's white handkerchief that presumably strangled her. Detective James R. Wood Jr. determined that Broadwell was murdered at the Buzzell Hotel and moved later to the garden.

An investigation revealed that Broadwell was unfaithful to her husband, Harry. She often visited a house of ill repute run by Mrs. Isabelle Parker, where she was having an affair with one of its residents, George R. Long (a pseudonym for George Rath). Long had an extensive criminal record. Circumstantial evidence tied him to the murder and, along with Parker, he was indicted by a grand jury. A jury eventually found Long guilty of second-degree murder, and he was sentenced to life imprisonment at Windsor State Prison. Parker pled guilty to conducting cheating parties at her "house of ill fame" and received a two-to-four-year jail sentence at the Women's Reformatory in Windsor. She died at the Rutland City Hospital two and a half years later.

Also in Barre: George Miles White (real name: George Bliss), a successful businessman, was at one time considered America's most notorious bank robber. He masterminded the robbery of the National Bank of Barre on July 6, 1875, and was best known for his theft innovation, the bank robber's mask. He got the idea from the White Masks, a precursor to the Ku Klux Klan.

More recently, on August 7, 2015, Jody Herring, a mother addicted to drugs and alcohol, blamed state social worker Lara Sobel, as well as a few of her own relatives, for causing her to lose custody of her then 9-year-old daughter. For revenge, Herring shot Sobel outside the state's Department for Children and Families in Barre and also murdered two cousins, sisters Rhonda and Regina Herring, and an aunt, Julie Falzarano, in their Berlin home. She was sentenced on November 17, 2021, to life without parole.

Belvidere: On July 14, 2001, in a town of 300 just forty miles from Burlington, state troopers discovered four people—Jessica Bishop (18), her father Mitchell Bishop Jr. (46), Derrick Davis (23), and Jessica's boyfriend, George Weatherwax (19), shot to death in a mobile home on rural Route 109. On Saturday, Douglas Provost, 34, of Fairfax, was arrested on murder charges for the shootings, precipitated by a gun-for-drugs deal gone bad. Provost claimed he shot the first victim by accident and then the others in self-defense. In 2003, he was convicted on four counts of first-degree murder and is currently serving four consecutive life terms in Tennessee.

Bennington: In 1900, 17-year-old Mary Mabel Bennett married Marcus Rogers but later grew disenchanted. The next year, she gave birth to a daughter, but six months later, she dropped baby Helen, who died of a fractured skull. Rogers' family questioned the "accident," especially after Marcus became violently ill after drinking a cup of tea prepared by his wife.

Marcus took work out of state and urged Mary to move with him, but she refused, instead enjoying the attention of several men, including Morris Knapp as well as two brothers, Leon and Levi Perham. Mary soon moved in with the Perhams. In July, when the family relocated, Morris Knapp and

VACATIONS CAN BE MURDER

Mary joined them. It is suspected Mary was sleeping with all three men.

Mary asked Levi to help murder her husband in exchange for $500 of the insurance money. He turned her down, but Leon agreed. At a supposed reconciliation picnic at Morgan's Grove, Mary watched as Leon bound her husband's hands, and then she sedated him with chloroform. Together, they rolled him into the Walloomsac River, where he drowned. They tried to pass the death off as suicide, but Perham confessed and testified against Mary, which helped him avoid a death sentence. Mary was convicted of first-degree murder.

Following inappropriate sexual activity between her and the prison staff, Mary was hanged on December 8, 1905, making her the last woman legally executed by the state of Vermont. That's because the hanging didn't go as planned—it took fourteen minutes for her to die by strangulation rather than instantly, had her neck snapped—which was instrumental in the state abolishing the death penalty.

Between 1920-1950, several people disappeared from what author Joseph Citro has coined the "Bennington Triangle," a small section of woods that's part of the 274-mile Long Trail on Glastenbury Mountain. It's estimated that up to forty people have gone missing, with the remains of only one person recovered, that of 53-year-old Frieda Langer. People claim to have seen UFO activity and Bigfoot in the area.

Burlington: H.H. Holmes, a man often referred to as America's first serial killer, has a Vermont connection. He committed most of his murders in Chicago, but in the fall of 1894, he hid from insurance investigators in Burlington under a fake name. He rented a property for his associate's wife, Carrie Pitezel, and her two children and stayed briefly at the Burlington Hotel. Unbeknownst to Carrie, Holmes had already killed her husband Benjamin, three of their children, and was aiming for her when he asked her to retrieve an explosive bottle of nitroglycerin from a booby-trapped basement. Carrie was too smart for Holmes, though, and the plot backfired. The murder of her husband, Benjamin Pitezel, eventually led to Holmes' conviction and execution.

Also in Burlington: on July 20, 1971, Rita Curran (24), a second-grade teacher, was discovered nude in her bedroom, sexually assaulted, beaten, and strangled to death. Police initially suspected mass murderer Ted Bundy, who had been in the area at that time, the attack matching his *modus operandi*. However, on February 21, 2023, the Burlington Police named Curran's neighbor from two floors above, William DeRoos, as her killer. Thanks to DNA testing done five decades after the incident, a cigarette butt found near the body connected DeRoos to the murder. Unfortunately, he went unpunished; he'd died of a drug overdose in 1986.

Most recently, in a possible hate crime spurred by the Israel-Hamas war in Gaza, Jason J. Eaton (48), a Syracuse transplant, is suspected of shooting three Palestinian college students on November 25, 2023. He pleaded not guilty to three charges of attempted murder in the second degree. Authorities found a gun during an apartment search that connected Eaton to the attack.

Finally, Burlington is the birthplace of serial killer Ted Bundy. He was born Theodore Robert Cowell on November 24, 1946, at the Lund Home, previously called Elizabeth Lund Home for Unwed Mothers. However, in her book *True Crime Stories of Burlington, Vermont*, author Thea Lewis called it the "Home for Friendless Women."

Duxbury: In the spring of 1879, Emeline Lucy Meaker and her family were living at the Somerville Farm in the Mutton Hollow section of Duxbury. Emeline did not appreciate her husband taking in his orphaned and destitute niece Alice and nephew Harry for the sum of $400. (Some references list Alice as Meaker's half-sister, not his niece.) She mistreated Alice terribly and eventually enlisted the help of her dimwitted son Almon to kidnap and poison the girl with strychnine in a remote area outside Waterbury, near what is now Little River State Park. They buried her there.

When the local sheriff investigated Alice's disappearance, Almon confessed, and her body was unearthed and tested, revealing she had been poisoned. Both he and Emeline were sentenced to death by hanging, but Almon's sentence was later commuted. Emeline was incarcerated at the Vermont State Prison in Windsor County and was the first woman executed by the state of Vermont.

Essex: Israel Keyes was an Alaska-based handyman and serial killer whose 8+ murders spanned the entire country. (Some accounts estimate he murdered 11 people between 2001-2012.) In a confession, he admitted to targeting Bill and Lorraine Currier of Essex. Two years prior to the crime, he said he'd hidden a "murder kit" near their home as he did for his other victims. It included a handgun, ammunition, Drano to hasten human decomposition and other supplies. To commit the murders, he claimed that on June 2nd, 2011, he'd flown to Chicago to cover his tracks and driven 1,000 miles to Vermont, Then, on the night of June 8th, he broke into the Currier's home, tied them up, and drove them to an abandoned farmhouse on Route 15 with a For Sale sign. There, he fatally shot Bill Currier and sexually assaulted and strangled Lorraine. Their bodies have never been recovered. While awaiting trial for another murder, Keyes committed suicide and was never convicted.

Hardwick: On July 15, 1977, two murders—the first since the early sixties—shook the sleepy town of Hardwick. First, the body of Joan Gray Rogers was found in a hay field, the victim of manual strangulation. She was last seen by a couple the same evening at 7:30 p.m., after having dropped off one of her sons at the movies. Next, the robbery and strangulation death of Bernard D. Ewen (64) created further panic among the townspeople, even though police contended the two murders were unrelated.

Jericho: On June 11, 1978, Michael Reapp reported his wife Grace (32) and daughter Gracie (5) missing, having left a note that they never planned to return. He filed for divorce ten days later on grounds of abandonment.

He then remarried his former babysitter and moved to Florida with his two remaining sons. However, in 1996, he too went missing after learning that Vermont police were searching the grounds of his former home. In 2006, the State of Vermont issued an arrest warrant for Michael Reapp, charging him with one count of first-degree murder and one count of second-degree murder. In 2012, they discovered he'd committed suicide in Arizona in 1997 after being pursued by police for an armed carjacking. At that time, he'd been listed as a John Doe. The remains of his wife and daughter have yet to be recovered.

Middlebury: Lynn Schulze, a freshman at Middlebury College, disappeared on December 10, 1971. Some people believe they saw her hitchhiking when she was supposed to be taking an exam. Though she had told a few people she was considering dropping out of society and starting over, foul play is suspected. Accused murderer Robert Durst is considered a strong person of interest, but as of this writing, the case remains unsolved.

Montgomery: Brianna Maitland (17) was seen leaving the Black Lantern Inn after her shift on March 19, 2004. Her green 1985 Oldsmobile was found the next day, backed into an abandoned house about a mile away. No further information exists, but multiple rewards are still being offered for information pertaining to the case.

Morrisville: Cheryl Peters (42) was a mother of five and worked at Copley Hospital. She was in the throes of her third divorce, this one from Carroll Peters, and was living with her cousin, Richard. On September 2, 1993, Richard discovered Cheryl's body in their home, shot to death by a single gunshot wound. A witness told police that the previous day, they'd seen a white, dark-haired, and mustached male of 170-200 pounds enter the residence and, five or six minutes later, leave carrying a large bag.

Court records show that Carroll Peters had shown up unannounced at the home in the past. He had written a letter admitting to sexually assaulting Cheryl without her knowledge. While the case remains unsolved, in June

1996, her daughter Raemarie Pecor and her siblings filed a civil suit against Carroll Peters on behalf of their late mother, accusing him of wrongful death, sexual assault, and battery. The statute of limitations had run out on the wrongful death claim, but a jury hearing sexual assault and battery claims awarded Peters' family $125,000 in compensatory damages and $480,000 in punitive damages.

On September 20, 2024, Carroll Peters (now 70) was arrested and pleaded not guilty to first-degree murder in connection with Cheryl Peters' death, even though Lamoille County state's attorney Aliena Gerhard said there's no evidence in the case. He is being held without bail.

Newbury: Orville Gibson, a wealthy dairy farmer, disappeared on December 31, 1957. He resurfaced—literally—nearly three months later in the Connecticut River, his body bound. It was speculated that town vigilantes killed Gibson as punishment for beating sickly farmhand Eri Martin after he had spilled milk. Gibson contended that Martin had come to work drunk, spilled the milk purposely, and tripped over a cart, fracturing his ribs. Locals Robert "Ozzie" Welch and Frank Carpenter were arrested for the crime due to circumstantial evidence but were later acquitted.

Richmond: Michelle Gardner-Quinn (21), a senior at the University of Vermont in Burlington, was found on October 13, 2006, at Huntington Gorge in Richmond, her dead body stuffed into a rock crevice and covered with leaves. She had been sexually assaulted and strangled, and her skull showed blunt force trauma. Jewelry store security camera footage from October 7th caught an image of Gardner-Quinn with Brian L. Rooney, a former construction worker. Rooney had federal charges filed against him for the sexual assault of two other women, one a minor. Semen found inside Gardner-Quinn's body linked him to her murder. In 2008, he was convicted and sentenced to life in prison without the possibility of parole, despite attempts at appeal. He is currently housed at a correctional facility in Kentucky.

Saxtons River: In April of 1986, Steven Moore came home to find his wife, Lynda Moore, dead in their living room. Another victim, a 36-year-old nurse named Barbara Agnew, disappeared from a highway rest stop in Hartford, VT, less than fifty miles away, and her remains were found near Advent Hill Road in Hartford on March 18, 1987. Both women suffered multiple stab wounds, and their throats had been slit. Michael Nicholaou is the suspected murderer. Though he lived in Massachusetts, his wife had relatives in Vermont, giving him a reason to visit. In December of 2005, in West Tampa, Florida, Nicholaou committed suicide after killing his wife and stepdaughter.

Shelburne: The remains of a six-week-old baby, killed in a Shelburne campground in July of 1999, were found in 2002, after the abandoned camper of Jason Michael Hann was sold at auction in Lake Havasu City, Arizona. Evidence showed that the baby's head had been smashed against a crib, and he died shortly afterwards. Hann and the baby's mother, Krissy Werntz, arrived in Vermont in 1998, and she had been working at multiple jobs through Westaff, including Magic Hat Brewery, Rhino Foods, and a bakery.

The couple had stored the baby's remains in a plastic container and traveled around for 18 months before abandoning the camper in Arizona. They were apprehended in Portland, Maine, in April of 2002, with a five-week-old son on the brink of death, suffering from multiple broken bones, blood clots on his brain, hearing loss, and eye damage. He was later renamed and adopted.

While serving a 27-to-30-year sentence for that crime, Hann was also found guilty of killing his 2-month-old daughter, Montana, while in Desert Hot Springs, CA. in 2001 and leaving the remains in a Wynne, Arkansas storage unit. Both he and Werntz were charged, and the jury recommended the death sentence for first-degree murder and assault on a child. In 2019, while on death row in San Quentin, an all-male facility, Hann changed names and gender identity and is now known as Jessica Marie Hann. Werntz was sentenced to 15 years to life, which she is serving at a prison in Chowchilla, CA.

Springfield: In 1952, Donald DeMag and fellow prisoner Francis Blair escaped from the state prison in Windsor, where DeMag had been sentenced to life imprisonment for the 1948 murder of Francis Racicot (81). They stopped to commit a robbery en route, during which they attacked Elizabeth Weatherup and her husband Donald in the Goulds Mill neighborhood of Springfield, beating the couple with a lead pipe. Elizabeth died from her injuries.

Two days after their escape, they were recaptured and tried for first-degree murder. They were both sentenced to death by the electric chair, with Blair's execution occurring on February 8, 1954, followed by DeMag's nine months later on December 8. DeMag was the last person to be executed in Vermont; the death penalty was abolished by the state in 1965.

Also in Springfield, Gary Lee Schaefer—an arsonist who had also been charged with illegal gun possession while in the Navy—kidnapped, raped, and murdered 13-year-old Sherry Nastasia in 1979, and then Theresa Fenton, in 1981. The following year, Deana Buxton (17) survived an attack from Schaefer in Brattleboro, but police lacked enough evidence to charge him. He struck again on April 9, 1983, when he abducted Catherine Richards (11) back in Springfield, sexually assaulted her, and then crushed her skull with a stone. Her body was found the next day, and descriptions from witnesses tied him to the Buxton assault of the previous year. An open letter from Richards' mother, invoking the precepts of his church, prompted him to confess to the two murders and rape. As part of a plea bargain, the Fenton murder was dismissed, but Schaefer was still sentenced to 30 years to life at Leavenworth in Kansas on the remaining counts. He died in prison in November of 2023.

Thetford (Post Mills): Louis (Doris) Maxfield (46), was found murdered at her home on January 3, 1977. Though foul play was not originally considered, the medical examiner ruled the death a homicide by asphyxiation caused by manual strangulation. Her husband was driving a school bus at the time of her death. The case remains cold as of this writing.

Vernon: On March 4, 1999, a passing motorist found the nude body of Springfield, MA resident Mary Morales, dumped alongside a guardrail on Interstate 91. It is believed she accepted a ride home after leaving her job at Unicare, Inc. the prior day. It is also suspected that she knew her murderer. Morales' husband Edgardo was suspected of drug activity, and Mary's death may have been retaliation for a deal gone bad. On March 19, newspapers reported that Edgardo Morales was picked up by police in Puerto Rico, but was cooperative when questioned. The murder remains unsolved.

West Charleston: In 2009, Christine Billis, tired of a life of abuse from her husband Charles, attempted to murder them both by slamming their car into a giant pine tree. He died, but she survived. She later confessed to Kevin Leland, a man she met on the OK Cupid dating site, that the crash was not the accident people believed it to be. He recorded the confession when they met in person and then went to the police. Billis was charged with first-degree murder but plea-bargained the charge down to manslaughter, buying her seven to fifteen years in jail. Her minimum sentence ended on June 25, 2018. In June 2019, she assaulted and threatened to kill her boyfriend at a home in Barton. She was sentenced in 2021 to serve 16 to 18 months for domestic assault.

West Guilford: Walter and Katherine Nichols, aged 27 and 21, respectively, were murdered by their alcoholic farmhand, Erving Wrisley, on October 9, 1913, who then committed suicide by shotgun. It is speculated that theft might have been a motive, also possibly revenge because it later came out that he had been discharged. However, that doesn't explain why Wrisley killed himself afterward.

White River Junction: Connecticut resident Jan Albert Zepka, 25, who had traveled to Vermont to go camping, was found dead off the side of Interstate 91. His skull had been fractured, and his wallet and valuables were missing. It's believed he was killed elsewhere a few days prior, his body then disposed of near the entrance/exit ramp.

Want more Vermont crime? Check out Murderpedia at http://www.murderp edia.org/ and also True Crime Stories of Burlington, Vermont by Thea Lewis (History Press, 2023).

Read Before You Leave: A Sampling of Vermont True Crime Books

(listed alphabetically by author)

Note: Some of these books may cover crimes not discussed elsewhere in this guide.

- Belding, Patricia Wyman. *One Less Woman*. Potash Brook Pub., 2006.
- Bellamy, John Stark III. *Vintage Vermont Villainies*. Countryman Press, 2007.
- Hunter, JT. *Devil in the Darkness: The True Story of Serial Killer Israel Keyes*. Pedialaw Publishing, 2020
- Kendrick, Patrick. *American Ripper: The Enigma of America's Serial Killer Cop*.Bluewaterpress LLC, 2020.
- Lewis, Thea. *True Crime Stories of Burlington, Vermont*. The History Press, 2023.
- Martin, Stephen B. *Orville's Revenge: The Anatomy of a Suicide*. L. Brown and Sons, 2014.
- Meyer, Peter. *Death of Innocence*. Berkley, 1986.
- Overacker, Gregory. *The Hunt for Brianna Maitland*. Bloated Toe Publishing, 2023.
- White, George M. *From Boniface to Bank Burglar; Or the Price of Persecution*. Good Press, 2019 (reprint).

Accommodations and Restaurants that are Crime/Prison-Related or Haunted

While there were no converted prisons or courthouse-type hotels or restaurants in Vermont that I could find, here is a list of accommodations that are rumored to be haunted. Where there are unsettled spirits, could murder be far behind?

Haunted Accommodations

Manchester Village
  Equinox Golf Hotel & Spa
  3567 Main Street, Manchester Village
  802-362-4700
  contactus@equinoxresort.com
  https://www.equinoxresort.com
  Guests claim to have seen the spirit of Mary Todd Lincoln, Abraham Lincoln's wife, strolling through the hotel.

Montgomery
  Black Lantern Inn and Restaurant
  2057 North Main Street, Montgomery
  802-326-3269
  blacklanternvt@gmail.com
  https://blacklanternvt.com

The ghost in Room 3 likes to take quick showers.

Proctorsville (near Ludlow)

Golden Stage Inn

399 Depot Street, Proctorsville

802-226-7744

innkeeper@goldenstageinn.com

https://www.goldenstageinn.com

Built in 1788, one male and one female apparition have been spotted here.

Norwich

The Norwich Inn and Jasper Murdock's Alehouse

325 Main Street, Norwich

802-649-1143

innkeeper@norwichinn.com

https://www.norwichinn.com

Mary "Ma" Walker, the former owner who served liquor illegally during Prohibition, has been seen visiting Rooms 20 and 32.

Quechee

Inn at Clearwater Pond

984 Quechee-Harland Road, Quechee

802-295-0606

innatclearwaterpond@gmail.com

https://innatclearwaterpond.com

The hotel is haunted by Mr. Tewksbury, who committed suicide here. He walks the hallways, family room, and garden, interacting with guests and breaking things.

The Quechee Inn at Marshland Farm

1119 Quechee Main Street, Quechee

802-295-3133

info@quecheeinn.com

https://www.quecheeinn.com

The spirits of former owners John and Jane Porter reportedly haunt the premises, along with someone named Patrick Marsh.

St. Albans

Back Inn Time Bed & Breakfast

68 Fairfield Street, St Albans

802-527-5116

reservations@backinntimevt.com

https://www.backinntimevt.com

Reportedly haunted by Lora Weaver, wife of a former owner, as well as an anonymous male spirit.

Springfield

Hartness House and Hotel

109 Front Street (formerly 30 Orchard St.) Springfield

802-885-8022

contact@hartnesshouse.com

https://www.hartnesshouse.com

The spirit of former owner James Hartness has been known to move guests' possessions, but they always turn up.

Stowe

Brass Lantern Inn

717 Maple Street, Stowe

802-253-2229

info@brasslanterninn.com

https://brasslanterninn.com

Listen in as the ghosts talk and laugh in rooms that are reportedly empty.

Green Mountain Inn

18 Main Street, Stowe

802-253-7301 or 800-253-7302
info@gminn.com
https://greenmountaininn.com

The ghost of Boots Berry, who was born in the servant's quarters here in 1840, apparently never left. He spent time in prison in New Orleans, where he learned to tap dance. Back in Stowe, he rescued a girl from the roof of the Inn, right above Room 302, and died on the way down. When he isn't stealing guests' keys, he visits the Main Street Dining Room but hasn't yet appeared in the Whip Bar and Grill. On snowy nights, he tap-dances on the roof.

Waterbury

The Old Stagecoach Inn
18 N. Main Street, Waterbury
802-244-5056 or 800-262-2206
lodging@oldstagecoach.com
https://oldstagecoach.com

Room 2 seems to be the locus of haunting by a former resident.

West Dover

The Gray Ghost Inn
290 Route 100 North, West Dover
802-464-2474 or 800-745-3615
grayghostinn@gmail.com
https://www.grayghostinn.com

This inn has a history involving gangsters, a prison break, and an FBI chase.

White River Junction

Comfort Inn
56 Ralph Lehman Drive, White River Junction
802-295-3051
https://www.choicehotels.com/en-in/vermont/white-river-junction/

comfort-inn-hotels

A woman committed suicide in Room 112; her spirit never left.

Hotel Coolidge

39 South Main Street, White River Junction

802-295-3118

hotelcoolidgevt@gmail.com

https://www.hotelcoolidge.com

Considered to be one of the most haunted hotels in the state. Farmer and bootlegger Ezra "Wrench" Magoon died here and then stayed on.

Wilmington

The White House Inn

178 VT-9, Wilmington

844-931-3242

hello@whitehouseinnvt.com

https://whitehouseinnvt.com

Original owner Clara Brown mourns her deceased husband Martin for eternity from Room 9.

Haunted Restaurants

Burlington

Shanty on the Shore

181 Battery Street, Burlington

802-864-0238

info@shantyontheshore.com

https://www.shantyontheshore.com

Isaac Nye, an eccentric who owned a storefront on this site, was a hermit who was obsessed with funerals. He shuttered his store in 1840 and allowed his goods to rot. When he died in 1871, he asked to be laid out on the counter with the rancid food and 40 years' worth of dust. His ghost reportedly never left, turning on lights, rattling glasses, and rearranging furniture.

American Flatbread
   115 St. Paul Street, Burlington
   802-861-2999
   contact@flatbreadhearth.com
   https://americanflatbread.com/locations/burlington-vt
   The restaurant's former iteration as "Carbur's" was visited by spirits after a cook took his own life following service one night. Others believe the ghosts arrived earlier, when rumrunners operated in the tunnels beneath Burlington. Flying wreaths, doors locked (that have no lock), a server locked in a cooler—proof that the poltergeists are not especially welcoming here.

The Norwich Inn (Norwich), which houses Jasper Murdock's Alehouse, and the Green Mountain Inn (Stowe), both listed in the Accommodations section, also feature restaurants that are rumored to be haunted.

Crime Tours and Paranormal/Haunted House Tours

Burlington

Queen City Ghostwalk Tours are true crime walking tours through the city streets. The tours share Burlington's history of serial killers, crimes, and criminal plots and are led by Holli Bushnell, who took over from the company's founder, author and local historian Thea Lewis. Some of the sights might include those described in Lewis's book True Crime Stories of Burlington, Vermont, including the beheading of Israel Freeman in a multifamily house on the corner of Burlington's Cherry and Water Streets (known as Battery Street today); the disembowelment of Irish laborer Frank McCullough; the pickpocketing exploits of con artist John Larney (aka Mollie Matches) who used to stay at the Hotel Van Ness on the corner of Main and St. Paul Street; the 1926 shooting of Beatrice Heed by her jealous husband Philip, who then attempted suicide inside Green Brother's Five and Ten on Burlington's Church Street; and the spot where Marilyn Dietl shot her daughter Judy outside of the Shalom Shuk thrift store behind the Ohavi Sedek Synagogue on North Prospect Street to supposedly save her from a life of prostitution after dating a suspected pimp. (Note: Most of these crimes and locations are not covered in the "Itineraries" of this guide). One hour, $25 plus fees, ages 10+, departs 7:00 p.m. from Courthouse Plaza, 199 Main Street.

Other tours by this company include:

- Darkness Falls: 1 hour, $25 plus fees, ages 10+, departs 7:00 p.m. from Courthouse Plaza, 199 Main Street.
- Ghosts & Legends of Lake Champlain: 1 hour, ages 10+. $25 plus fees, departs at 7:00 p.m. from Union Station, 1 Main Street.
- Fright by Flashlight: 1 hour, ages 8+, $18-$25 plus fees, departs 6:00 p.m. from Louisa Howard Chapel at Lakeview Cemetery, 455 North Avenue.
- Elmwood Cemetery Tour: 1 hour, ages 10+. $25 plus fees, departs 6:00 p.m. from the main gate of Elmwood Cemetery on Elmwood Avenue.
- Lakeview Cemetery Tour: 1 hour, ages 10+. $25 plus fees, departs 6:00 p.m. from Louisa Howard Chapel at Lakeview Cemetery, 455 North Avenue.
- True Crime Burlington Bus Tour: length, price TBA, ages 16+, departs from 345 Pine Street (park at the lot used by the Burlington Farmers Market).
- UWM's Most Haunted Bus Tour: 2 hours, ages 14+, price TBA, departs at 7:00 p.m. from 345 Pine Street (park at the lot used by the Burlington Farmers Market).

Contact them at 802-324-5467, https://queencityghostwalk.com. Some tours may be seasonal.

All prices are per person. Tour offerings, prices, times, age restrictions, and meeting locations are subject to change.

Police/Crime/Prison/Courthouse Museums and Other Attractions

None currently exist in Vermont.

State and Federal Prisons of Note in Vermont

Newport

Northern State Correctional Facility
  2559 Glen Road, Newport

St. Albans

Northwest State Correctional Facility
  3649 Lower Newton Road, St. Albans

St. Johnsbury

Northeast Correctional Complex
  1266-1270 US Route 5, St. Johnsbury
  Consists of two facilities: Northeast Correctional Facility (NERCF) and Caledonia Community Work Camp (CCWC).

South Burlington

Chittenden Regional Correctional Facility
7 Farrell Street, South Burlington
Vermont's only prison for women, site of allegations of sexual misconduct. Notable inmates include Beatrice Heed for alienation of affection long after her husband attempted to murder her and Marilyn Dietl for murdering her daughter in Burlington.

Springfield

Southern State Correctional Facility
700 Charlestown Road, Springfield

Windsor

On August 7, 1975, the Southeast State Correctional Facility officially closed after 166 years of operation. A development group paid $27,050 to buy what was once the first state prison of its kind. What stands there now is Windsor Village Apartments (administrative offices at 65 State Street, formerly called Olde Windsor Village), with the prison's classic Federalist architecture preserved. While most of the inside was gutted, some cells from the 1870s, including their barred doors, are still intact in the basement and are now used for storage.

Notable Crime-and-Justice-Related Burial Sites

Plot locations included where available, burial sites not always included in itineraries.

Andover

Simonsville Cemetery
  104 Middletown Road, Andover
  Burial Site of Henry Filmore Wiggins and Georgia Ann Forbes Wiggins. Also buried here: their son-in-law and murderer, George Edward Warner, who was the first of only five people who have died in Vermont's electric chair.

Brattleboro

West Brattleboro Cemetery
  Mather Road, Brattleboro
  Burial site of Walter Herbert Nichols and Katherine Erma Moore Nichols, murdered by their farmhand Erving Wrisley.

Meeting House Hill Cemetery
  580 Orchard Street, Brattleboro
  Burial Site of murderer Erving Wrisley (gravestone incorrectly reads

"Irving").

Burlington

Old Mount Calvary Cemetery
253 Archibald Street, Burlington
Burial site of Francis Racicot (unmarked grave, area A-002), murdered by Donald DeMag.

Cabot

Durant Cemetery
1019-1363 VT-215N, Cabot
Burial site of Bernard D. Ewen, strangled by an unknown murderer.

Essex Junction

Holy Family Cemetery
Lincoln Street, Essex Junction
Burial site of Donald Edward DeMag (no marker, but reportedly buried in the NW corner of the DeMag lot near David DeMag)

Johnson

Lamoille View Cemetery
153 Clark Avenue, Johnson
Burial site of Lucina Courser Broadwell, murdered by George Long, aka George Rath.

Middlesex

Middlesex Center Cemetery
  485 Center Road, Middlesex
  Burial Site of Rhonda Jean Herring, Regina Lynn "Gina" Herring, and Julie Ann Boyce Falzarano, relatives and victims of murderer Jody Herring.

Milton

Saint Ann's Cemetery
  Corner of Middle Road and Railroad Street, Milton
  Burial Site of Rita Curran, murdered by William DeRoos.

Montpelier

Green Mount Cemetery
  250 State Street, Montpelier
  Burial Site of Lara Sobel, victim of Jody Herring.

Morristown

Plains-Green Lawn Cemetery
  26 Needles Eye Road, Morristown
  Burial site of Cheryl Anne Degree Peters, shot in her home by an unnamed assailant.

Newbury

Oxbow Cemetery
  4220 US-5, Newbury
  Burial site of Orville Albert Gibson, the dairy farmer reportedly murdered by members of his town.

Saxtons River

Saxtons River Cemetery
  Westminster Street, Saxtons River
  Burial site of Lynda Ann Marine Moore, murdered by an unnamed assailant.

Springfield

Oakland Cemetery
  251 River Street, Springfield
  Burial Site of Elizabeth Chase Weatherup, murdered by Donald DeMag.

West Windsor

Brownsville Cemetery
  Brownsville-Hartland Rd (across the street from the Albert Bridge School at 108 Brownsville-Hartland Road), West Windsor
  Burial site of Charles Bronson (star of the Death Wish movies).

Westminster

Old Westminster Cemetery
  Old Cemetery Road, Westminster
  Burial Site of George Miles White (Lot 204), a businessman-turned-bank robber.

Putting it All Together: Itineraries

Itinerary: True Crime Tour of Southern Vermont

Start your tour in the southwest corner of the state in Manchester County. In **Bennington**, you can visit the north end of Safford Street, where Mary Mabel Rogers lived with the Perham family along with Morris Knapp. The Bennington Triangle is a small, wooded area that's part of the 274-mile Long Trail on Glastenbury Mountain, where up to forty people have gone missing. While in Manchester County, why not stay at the Equinox Golf Hotel & Spa to the north in **Manchester Village** at 3567 Main Street, rumored to be haunted.

Next head north to **Middlebury**, where Lynn Schulze was abducted from Middlebury College (14 Old Chapel Road is the college's main address). She was last seen hitchhiking on Route 7 southbound. Further northeast in **Waterbury** (a side trip), Emeline Lucy Meaker and her son poisoned her husband's niece near what is now Little River State Park. While there, visit the Old Stagecoach Inn at 18 N. Main Street, which is also haunted.

Heading southeast, **Newbury** is where Orville Gibson disappeared after a group of vigilantes murdered him in his barn on Route 5 and tossed him off a bridge into the Connecticut River. He was found near Bradford and buried at the Oxbow Cemetery at 4220 US-5. The unincorporated community of Post Mills in **Thetford** to the south is where Louis (Doris) Maxfield was found murdered in her home (no street address available.)

Further southwest in Windsor County, be prepared to make several stops. The Norwich Inn, 325 Main Street, **Norwich,** with its resident ghosts, might be one stop, followed by **White River Junction**, where Jan Albert Zepka was found dead 200 feet west of the highway near the I-91 southbound onramp. Both the Comfort Inn (56 Ralph Lehman Drive) and Hotel Coolidge (39 South Main Street) are rumored to harbor spirits.

Moving on to **Windsor**, you can drive by the Windsor Village Apartments at 65 State Street, once the home of the Southeast State Correctional Facility. Slightly west in **West Windsor**, *Death Wish* star Charles Bronson is buried at Brownsville Cemetery on Brownsville-Hartland Road.

Continue driving south to **Springfield,** where Donald DeMag and Francis Blair attacked Elizabeth Weatherup and her husband in their Goulds Mill home, estimated to be 350 feet off VT-Route 11. She is buried at the Oakland Cemetery at 251 River Street. This town is also where Gary Lee Schaefer kidnapped, raped, and murdered 13-year-old Sherry Nastasia in 1979, and then beat and buried Theresa Fenton in the woods near Mile Hill Road in 1981. Later, he abducted Catherine Richards from Pedden Acres Road and VT-106, where she'd been walking with friends. Her body was later found in a wooded area off of Baltimore Road. Next, you can drive by the Southern State Correctional Facility at 700 Charlestown Road, then visit ghosts overnight at the Hartness House & Hotel at 109 Front Street (formerly 30 Orchard St.). Alternatively, there's another haunted hotel, the Golden Stage Inn, at 399 Depot Street, in nearby **Proctorsville**.

In the hamlet of **Simonsville** to the southwest, Vermont's former Representative Henry Wiggins and his wife Georgia were found murdered on their property on Howard Hill Road by their son-in-law, George Edward Warner. Warner was the first of only five people who died in Vermont's electric chair. Their three graves can be visited at the Simonsville Cemetery at 104 Middletown Road.

Rounding out your Southern Vermont crime tour, head southeast to Windham County for a series of short stops. Lynda Moore was murdered in the home she shared with her husband on Route 121 in **Westminster** outside of the Village of **Saxtons River**. She is buried at the Saxtons River Cemetery on Washington Street. Also in Westminster, the grave of bank robber George Miles White is at the Old Westminster Cemetery on Old Cemetery Road.

Drive south to **Brattleboro**, where alcoholic farmhand Erving Wrisley committed suicide by shotgun and is buried in the Meeting House Hill Cemetery at 580 Orchard Street. To the west, Walter and Katherine Nichols are buried at the **West Brattleboro** Cemetery on Mather Road, after they were murdered by Wrisley. The site of the murders is to the west in **West Guilford** on what was likely Hayes Road. The tour ends to the southeast to **Vernon**, where the nude body of Mary Morales was dumped alongside a guardrail on Interstate 91 near Mile Marker 4.

Missing from this tour: the site near where Barbara Agnew's remains were found in Hartford, and stops near Hartford in Quechee, including two haunted hotels: the Quechee Inn at Marshland Farm, and the Inn at Clearwater Pond. Also omitted: the haunted Gray Ghost Inn in West Dover and the White House Inn in Wilmington.)

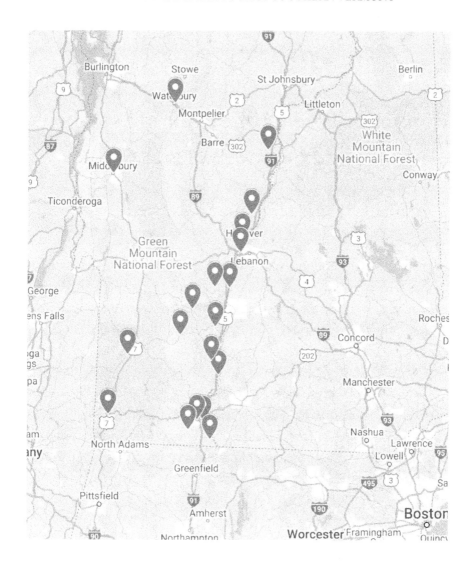

Itinerary: True Crime Tour of Northern and Central Vermont

Start your tour in Chittenden County in **Shelburne**, home to the campground where Jason Michael Hann murdered his infant son. The baby's mother, Krissy Werntz, worked at both Magic Hat Brewery on Flynn Avenue in Burlington's South End and Rhino Foods on Queen City Park Road.

Move on to **Burlington**, where serial murderer H.H. Holmes rented an apartment for his associate's wife, Carrie Pitezel, and her two children on 26 North Winooski Avenue and stayed briefly at the Burlington Hotel on College Street. He also purchased the nitroglycerine meant to kill Carrie at a pharmacy on St. Paul Street. Francis Racicot, 81-year-old victim of Donald DeMag, was murdered at his shop at 24 Center Street, and later buried at the Old Mount Calvary Cemetery on 253 Archibald Street. Also in this city, teacher Rita Curran was murdered in the bedroom of her apartment at 17 Brookes Avenue.

On North Prospect Avenue, Jason J. Eaton is suspected of shooting three Palestinian college students. Finally, Burlington is the birthplace of serial killer Ted Bundy, who was born Theodore Robert Cowell on November 24th, 1946, at what's now called the Lund Home at 50 Joy Drive in **South Burlington**. Both Beatrice Heed and Marilyn Dietl served time at Chittenden Regional Correctional Facility at 7 Farrell Street in

South Burlington if you'd like to drive past. For a guided walking tour of Burlington, check out Queen City Ghostwalk Tours, which covers Burlington crime sites not listed in this section. Before or after a tour, you might like to grab a bite at one of the city's two reportedly haunted restaurants: Shanty on the Shore at 181 Battery Street or American Flatbread at 115 St. Paul Street.

On the 0-50 block of Colbert Street in **Essex Junction** stands the house from which Bill and Lorraine Currier were abducted by Israel Keyes and killed in an abandoned farmhouse on Route 15. (Oddspots.com puts the home at 15 Upper Main Street, where there's now an empty lot.) Also in Essex Junction, the unmarked grave of Donald DeMag is at Holy Family Cemetery on Lincoln Street, at the northwest corner of the DeMag lot. And to the east in **Jericho**, Grace Reapp and her daughter Gracie were reported missing from their home on Hanley Lane.

Heading north, you can visit the haunted Back Inn Time Bed & Breakfast in **St. Albans** at 68 Fairfield St, as well as drive by the Northwest State Correctional Facility at 3649 Lower Newton Road. Marietta Ball, victim of Joseph LaPage (see the New Hampshire chapter) is buried in Greenwood Cemetery on South Main Street (US Route-7). To the northwest in **Montgomery**, Brianna Maitland was seen leaving the Black Lantern Inn at 2057 North Main Street after her shift and was never seen again. You, too, can stay here; the Inn is said to be haunted. According to Oddspots.com, Maitland's car was found around 10 miles to the west at 3451 North Main Street in **Enosburg Falls**.

Heading east, the Northern State Correctional Facility is in **Newport** at 2559 Glen Road. Southeast in **West Charleston**, Christine Billis slammed her car into a pine tree on Route 5A at the intersection of Line Farm Road, which killed her abusive husband.

Next, you can head southwest to visit **Belvidere**, where four people were found shot to death by Douglas Provost in a mobile home on rural Route 109, just northeast of Belvidere Center. Turning southeast, in **Johnson**, Lucina Courser Broadwell is buried at Lamoille View Cemetery at 153 Clark Avenue, and further southeast in **Morrisville**, Cheryl Peters was found in her rental home on Washington Highway by her cousin/roommate, shot to death by a single bullet.

Further southeast, the body of Joan Gray Rogers was found in **Hardwick**, in a hay field on the Old Bagley Farm along Highway 45. On the same day, Bernard D. Ewen was found strangled in Bemis Block Housing (aka Bemis Block-Elderly) at 41 South Main Street.

The last stops on the tour include **Barre** to the south, where Lucina Courser Broadwell was murdered at the Buzzell Hotel, then located at 28 Pearl Street, and her body dumped in the Wheelock Garden off North Main Street. You can also see the location of Isabelle Parker's cheating parties at 110 South Main Street. George Miles White masterminded the robbery of the National Bank of Barre, which was located on the corner of Elm and Main Streets. And Jody Herring murdered social worker Lara Sobel outside the state's Department for Children and Families at 255 North Main Street. Finally, northwest in **Duxbury**, Emeline Lucy Meaker and her son Almon lived with her husband's relative Alice, whom they kidnapped, poisoned, and then buried in nearby Waterbury.

(Omitted from this tour: Richmond, where the body of Michelle Gardner-Quinn was found at the Huntington Gorge; Stowe, where ghosts haunt both the Brass Lantern Inn at 717 Maple Street and the Green Mountain Inn at 18 Main Street; the burial site of Bernard D. Ewen in Cabot, and St. Johnsbury to drive by the Northeast Correctional Complex at 1270 US-5.)

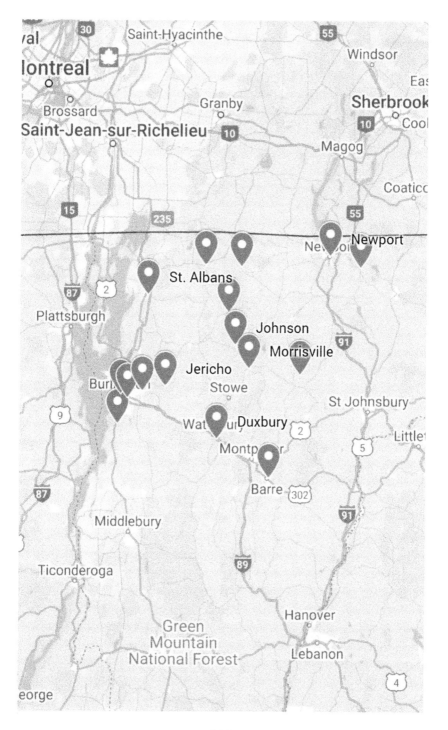

Vermont Victim Resources

This is a noncomprehensive summary of services available to victims of crime in Vermont. Information was taken directly from their websites. Visit/contact agencies for complete information and note that some programs offered by certain contractors focus on specific geographic areas. Some resource categories and content may overlap. Inclusion does not equate to recommendation.

Victim Services

- Dial 211: For information and Referral Specialists from United Way of Vermont, see www.vermont211.org.
- Vermont Center for Victim Services: 800-750-1213 or 802-241-1250, see https://ccvs.vermont.gov.
- Vermont Network (links to many resources): see https://www.vtnetwork.org.

Crime-centric List of Resources

Child Abuse

- KidSafe Collaborative: A community partnership of over 30 organizations, agencies, and individuals working together to improve the community's response to child abuse and neglect, 800-649-5285, see

https://www.kidsafevt.org.
- Prevent Child Abuse VT: Statewide organization that conducts prevention education on sexual abuse and abusive head trauma and leads Nurturing Parent classes and Parents Together support groups throughout the state, 800-244-5373, or DCF Central Intake Line at 800-649-5285, see https://www.pcavt.org.
- Child Safe Clinic: University of Vermont Children's Hospital clinic serving children and families where child abuse/child sexual abuse is suspected or diagnosed, 802-847-8200, see https://www.uvmhealth. org/childrens-hospital/pediatric-specialties/child-safe-program.

Civil Legal Help for People with Low Income

- Vermont Legal Aid: 800-889-2047 (Northern VT) 802-863-5620 Voice/TTY Helping adults with disabilities get assistance under the Rehabilitation Act. All counties in VT. See https://www.vtlegalaid.org or VTLawHelp.org.

Domestic Violence

- Domestic Shelters: For a list of resources and more, see https://www. domesticshelters.org/help
- National Domestic Abuse Hotline: 800-799-7233 or 800-228-7395, or text START to 88788, see https://www.thehotline.org/?utm_sour ce=youtube&utm_medium=organic&utm_campaign=domestic_viol ence,
- Aware Domestic & Sexual Violence Services: dedicated to resolving the causes and effects of domestic violence and sexual assault in the greater Hardwick area, 802-472-6463, see https://www.awarevt.org.
- Circle: Shelter service and advocacy for anyone experiencing intimate partner violence in the Washington County area.877-543-9498, info@circlevt.org, see https://www.circlevt.org.

Drunk Driving Victims

- Mothers Against Drink Driving Vermont: 877-623-3435 or 877-275-6233, see https://madd.org/vermont.

Elder Abuse

- National Special Victim Hotline (NSV): (support provided by the National Domestic Violence Hotline), 888-805-0122, see https://specialvictims.org/seniors/.
- Adult Protective Services (APS): 877-623-3435, https://madd.org/vermont.
- Vermont Area Agencies on Aging Helpline: 800-642-5119, see https://www.vermont4a.org.
- Vermont 211/United Way of Vermont: 866-652-4636 or 802-652-4636, text 988 or chat 988Lifeline.org, see https://vermont211.org.

Fraud

- State of Vermont, Department of Financial Regulation: Many resources for various types of fraud, see https://dfr.vermont.gov/avoid-scams-and-frauds.

Identity Theft

- Identity Theft Resource Center: see https://www.idtheftcenter.org.
- Vermont Attorney General's Consumer Assistance Hotline: 800-649-2424, or report identity theft at 802-828-2865 or 866-828-2865, see https://tax.vermont.gov/help/identity-theft.
- Annual Credit Report Request Service from Annual Credit Report.com: see https://www.annualcreditreport.com/protectYourIdentity.action,
- National Consumers League Fraud Center (not limited to Vermont):

see https://fraud.org.

Online Criminal Case Status, Inmate Status, and Sex Offender Registry

- Free Access to Court Electronic Records (PACER): See https://pcl.usco urts.gov/pcl and https://pacer.uscourts.gov/register-account/pacer-case-search-only.
- Vermont Court Records and Case Search Online: see https://vermon t.thepublicindex.org/court-records.
- Vermont Criminal Conviction Record Internet Service: see https://se cure.vermont.gov/DPS/criminalrecords.
- Vermont Offender Locator: see https://vermontcourtrecords.us/cri minal-court-records.
- Vermont Sex Offender Registry: see https://vcic.vermont.gov/sor.

Sexual Assault

- National Sexual Assault Hotline: 800-656-4673, see https://rainn.org.
- VT Sexual Violence Hotline: 800-489-7273, see https://humanservic es.vermont.gov/help-and-resources/domestic-violence.
- National Human Trafficking Hotline: 888-373-7888 or text 233733 or email help@humantraffickinghotline.org, see https://humantraffi ckinghotline.org/en.
- Hope Works: Advocates and survivor support: 802-863-1236, see https://hopeworksvt.org.
- Mosaic Vermont: Helping people heal from sexual harm, see https://m osaic-vt.org.

Survivors of Homicide

- Survivors of Homicide: 860-257-7388 (main office) or 860-324-5679 (Fairfield and New Haven County). Offers one-on-one counseling, support groups, court support throughout the judicial process, personal advocacy in working with law enforcement and other community agencies, and planning and business meetings to further our advocacy and educational goals, Based in Connecticut but available to survivors everywhere. See https://www.survivorsofhomicide.com/about-us.

Victim Advocacy

- Vermont Center for Crime Victim Services: see https://ccvs.vermont.gov/about-us.
- Vermont Legal Aid: see https://www.vtlegalaid.org/legal-projects/victims-rights.

Victim Compensation

- Vermont Center for Crime Victim Services/Victims Compensation Program: see https://ccvs.vermont.gov/victims-compensation.

Victim Notification System

- Vermont Automated Notification Service: 866-976-8267, see https://doc.vermont.gov/van.

Victim Rights and Services Complaints

- Office of the Victims' Rights Ombudsman (National): Victims can file a complaint with the Office of the Victims' Rights Ombudsman, who will then forward the complaint to the relevant office, see https://www.justice.gov/usao/crime-victims-rights-ombudsman-victims-rights.

Victim/Witness Assistance Program

- U.S. Attorney's Office District of Vermont Victim Witness Assistance:

see https://www.justice.gov/usao-vt/victim-witness-assistance.
- OVC Help Series for Crime Victims: see https://ovc.ojp.gov/sites/g/files/xyckuh226/files/pubs/helpseries/HelpBrochure_Homicide.html.

Programs subject to change or end without notice.

Notes

Chapter 1: Connecticut

1. "About | Market Place Tavern Litchfield," markethospitalitygroup.com, accessed April 24, 2024, https://mptavern.com/litchfield/about.
2. Mullen, Matt. "Sandy Hook School Shooting." HISTORY, December 11, 2019. https://www.history.com/this-day-in-history/gunman-kills-students-and-adults-at-newtown-connecticut-elementary-school.
3. Psychology Today Staff. "Bystander Effect." *Psychology Today*. Accessed April 12, 2024. https://www.psychologytoday.com/us/basics/bystander-effect.
4. History Editors, "Kitty Genovese," History.com, January 5, 2018, https://www.history.com/topics/crime/kitty-genovese.

Chapter 3: Massachusetts

1. "The ALLY Foundation | About," The ALLY Foundation | about, accessed April 23, 2024, https://www.theallyfoundation.org/about/history/.

Chapter 4: New Hampshire

1. crimestats.dos.nh.gov. "Violent Crime 2022," Accessed April 15, 2024. https://crimestats.dos.nh.gov/tops/report/violent-crimes/new-hampshire/2022.
2. freepages.rootsweb.com. "Eliphaz DOW." Accessed April 15, 2024.

https://freepages.rootsweb.com/~laplante/genealogy/PS36/PS36_414.HTM.

Chapter 5: Rhode Island

1. Ramsland, Katherine. "Mike DeBardeleben: Serial Sexual Sadist — The Trap — Crime Library," n.d. https://www.crimelibrary.org/serial_killers/predators/debardeleben/index_1.html.
2. Breton, Tracy, and Wayne Miller. "How Billy Sarmento Fell through the Cracks State Missed Its Chances to Stop 2 Killings." *Providence Journal*, March 19, 1989, A-01.

Bibliography

Chapter 1: Connecticut

- "Ad for South End Seaport Restaurant." Hartford Courant, October 1, 1989. https://www.newspapers.com/image/374093937/?match=1&terms=South%20End%20Seaport.
- Ahein075. "Was It Just One Man?" Truth or Scares? August 10, 2021. https://www.truthorscares.com/post/was-it-just-one-man.
- Ahles, Dick. "One Law and the Violent History behind It." The New York Times, August 10, 2003. https://www.nytimes.com/2003/08/10/nyregion/one-law-and-the-violent-history-behind-it.html.
- Aiello, Tony. "Michelle Troconis Trial: Jury Sees Evidence Retrieved from Trash Believed to Have Been Used to Hide Jennifer Dulos' Death." www.cbsnews.com, January 24, 2024. https://www.cbsnews.com/newyork/news/michelle-troconis-trial-jury-sees-evidence-retrieved-from-trash-believed-to-have-been-used-to-hide-jennifer-dulos-death/.
- AP News. "Former Death Row Inmate Pleads Guilty to Murder and Is Sentenced to Decades in Connecticut Prison." August 29, 2023. https://apnews.com/article/ashby-death-row-murder-plea-97501b70d8c7b20207e0416c79f0683e.
- Apruzzese, Art. "I Remember New Britain." www.facebook.com, December 15, 2019. https://www.facebook.com/groups/artap5/posts/2578134392222646/.
- "Arsenic and Old Lace: Diving Deeper: The Brewster Sisters." Virginia Stage Company, August 14, 2024. https://www.vastage.org/blog/2024/8/12/arsenic-amp-old-lace-diving-deeper-the-brewster-sisters.
- Associated Press. "Kennedy Cousin Skakel Won't Be Retried in 1975

Killing." Los Angeles Times, October 30, 2020. https://www.latimes.c om/world-nation/story/2020-10-30/kennedy-cousin-michael-skake l-will-not-be-retried.

- Associated Press. "'Sesame Street' Actor's Property Caretaker Charged with Jogger's Murder." Fox News, March 25, 2015. https://www.foxn ews.com/story/sesame-street-actors-property-caretaker-charged-wit h-joggers-murder.
- "Bandit Kills E. Hartford Store Owner." Meriden Record-Journal, December 27, 1956. https://www.newspapers.com/image/67740 2605/?match=1&terms=samuel%20cohn.
- Beach, Randall. "Retired North Haven Cop Recalls Grisly Scene of Slayings." New Haven Register, January 17, 2005. https://www.nhregi ster.com/news/article/Retired-North-Haven-cop-recalls-grisly-scen e-of-11648624.php.
- Bendici, Ray. "Fairfield Hills State Hospital, Newtown – Damned Con- necticut." Damned Connecticut, accessed April 12, 2024. https://ww w.damnedct.com/fairfield-hills-state-hospital-newtown/.
- Breese, Amber. "Inside the Cheshire Murders, the Deadly Home Invasion That Rocked Connecticut in 2007." All That's Interesting, April 30, 2023. https://allthatsinteresting.com/cheshire-murders.
- Brown, Tina A., and John Springer. "Can Police Connect the Cases?" Hartford Courant, September 22, 2000. https://www.newspapers.co m/image/176831163/.
- Burgard, Matt, and Tina Brown. "Gunfire in City Claims 2 Lives." The Hartford Courant, September 3, 2003. https://www.newspapers.com /image/256516057/.
- Caruso, Beth. "Alice 'Alse' Young – First Witch Hanging Victim in Colonial America – Legends of America." www.legendsofamerica.com, Accessed April 12, 2024. https://www.legendsofamerica.com/alse-yo ung-witch/.
- Christofferson, John. "Conn. Lawyer Who Stabbed Neighbor Insists Daughter Was Molested." Hartford Business Journal, October 29, 2007. https://www.hartfordbusiness.com/article/conn-lawyer-who-stabbe

d-neighbor-insists-daughter-was-molested.

- "Connecticut Crime Rates and Statistics." Neighborhoodscout.com, Accessed April 12, 2024. https://www.neighborhoodscout.com/ct/crime.

- "Connecticut Murderers List." Murderpedia.org, Accessed April 12, 2024. https://murderpedia.org/usa/connecticut.htm.

- "Connecticut's 20 Safest Cities of 2020." SafeWise.com, April 8, 2020, https://www.safewise.com/blog/safest-cities-connecticut/.

- "Connecticut's Real Haunted Hotels." www.cthauntedhouses.com, accessed April 13, 2024. https://www.cthauntedhouses.com/real-haunts/hotels.aspx.

- Dapper, Don. "Investigation into Boxer's Murder Stalled after Death of Turncoat Hartford Mobster." Five Families of New York City, September 2, 2013. https://www.fivefamiliesnyc.com/2013/09/investigation-into-boxers-murder.html.

- "Department of Correction Inmate Information Search." PMG/Department of Correction, State.ct.us, 2024. http://www.ctinmateinfo.state.ct.us/detailsupv.asp?id_inmt_num=171508.

- Devlin, Robert J. 'State v. Webb." Connecticut Superior Court Judicial District of Fairfield at Bridgeport, May 6, 2008. https://casetext.com/case/state-v-webb-no-cr07-022-20-67-t-may.

- Dignam, John. "Missing Woodstock Woman Found Dead." The Worcester Telegram & Gazette, December 13, 2005. https://www.telegram.com/story/news/state/2005/12/13/missing-woodstock-woman-found-dead/53150667007.

- Farragher, Thomas. "Police Believe Arrest Lays Bare Grisly Trail." The Day, June 29, 1984. https://www.newspapers.com/image/970459515/.

- Fortier, Bill. "Deojay Given Life Sentence for Murder." The Worcester Telegram & Gazette, March 9, 2007. https://www.telegram.com/story/news/local/south-west/2007/03/10/deojay-given-life-sentence-for/52953855007/.

- Fowler, Andrew. "The Connecticut Witch Trials." Yankee Institute,

October 20, 2023. https://yankeeinstitute.org/2023/10/20/the-conn
ecticut-witch-trials/.

- Gangland Wire. "Wild Guy William Grasso." Spreaker, 2020. https://w
ww.spreaker.com/episode/wild-guy-william-grasso—49258050#.

- "Garner Inmates Included the Infamous." News-Times, February 2,
2010. https://www.newstimes.com/local/article/Garner-inmates-inc
luded-the-infamous-347635.php.

- Gorosko, Andrew. "Richard Crafts Moved to Homeless Shelter for
Veterans." www.newtownbee.com, January 30, 2020. https://www.ne
wtownbee.com/01302020/richard-crafts-moved-to-homeless-shelter
-for-veterans/.

- Griffin, Leeanne. "CT Restaurants' Past Lives: Former Banks, Jails and
Gas Stations among Today's Eateries." *CT Insider*, February 27, 2024.
https://www.ctinsider.com/living/food/article/ct-restaurants-jails-b
anks-gas-stations-18648929.php.

- Habas, Cathy. "Connecticut's 20 Safest Cities of 2020." SafeWise, April
8, 2020. https://www.safewise.com/blog/safest-cities-connecticut/.

- Healion, James. "Reputed Mobster Frank Piccolo, Indicted for Allegedly Conspiring To…". UPI, September 19, 1981. https://www.upi.
com/Archives/1981/09/19/Reputed-mobster-Frank-Piccolo-indicte
d-for-allegedly-conspiring-to/9760369720000/.

- "High Crime Rate: What States Are the Most Dangerous, with Most
Violent Crimes per Capita?" USAToday.com, Accessed April 12, 2024.
https://www.usatoday.com/picture-gallery/money/2020/01/13/mos
t-dangerous-states-in-america/40969391/.

- History Editors. "Kitty Genovese." History.com, January 5, 2018.
https://www.history.com/topics/crime/kitty-genovese.

- Hoffman, Christopher. "Operation Richmart." September 28, 2009.
https://www.newhavenindependent.org/article/operation_richmart.

- Hoffman, Christopher. "Midge Renault & the Heyday of the Mob."
New Haven Independent, August 25, 2010. https://www.newhavenin
dependent.org/article/midge_renault_the_heyday_of_the_mob.

- "Java Jeopardy Answer: Bonnie Elbe of East Hartford Wins." The

Hartford Courant, July 2, 2004. https://www.newspapers.com/image/256656121/?terms=alse%20young&match=1.

- "Kitty Genovese (1935-1964). Findagrave.com, Accessed April 12, 2024. https://www.findagrave.com/memorial/7195328/kitty-genovese.

- Kotler, Hannah, and Kenisha Mahajan. "Qinxuan Pan Pleads Guilty to Murder of Kevin Jiang ENV '22." Yale Daily News, March 1, 2024. https://yaledailynews.com/blog/2024/02/29/qinxuan-pan-pleads-guilty-to-murder-of-kevin-jiang-env-22/.

- Krieg, Andrew, "Mob Boss Piccolo Gunned Down on Street." Hartford Courant, September 20, 1981, https://www.newspapers.com/image/368717792/?clipping_id=118403973&fcfToken

- "List of Serial Killers in Connecticut." Connecticut Bail Bonds Group, Accessed April 12, 2024. https://www.connecticut-bailbonds.com/connecticut-life/list-of-serial-killers-in-connecticut/.

- Little, Becky. "'Arsenic and Old Lace': The Real Murders behind the Halloween Classic Film." History, October 25, 2021. https://www.history.com/news/arsenic-old-lace-real-murders.

- "Lottery Victim Begged for His Life." CBSNews.com, March 7, 1998. https://www.cbsnews.com/news/lottery-victim-begged-for-his-life/.

- "Lydia Sherman: The Derby Poisoner." Connecticut History.org, March 10, 2020. https://connecticuthistory.org/lydia-sherman-the-derby-poisoner/.

- Maag, Christopher. "Former M.I.T. Student Pleads Guilty in 2021 Killing of Yale Student." The New York Times, March 1, 2024. https://www.nytimes.com/2024/02/29/nyregion/qinxuan-pan-mit-yale-killing.html.

- "MacDougall-Walker CI." CT.gov, accessed April 13, 2024. https://portal.ct.gov/DOC/Facility/MacDougall-Walker-CI.

- "Man Accused of Abducting Dead Jogger." NBC News, December 14, 2005. https://www.nbcnews.com/id/wbna10468647.

- "Maple Ave. Man Alone When Shot." The Hartford Courant, January 27, 1957. https://www.newspapers.com/image/367944797/.

- Mason Jr., Johnny. "Father Hopes Increased Reward Helps Solve Son's Killing." Hartford Courant, July 17, 1999.
- https://www.newspapers.com/image/177127422/?match=1&terms= Eric%20Miller.
- "Matthew Steven Johnson." Murderpedia.org. accessed April 13, 2024. https://murderpedia.org/male.J/j/johnson-matthew-steven.htm.
- "Memorial to Alse Young and Lydia Gilbert." Atlas Obscura, Accessed April 12, 2024. https://www.atlasobscura.com/places/memorial-alse-young-and-lydia-gilbert.
- Morrison, Sara. "Two More Victims of Conn. Serial Killer Identified." www.boston.com, May 13, 2015. https://www.boston.com/news/loc al-news/2015/05/13/two-more-victims-of-conn-serial-killer-identif ied/.
- Munoz, Hilda. "At Murder Trial, Boyfriend Testifies." Hartford Courant, January 25, 2007. https://www.newspapers.com/image/ 244036395/.
- "OVS Victim Resources." Jud.CT.gov, Accessed April 12, 2024. https://www.jud.ct.gov/crimevictim/resources.htm.
- Pagliuco, Chris. "Connecticut's Witch Trials." Wethersfield Historical Society, 2007. https://www.wethersfieldhistory.org/articles/connecti cuts-witch-trials/.
- Palmer, J. "State of Connecticut v. Matthew Steven Johnson." Supreme Court of Connecticut, November 11, 2008. https://caselaw.findlaw.c om/court/ct-supreme-court/1123589.html.
- Psychology Today Staff. "Bystander Effect." Psychology Today, 2019. https://www.psychologytoday.com/us/basics/bystander-effect.
- Puffer, Michael. "Hartford Developer Takes on Transformation of Antique Litchfield Courthouse into Boutique Hotel." Hartford Business Journal, April 17, 2023. https://www.hartfordbusiness.c om/article/hartford-developer-takes-on-transformation-of-antique-litchfield-courthouse-into-boutique.
- Rierden, Andi. "Coping with Life When Its Wounds Never Seem to Heal." The New York Times, February 21, 1993. https://www.nytime

s.com/1993/02/21/nyregion/coping-with-life-when-its-wounds-nev
er-seem-to-heal.html.

- Schier, Anna. "Fairfield Woman Hanged for Witchcraft to Be Honored with Memorial." Fairfield, CT Patch, August 15, 2019. https://patch.c om/connecticut/fairfield/memorial-honor-fairfield-woman-hanged-witchcraft.
- Schroder, Jan. "11 Hotels and Breweries That Used to Be Prisons." Fodors Travel, December 27, 2017. https://www.fodors.com/news/p hotos/from-prisons-to-pints-and-pillows-11-former-jails-where-yo ull-want-to-serve-time.
- Singer, Stephen. "In Call, Shooter Says He 'Handled the Problem.'" NBC News, August 5, 2010. https://www.nbcnews.com/id/wbna385 83491.
- Smart, Martha, and Gillie Johnson. Letter to Dawn Barclay. "William Beadle Address Inquiry." Email, May 11, 2024.
- "State of Connecticut v Michael Skakel." CT.gov, Accessed April 12, 2024. https://portal.ct.gov/DCJ/Latest-News/State-v-Skakel/State-o f-Connecticut-v-Michael-Skakel.
- "The Story of the Murder of the Beadle Family by William Beadle." Wethersfield Historical Society, Accessed April 12, 2024. https://ww w.wethersfieldhistory.org/articles/the-story-of-the-murder-of-the-b eadle-family-by-william-beadle/.
- "The Top 15 Mob Murders in Connecticut." The Original Gang-sters Podcast, Scott Burnstein, host, and James Buccellato, co-host. www.youtube.com, July 26, 2023. https://www.youtube.com/watch?v =D-nR8w_jCZI.
- "These Are the Most Dangerous Cities, Towns in Connecticut, Study Finds." WTNH.com, December 28, 2023. https://www.wtnh.com/ne ws/connecticut/these-are-the-most-dangerous-cities-towns-in-conn ecticut-study-finds/.
- "Timeline: The Deadliest Mass Shootings in the US." Al Jazeera, August 4, 2019. https://www.aljazeera.com/news/2019/8/4/timeline-the-de adliest-mass-shootings-in-the-us.

- "Timeline: The Disappearance of Jennifer Farber Dulos and the Investigation That Has Followed." The Hartford Courant, June 9, 2019. https://www.newspapers.com/image/571560556/.
- Tom, Michelle. "Amy Archer-Gilligan: Entrepreneurism Gone Wrong in Windsor." Windsor Historical Society, July 16, 2018. https://winds orhistoricalsociety.org/amy-archer-gilligan-entrepreneurism-gone-wrong-in-windsor/.
- "Top 6 Most Haunted Hotels in Connecticut." Hauntedrooms.com, January 29, 2020. https://www.hauntedrooms.com/connecticut/hau nted-places/haunted-hotels.
- "Unique Places to Stay-Connecticut's Most Unconventional Accommodations." CTvisit.com, Accessed April 12, 2024. https://ctvisit.com /articles/unique-places-stay-connecticuts-most-unconventional-acco mmodations.
- "Visit: Travel the Amistad Freedom-Seeking Story, Connecticut." Nps.gov, Accessed April 12, 2024. https://www.nps.gov/subjects/ travelamistad/visit.htm.
- "Where Does Connecticut Place in the U.S. News Best States Rankings?" USnews.com, 2020. https://www.usnews.com/news/best-states/con necticut.
- "William Devin Howell Pleads Guilty to Serial Murders." CT.gov, Accessed April 12, 2024. https://portal.ct.gov/DCJ/Archives/Arc hived/William-Devin-Howell-Pleads-Guilty-to-Serial-Murders.
- "Woman Found Dead in Home." Hartford Courant, December 3, 2002. https://www.courant.com/2002/12/03/woman-found-dead-in-hom e/.
- Yardley, William. "DNA Samples Link 4 Murders in Connecticut." The New York Times, June 8, 2006. https://www.nytimes.com/2006/06/0 8/nyregion/08bridgeport.html.

Chapter 2: Maine

- "A List of Mass Killings in the United States since January." AP News,

October 26, 2023. https://apnews.com/article/mass-killings-united-s
tates-list-8eea3427796229eb127e052b3c66c691.

- Abel, Ann. "A New Reason to Visit Maine: The Press Hotel in Portland."
Forbes, August 24, 2015. https://www.forbes.com/sites/annabel/201
5/08/24/a-new-reason-to-visit-maine-the-press-hotel-in-portland/.

- "Admiral Peary Inn." Haunt ME, May 18, 2020. https://haunt-me.com
/admiral-peary-inn/.

- Alleman, Katie. Letter to Dawn Barclay. "Book Research." Email,
March 13, 2024. kalleman@mainehistory.org.

- Archie, Ayana. "What We Know about the Victims in the Lewiston,
Maine, Mass Shooting." NPR, October 27, 2023. https://www.npr.or
g/2023/10/27/1208896628/lewiston-maine-mass-shooting-victims.

- "Arline Lawless." Murderpedia.org, Accessed April 20, 2024. https://m
urderpedia.org/female.L/l/lawless-arline.htm.

- "Arline Lawless." Rage World, March 1, 2023. https://holistixrage.wor
dpress.com/tag/arline-lawless/.

- Armstrong, Jane, and Alan Freeman. "Slaying Suspect Had Past Brush
with Violence." The Globe and Mail, April 20, 2006. https://www.the
globeandmail.com/news/national/slaying-suspect-had-past-brush-w
ith-violence/article707045/.

- Barker, Meg. Letter to Dawn Barclay. "Research Request." Bath
Historical Society, March 10, 2024. info@bathhistorical.org.

- Blanco, Juan Ignacio. "Steven Oken." Murderpedia.org, 2024.
https://murderpedia.org/male.O/o1/oken-steven.htm.

- Bovsun, Mara. "How Notorious Serial Killer John Joubert's Days of
Slaying Children Came to an End." New York Daily News, September
17, 2017. https://www.nydailynews.com/2017/09/17/how-notoriou
s-serial-killer-john-jouberts-days-of-slaying-children-came-to-an-en
d/.

- Bovsun, Mara. "Justice Story: Mentally Ill Mother Commits Same
Horrific Crime Twice." New York Daily News, July 19, 2020. https://w
ww.nydailynews.com/2020/07/19/justice-story-mentally-ill-mother-
commits-same-horrific-crime-twice/.

- "Boy Scout Turned Serial Killer: The John Joubert Story I Dispatches from the Middle." Very Local on www.youtube.com, 2020. https://www.youtube.com/watch?app=desktop&v=XjuxkNmijIY.
- Briggs, Bob. *The Constance Fisher Tragedy.* AuthorHouse, 2011.
- Bryan, Shannon. "Murderer's Cave! Hiking Trails and Homicidal History at Thorne Head Preserve in Bath." Fit Maine, October 29, 2019. https://fitmaine.com/murderers-cave-hiking-trails-homicide-thorne-head-preserve-bath/.
- Campbell, Cindy. "The Scary Stories of 10 Maine Multiple Murderers & Their Victims." Q106.5, August 23, 2021. https://q1065.fm/the-scary-stories-of-10-maine-multiple-murderers-and-their-victims/.
- Cann, Christopher, and Adrianna Rodriguez. "Maine Mass Shooter Robert Card Had 'Traumatic Brain Injuries,' New Report Shows." USA Today, March 7, 2024. https://www.usatoday.com/story/news/nation/2024/03/07/robert-card-lewiston-maine-shootings-brain-injuries/72877485007/.
- Carmona, Vana. "Patience Boston 1711-1735." Atlantic Black Box, September 28, 2020. https://atlanticblackbox.com/2020/09/28/patience-boston-1726-1735/.
- Chantel. "Have You Eaten at These Three Haunted Restaurants in New England?" 94.9 HOM, April 7, 2023. https://949whom.com/new-england-haunted-restaurants/.
- "Christian Nielsen." Murderpedia.org, Accessed April 23, 2024, https://murderpedia.org/male.N/n/nielsen-christian.htm.
- Ciampi, Raquel. "Accused Bowdoin, I-295 Shooter Joseph Eaton Withdraws Insanity Plea." WMTW, December 27, 2023. https://www.wmtw.com/article/bowdoin-295-shooter-joseph-eaton-withdrawals-insanity-plea/46235515.
- Csernyik, Rob. "How Sex Offender Registries Can Result in Vigilante Murder." Vice.com, March 28, 2018. https://www.vice.com/en/article/ne9ew7/how-sex-offender-registries-can-result-in-vigilante-murder.
- Cummings Jr., Leigh E. "Letter to Dawn Barclay: Carl Lord Jr, North

St, Houlton Maine." March 1, 2024, leighandsandra@gmail.com.

- "Daniel Wilkinson." Murderpedia.org, Accessed April 21, 2024. https://murderpedia.org/male.W/w/wilkinson-daniel.htm.

- Dlsoucy. "The Purrinton Tragedy Augusta 1806." Maine History News (blog), March 2, 2012. https://touringmaineshistory.wordpress.com/2012/03/02/the-purrinton-tragedy-augusta-1806/.

- Dow, Charles, and Steve McCausland. "AG, State Police Close Investigation of 2003 New Sweden Poisonings; Conclude Bondeson Acted Alone." Maine.gov, accessed April 14, 2024. https://www.maine.gov/ag/news/article.shtml?id=48446.

- "Fairfield Mother Charged with Murder of Three Children." Portland Press Herald, July 2, 1996. https://www.newspapers.com/image/847904638/?terms=three%20children%20drowned&match=1.

- "Family Members Gather to Dedicate Monument to Murder Victims." The Lincoln County News, July 31, 2014. https://lcnme.com/currentnews/family-members-gather-to-dedicate-monument-to-murder-victims/.

- Florio, Brett. "FINE Brings New England Leaders to Maine Prisons." Farmtoinstitution.org, October 17, 2023. https://farmtoinstitution.org/blog/visit-to-maine-prisons.

- Fortier, Marc. "4 Shot to Death in Maine Home, 3 Shot While Driving on I-295; Man Facing Murder Charges." NECN, April 18, 2023. https://www.necn.com/news/local/part-of-i-295-in-maine-shut-down-due-to-police-response/2965421/.

- Fox, Cooper. "8 Shocking Maine Murders Guaranteed to Keep You Awake at Night." B98.5, March 18, 2023. https://b985.fm/maine-murders-shocking.

- Frary, John. "The Thayne Ormsby I Knew." The Franklin Journal and Farmington Chronicle, July 20, 2010. https://www.newspapers.com/image/1022856901/.

- Graham, Gillian, and Megan Gray. "Family from Away Found Deep Friendship in Maine Decades before Bowdoin Killings." Press Herald, April 20, 2023. https://www.pressherald.com/2023/04/20/family-fr

om-away-finds-deep-friendship-in-maine-decades-before-bowdoin-killings/.

- Harrison, Judy. "2 Sex Offenders Slain in Milo, Corinth; Suspect from Canada Kills Himself in Boston." Bangor Daily News, April 17, 2006. https://www.bangordailynews.com/2006/04/17/news/2-men-slain-in-milo-corinth-suspect-from-canada-kills-himself-in-boston/.

- Harrison, Judy. "No Verdict after Jurors Deliberate 11 Hours in Triple Murder Trial." Sun-Journal, May 22, 2014. https://www.newspapers.com/image/831936343/?terms=Nicholas%20Sexton&match=1.

- "Horrid Murder! The James Purrington Family Massacre." Murder, She Told, Accessed April 20, 2024. https://www.murdershetold.com/episodes/james-purrington.

- "Hoyt Brook Cemetery, an Argyle, Maine Cemetery." Funerals360.com, Accessed April 21, 2024. https://www.funerals360.com/cemetery/ME/Maine/126026-hoyt-brook-cemetery/.

- Hughes, Trevor. "Live Updates on Shooting on I-295 in Maine: 4 Dead, 3 Injured, Man Arrested." USA Today, April 18, 2023. https://www.usatoday.com/story/news/nation/2023/04/18/maine-shooting-interstate-295-highway-live-updates/11688716002/.

- Humphrey, J. "State of Maine v. Nicholas Sexton." Supreme Judicial Court of Maine, April 6, 2017. https://caselaw.findlaw.com/court/me-supreme-judicial-court/1855852.html.

- Ilic, Srdjan. "10 Most Dangerous Cities in Maine 2024: Exploring the Darker Side of Vacationland." Southwest Journal, July 6, 2023. https://www.southwestjournal.com/us/maine/most-dangerous-cities-in-maine/.

- Journal Tribune. "Victim Had Nightmare of Violent Death." November 18, 1987. https://www.newspapers.com/image/853291772/.

- Kolmar, Chris. "Most Dangerous Cities in Maine for 2024." RoadSnacks, January 17, 2024. https://www.roadsnacks.net/these-are-the-10-most-dangerous-cities-in-maine/.

- Lobkowicz, Sally. "Coach Stop Inn." www.americanghostwalks.com, Accessed April 21, 2024. https://www.americanghostwalks.com/artic

les/coach-stop-inn.

- Lynds, Jen. "Suspect in Amity Slayings Arrested in New Hampshire." The Bangor Daily News, July 3, 2010. https://www.newspapers.com/image/665148712/.
- "Maine-Based Resources," AMHC, Accessed April 13, 2024. https://www.amhcsas.org/maine.html.
- "Maine Crime Index City Rank." USA.com, Accessed April 20, 2024. http://www.usa.com/rank/maine-state—crime-index—city-rank.htm.
- "Maine Crime Rates and Statistics." Neighborhoodscout.com, accessed April 15, 2024. https://www.neighborhoodscout.com/me/crime.
- "Man Who Confessed to Killing 4 People, Including Parents, Is Sentenced to Life in Maine." NECN, July 2024. https://www.necn.com/news/local/maine-man-who-confessed-to-killing-parents-2-others-will-enter-pleas-to-settle-case-lawyer-says/3271672/.
- McDaniel, Justine, Arelis R. Hernández, and Perry Stein. "Maine Gunman Who Killed 18 Was Found in Third Search of Recycling Center." Washington Post, October 29, 2023. https://www.washingtonpost.com/nation/2023/10/28/maine-shooting-robert-card-lewiston/.
- Megan. "Dine with a Ghost at These 13 Haunted New England Restaurants." 97.5 WOKQ, April 6, 2024. https://wokq.com/haunted-new-england-restaurant/.
- Michelle. "There's a Farm-To-Table Restaurant inside a Former Maine Jail Garage, and It'd Be a Crime Not to Visit." OnlyInYourState, February 25, 2021. https://www.onlyinyourstate.com/maine/restaurant-former-jail-me/.
- Morrison, Meghan. "Empire Live Entertainment Venue Is Now Open in Portland, Maine." Q97.9, April 5, 2023. https://wjbq.com/empire-live-entertainment-venue-is-now-open-in-portland-maine/.
- Ordway, Renee. "Hicks Enters Guilty Plea." The Bangor Daily News, November 18, 2000. https://www.newspapers.com/image/664833812/.

- "Patience Sampson." Murderpedia.org, Accessed April 20, 2024. https://murderpedia.org/female.S/s/sampson-patience.htm.
- Peavey, Elizabeth. "Empire Chinese Kitchen." Down East Magazine, March 24, 2014. https://downeast.com/food-drink/empire-chinese-kitchen/.
- "Police Investigate Sex Offender Slayings." NBC News, April 17, 2006. https://www.nbcnews.com/id/wbna12346578.
- Ramer, Holly, Lisa Rathke, Kathy McCormack, David R. Martin, and David Sharp. "A Teen Bowler, a Shipbuilder, and a Sign Language Interpreter are among the Maine Shooting Victims." AP News, October 26, 2023. https://apnews.com/article/maine-shooting-victims-1be7d14e90ef6c91ca23819163d29f3e.
- "Rampage Suspect Showed No Emotion When Arrested According to His Uncle." Morning Sentinel, July 19, 2015. https://www.newspapers.com/image/924170200/.
- Saufley, C.J. "State of Maine vs. Anthony Lord." Maine Supreme Judicial Court, May 30, 2019. https://law.justia.com/cases/maine/supreme-court/2019/2019-me-82.html.
- Scee, Trudy Irene. Tragedy in the North Woods. Arcadia Publishing, 2009.
- Sharp, David. "Police Documents Shed Light on Maine Sex Offender Killer." Times Argus, November 4, 2006. https://www.timesargus.com/news/police-documents-shed-light-on-maine-sex-offender-killer/article_8df32109-7d40-5bdd-81cb-20f9d0ce9239.html.
- Sharp, David, Patrick Whittle, Holly Ramer, and Michelle R. Smith. "Amid Massive Search for Mass Killing Suspect, Maine Residents Remain behind Locked Doors." AP News, October 27, 2023. https://apnews.com/article/maine-shooting-lewiston-fed5ab0aaee9d7d4c0f0fccb3d301bb7.
- "Shooting Rampage." Sun Journal, July 18, 2015. https://www.newspapers.com/image/832555310/.
- Stackhouse, Terry. "FBI Data Shows Maine Has Nation's Lowest Rate of Violent Crime." WMTW, October 17, 2023. https://www.wmtw.co

m/article/fbi-data-shows-maine-has-nations-lowest-rate-of-violent-crime/45563922.

- Staff, WBZ-News. "Joseph Eaton in Court: Police Describe Grisly Discovery in Maine Shootings." www.cbsnews.com, April 20, 2023. https://www.cbsnews.com/boston/news/joseph-eaton-maine-shooting-suspects-family-parents-bowdoin/.

- "State of Maine vs. James Hicks." Supreme Judicial Court of Maine. July 9, 1985. https://law.justia.com/cases/maine/supreme-court/1985/495-a-2d-765-0.html.

- "Stephen A. Marshall." Murderpedia.org, Accessed April 20, 2024. https://murderpedia.org/male.M/m/marshall-stephen.htm.

- Stevens, Emery. "Suspect Sought in Boy's Death." Evening Express, August 24, 1982. https://www.newspapers.com/image/853259334/.

- "Suspect Accused of Sex Assault." Sun-Journal, July 23, 2015. https://www.newspapers.com/image/832549460/.

- Terhune, John. "People Are No Longer Walking This Earth because of Me.'" Press Herald, June 25, 2023. https://www.pressherald.com/2023/06/25/people-are-no-longer-walking-this-earth-because-of-me/.

- "The Bolduc Family Murders." Strange Deranged Unexplained, 2023. https://www.youtube.com/watch?v=e6904ImAcAI.

- "The Deadly Web of Maine Serial Killer James Hicks." Murder, She Told, Accessed April 16, 2024. https://www.murdershetold.com/episodes/1-james-hicks.

- "The Haunted East Wind Inn in Maine." Haunted-Places-To-Go.com, 2018, www.haunted-places-to-go.com/east-wind-inn.html.

- "The Minister's Black Veil & Patience Boston." Strange New England, October 24, 2023. https://strangenewengland.com/podcast/the-ministers-black-veil-patience-boston/.

- "The Most Haunted Hotels in Maine." Hauntedrooms.com, January 29, 2020. https://www.hauntedrooms.com/maine/haunted-places/haunted-hotels.

- "Thorne Head, Bath." Kennebec Estuary Land Trust, Accessed April 20, 2024. https://www.kennebecestuary.org/thorne-head-bath.

- Turner. "York, Maine & Patience Boston (Samson)." The Gene Genie, December 31, 2016. https://thegenegenieblog.wordpress.com/2016/12/31/york-maine-patience-boston-samson/.
- Van Sambeck, Becca. "'She Was Clearly Stomped On': Serial Killer Crushing Women's Skulls Terrorized Connecticut." Oxygen Official Site, April 16, 2022. https://www.oxygen.com/mark-of-a-serial-kille r/crime-news/serial-killer-matthew-steven-johnson-crushed-victims -skulls.
- "Violence Prevention Resources." Maine DHHS, Accessed September 9, 2024. https://www.maine.gov/dhhs/ocfs/support-for-families/vio lence-prevention-resources.
- "Exploring Maine's Haunted Inns and Lighthouses." Visitmaine.net, March 21, 2022. https://www.visitmaine.net/haunted-maine-inns-lig hthouses/.
- Voornas, Lori. "5 Very Haunted Maine Restaurants." Q97.9, April 8, 2021. https://wjbq.com/5-very-haunted-maine-restaurants/.
- Walsh, Barbara. "Bechard's New Home Strictly Controlled." Kennebec Journal, October 21, 1996. https://www.newspapers.com/image/859 515650/.
- Weber, Tom. "Closing Arguments Slated Thursday in Murder Trial of James Hicks." The Bangor Daily News, March 22, 1984. https://www. newspapers.com/image/664785649/.
- Werner, Laurie. "4 Redesigned Maine Captains' Houses Are Opening for Stays This Spring." Forbes, March 24, 2021. https://www.forbes.c om/sites/lauriewerner/2021/03/24/4-redesigned-maine-captains-ho uses-are-opening-for-stays-this-spring/.
- Whittle, Patrick. "Jury Convicts Two Men in Murder Trial." Sun-Journal, May 29, 2014. https://www.newspapers.com/image/831936 382/.
- Whittle, Patrick, and David Sharp. "Police: Maine Man Killed Parents before Firing on Motorists." AP News, April 20, 2023. https://apnews. com/article/bowdoin-maine-shooting-highway-939417fcf2eb858cf7 d82361860f5253.

Chapter 3: Massachusetts

- "25 Most Haunted Inns in New England." www.orleansinn.com, July 3, 2013. https://www.orleansinn.com/25MostHauntedInnsinNewEngl and.html.
- "Alfred Gaynor." Murderpedia.org, Accessed April 23, 2024. https://m urderpedia.org/male.G/g/gaynor-alfred.htm.
- "America's First Murderer Was Executed for Killing Fellow Plymouth Settler." Mayflower 400, Accessed April 24, 2024. https://www.mayfl ower400uk.org/education/who-were-the-pilgrims/2020/may/john-billington/.
- America's Most Wanted. "AMW | Fugitives | Jacob Robida | Case." August 13, 2012. https://web.archive.org/web/20120813151117/http ://www.amw.com/fugitives/case.cfm?id=37291.
- Amore, Anthony. "Gardner Museum Theft." Gardnermuseum.org. 2019. https://www.gardnermuseum.org/organization/theft.
- Associated Press. "Report: Wakefield Shooting Suspect Owed IRS Less than $5K." Portsmouth Herald, January 3, 2001. https://www.seacoast online.com/story/news/2001/01/03/report-wakefield-shooting-sus pect-owed/51305385007/.
- Associated Press. "Story of Accused Killer Depends on Whom You Ask." New Haven Register, December 29, 2000. https://www.nhregist er.com/news/article/Story-of-accused-killer-depends-on-whom-you -ask-11713389.php.
- Associated Press. "Trooper Recalls Screams, Blood." Cape Cod Times, January 5, 2011. https://archive.ph/20240108033015/https://www.c apecodtimes.com/story/news/2003/09/23/trooper-recalls-screams-blood/50952808007/#selection-411.0-411.30.
- Baker, Ed. "Local Author Recounts 1860 Weymouth Murder." Wicked Local, May 13, 2020. https://www.wickedlocal.com/story/weymouth -news/2020/05/12/local-author-recounts-1860-weymouth/6469790 4007/.
- Ballou, Brian. "Bristol DA Says Robida Shot Self." Boston Herald,

February 17, 2006. https://web.archive.org/web/20060217065254/h
ttp://news.bostonherald.com/localRegional/view.bg?articleid=12499
7.

- "'Boston Strangler' Albert DeSalvo Linked by DNA to Victim." BBC
  News, July 11, 2013. https://www.bbc.com/news/world-us-canada-2
  3280128.
- Black, Chris. "Slain Woman, a Student, 15, of Dorchester." Boston
  Globe, March 16, 1979. https://www.newspapers.com/image/43672
  6338/.
- Borelli, Joshua. "StackPath." www.officer.com, November 17, 2020.
  https://www.officer.com/active-shooter/article/21162999/the-wake
  field-massacre-attack.
- Bort, Ryan. "A Timeline of the Rise and Tragic Fall of Aaron Hernandez." Newsweek, April 19, 2017. https://www.newsweek.com/aaron-
  hernandez-found-dead-timeline-rise-fall-patriots-shooting-jail-5861
  31.
- "Boston Bombing Brings Twist to Cold Murder Case." ABC News,
  April 29, 2013. https://abcnews.go.com/Blotter/boston-bombing-bri
  ngs-twist-cold-murder-case/story?id=19063282&page=2#.UYgiLLW
  koXE.
- "Boston Crime, with Neighborhood Maps and Infamous Crimes."
  Celebrateboston.com, Accessed April 23, 2024. http://www.celeb
  rateboston.com/crime.htm.
- Boston25News.com Staff. "Boxing Day Marks 20-Year Anniversary of
  Edgewater Shooting in Wakefield That Left 7 Dead." Boston 25 News,
  December 27, 2020. https://www.boston25news.com/news/boxing-
  day-marks-20-year-anniversary-edgewater-shooting-wakefield-that-
  left-7-dead/IFI4OOXWWFBB3I7AP6HYGT6YUY/.
- "Boston Marathon Terror Attack Fast Facts." CNN, 2013. https://ww
  w.cnn.com/2013/06/03/us/boston-marathon-terror-attack-fast-fact
  s/index.html.
- Boyle, Maureen. "Accused Killer Keith Luke Appears in Court with
  Swastika on His Forehead." The Patriot Ledger, May 6, 2009. https://w

ww.patriotledger.com/story/news/2009/05/06/accused-killer-keith-luke-appears/40273755007/.

- "Brink's Robbery." Federal Bureau of Investigation, 2016. https://www.fbi.gov/history/famous-cases/brinks-robbery.
- Burnstein, Scott. "Mafia Art Heist Mystery - Part 1." The Gangster Report, November 28, 2014. https://gangsterreport.com/mafia-art-heist-mystery-part-1/.
- "Burnt Ziti Murder, 1995." Celebrateboston.com, Accessed April 24, 2024. http://www.celebrateboston.com/crime/burnt-ziti-murder.htm.
- Candiotti, Susan, Laura Dolan, and Ray Sanchez. "Aaron Hernandez Verdict: Guilty of Murder." CNN, April 16, 2015. https://edition.cnn.com/2015/04/15/us/aaron-hernandez-verdict/.
- "Cape Searchers Dig up Leg in Graves Vicinity." The Recorder, March 8, 1969. https://www.newspapers.com/image/840876396/.
- Cassidy, Tina. "Man Accused in Mutilation Reportedly Abused Spouse." Rutland Daily Herald, September 2, 1995. https://www.newspapers.com/image/535691299/.
- Commonwealth vs. William R. Horton & Others. Justia US Law, Accessed April 23, 2024. https://law.justia.com/cases/massachusetts/supreme-court/volumes/376/376mass380.html.
- Contreras, Cesareo. "Eerie Tales and Stories of Paranormal Activity at Stone's Public House in Ashland." MetroWest Daily News, October 25, 2021. https://www.metrowestdailynews.com/story/news/2021/10/25/ashland-ma-stones-public-house-halloween-haunted-inn-restaurant-paranormal-activity-ghost-lab/6055877001/.
- 'Craigslist Killer' Philip Markoff Died Amid His Fiancée's Photos." ABC News, August 16, 2010. https://abcnews.go.com/US/TheLaw/craigslist-killer-philip-markoff-spread-photos-fiance-died/story?id=11419551.
- "Crimes against Black Women: Four Cases." Journal de La Reyna (World News Today), August 29, 2007. https://httpjournalsaolcomjenjer6steph.blogspot.com/2007/08/crimes-against-black-women-four-

cases.html.

- Cullen, Kevin, and Brian McGrory. "Gunman Opens Fire in Brookline Clinics, Kills 2 and Wounds 5." Boston Globe, December 31, 1994. https://www.newspapers.com/image/440606226/.

- Daley, Christopher. "Mass Murder: Massachusetts' Most Infamous Murder Cases." www.daleyhistory.com. Accessed April 23, 2024. https://www.daleyhistory.com/mass-murder-massachusetts-most-in famous-murder-cases.

- Dame, Johathan. "Bank Robbery, Retold." Wicked Local, April 8, 2015. https://www.wickedlocal.com/story/medford-transcript/2015/04/0 9/bank-robbery-retold/64838001007/.

- Dan_nehs. "The Merry Widow Murder of 1936." New England Historical Society, November 18, 2016. https://newenglandhistor icalsociety.com/merry-widow-murder-1936/.

- "Death Penalty Sought for Nurse in Patients' Deaths." Los Angeles Times, May 16, 1999. https://www.latimes.com/archives/la-xpm-19 99-may-16-mn-37761-story.html.

- Deburro, Joe. "Ghost Hunters Set Sights on Theodores' Tavern in Springfield." Mass Live, August 19, 2008. https://www.masslive.com/ news/2008/08/ghost_hunters_set_sights_on_th.html.

- "Did Tamerlan Tsarnaev Kill His Jewish Friends?" Jewish Journal, April 23, 2013. https://jewishjournal.com/news/united-states/115919/.

- "Dining Off-Duty Cop Stops Fatal Stabbing Rampage in Massachusetts Mall." ABC News, May 11, 2016. https://abcnews.go.com/US/dining-off-duty-cop-stops-fatal-stabbing-rampage/story?id=39034337.

- "District of Massachusetts | Victim and Witness Assistance Program." Justice.gov., December 15, 2014. https://www.justice.gov/usao-ma/vi ctim-and-witness-assistance-program.

- Driscoll, Kathi Scrizzi. "'Stunned at the Sheer Brutality': Author Casey Sherman's 'Helltown' Explores Costa Serial Murders on Cape Cod." Cape Cod Times, May 31, 2022. https://www.capecodtimes.com/stor y/entertainment/2022/05/31/tony-costa-cape-cod-serial-murders-c asey-sherman-helltown-kurt-vonnegut-norman-mailer-provincetow n/9942373002/.

- Dunlap, David W. "5 Standish Street." Building Provincetown, January 2, 2010. https://buildingprovincetown.wordpress.com/2010/01/02/5-standish-street/.
- Dwyer, Dialynn. "11 Black Women Were Murdered in Boston 40 Years Ago. A Local Artist Is Remembering Them Across the City." www.boston.com, February 20, 2019. https://www.boston.com/news/local-news/2019/02/20/1979-boston-murders-estuary-projects/.
- Dwyer, Timothy. "Police Reconstructs Bits of Bobbie Graham's Life." Boston Globe, May 9, 1979. https://www.newspapers.com/image/437001950/.
- Edwards, Rebecca. "The Safest Cities in Massachusetts." SafeWise, August 20, 2019. https://www.safewise.com/blog/safest-cities-massachusetts/.
- Fargen, Jessica. "Cops Piece Together Chilling Details of Tragedy." Boston Herald, January 23, 2009. https://www.bostonherald.com/2009/01/23/cops-piece-together-chilling-details-of-tragedy/.
- Fargen, Jessica, and Joe Dwinell. "Cops Traced E-Mail to Philip Markoff." Boston Herald, April 22, 2022. https://web.archive.org/web/20090526041353/http://www.bostonherald.com/news/regional/view/2009_04_22_Cops_traced_e-mail_to_Philip_Markoff.
- Ferdin, Pamela, and Dan Eggen. "7 Die in Massachusetts Office Shooting." Washington Post, December 27, 2000. https://www.washingtonpost.com/archive/politics/2000/12/27/7-die-in-massachusetts-office-shooting/1b9f9c67-b2c3-482c-bf1b-fa869fc6c430/.
- "Final Report Regarding Police Involved Shooting of Arthur DaRosa at Taunton Galleria Mall." New Bedford Guide, October 26, 2016. https://www.newbedfordguide.com/final-report-darosa-taunton-mall-shooting/2016/10/26.
- Fitzgerald, Edward. "Sacco and Vanzetti at 100: The Quincy Connections." Quincy Historical Society, April 28, 2020. https://quincyhistory.org/blog/?p=89.
- "Five Found Slain at Boston Disco in Apparent Dispute over Drugs."

The New York Times, June 29, 1978. https://www.nytimes.com/1978 /06/29/archives/five-found-slain-at-boston-disco-in-apparent-dispu te-over-drugs.html.

- Flynn, Sheila. "The Terrifying Serial Killer Who Killed at Least Nine Women—and Got Away with It." The Independent, February 10, 2022. https://www.the-independent.com/news/world/americas/crime/tru e-cime-serial-killer-new-bedford-b2010282.html.

- Folsom, Beth. Letter to Dawn Barclay. "Cambridge Hospital." April 1, 2024. bfolsom@historycambridge.org.

- Ford, Leslie. "The Model Murder Case." Pittsburgh Sun-Telegraph, November 1, 1953. https://www.newspapers.com/image/524610476 /.

- Fraga, Brian. "Jurors View Key Locations in Aaron Hernandez Trial." Patriot Ledger, February 10, 2015. https://www.patriotledger.com/st ory/news/courts/2015/02/06/jurors-view-key-locations-in/351438 62007/.

- Frankfurter, Felix. "The Case of Sacco and Vanzetti." The Atlantic, March 1927. https://www.theatlantic.com/magazine/archive/1927/ 03/the-case-of-sacco-and-vanzetti/306625/.

- "GOAL - Massachusetts Leads Again – as the Most Violent State in New England," Goal.org, 2020. https://goal.org/Massachusetts-Leads-Agai n-As-the-Most-Violent-State-in-New-England#:~:text=GOAL%20% 2D%20Massachusetts%20Leads%20Again%20%E2%80%93%20As.

- Goldberg, Carey. "A Deadly Turn to a Normal Work Day." The New York Times, December 28, 2000. https://www.nytimes.com/2000/12 /28/us/a-deadly-turn-to-a-normal-work-day.html.

- Goodnough, Abby. "Medical Student Is Indicted in Craigslist Killing." The New York Times, June 22, 2009. https://www.nytimes.com/2009 /06/22/us/22indict.html.

- Gorenstein, Nathan. "The Millen-Faber Gang." Tommy Gun Winter, August 26, 2014. https://www.nathangorenstein.com/83-2/.

- "Great Brink's Robbery." Northendwaterfront.com, January 17, 2020. https://northendwaterfront.com/tag/great-brinks-robbery/.

- Grey, Dana. "Research Guides: Crime in Boston: Criminals & Crime." guides.bpl.org, Accessed April 25, 2024. https://guides.bpl.org/crimeinboston.
- Grigoriadis, Vanessa. "The Single-Mom Murder." NYMag.com, Accessed April 24, 2024. https://nymag.com/news/articles/02/worthington/index.htm.
- Guyon, Janet. "Aaron Hernandez's Brain Shows Why No One Should Play Football. Ever." Quartz, November 9, 2017. https://qz.com/1125605/footballs-aaron-hernandez-dead-at-27-had-the-worst-cte-of-anyone-his-age.
- "Haunted Restaurants and Bars Across Massachusetts." MAHaunted-houses.com, Accessed April 24, 2024. https://www.mahauntedhouses.com/real-haunts/restaurants-bars.aspx.
- "Highway Murders." Southcoast Murders & Mysteries, Accessed April 24, 2024. https://southcoastmurdersmysteries.weebly.com/highway-murders.html.
- "Historic Hotels of America." Historic Hotels Worldwide, Accessed April 24, 2024. https://www.historichotels.org/us/hotels-resorts/hawthorne-hotel/ghost-stories.php.
- History.com Editors. "Salem Witch Trials." History.com, November 4, 2011. https://www.history.com/topics/colonial-america/salem-witch-trials.
- Huffman, Zack. "Aaron Hernandez Acquitted of Drive-by Killings." Courthouse News Service, April 14, 2017. https://www.courthousenews.com/aaron-hernandez-acquitted-drive-killings/.
- Hunter, Brad. "Crime Hunter: Who Was Serial Killer Who Terrorized New Bedford?" Toronto Sun, July 25, 2020. https://torontosun.com/news/world/crime-hunter-who-was-serial-killer-who-terrorized-new-bedford.
- "Husband Charged in Wife's Death after Argument over Pasta." The Tennessean, August 31, 1995. https://www.newspapers.com/image/113238752/.
- Jagolinzer, Jordyn. "Rockafellas Restaurant a Popular Part of Salem's

Spooky History." www.cbsnews.com, October 31, 2023. https://www.cbsnews.com/boston/news/rockafellas-restaurant-salem-massachusetts/.

- Jake. "The Millen Gang Machine Gun Murders (Episode 170)." HUB History, February 2, 2020. https://www.hubhistory.com/episodes/the-millen-gang-machine-gun-murders-episode-170/.
- "James 'Whitey' Bulger." The Mob Museum, Accessed April 27, 2024. https://themobmuseum.org/notable_names/whitey-bulger/.
- "John Billington." Murderpedia.org, accessed April 22, 2024. https://murderpedia.org/male.B/b/billington-john.htm.
- Kaplan, Aline. "The Niles Building: Hub of a Financial Scandal." The Next Phase Blog, July 19, 2018. https://aknextphase.com/the-niles-building-hub-of-a-financial-scandal/.
- "Killer Nurse Gets Life." CBSNews.com, March 26, 2001. https://www.cbsnews.com/news/killer-nurse-gets-life/.
- Kolnos, Jason. "Serial Killer 'Jolly Jane' Still Fascinates." Cape Cod Times, October 25, 2010. https://www.capecodtimes.com/story/news/2010/10/25/serial-killer-jolly-jane-still/51426686007/.
- Kovaleski, Serge F., and Richard A. Oppel Jr. "In 2011 Murder Inquiry, Hints of Missed Chance to Avert Boston Bombing." The New York Times, July 10, 2013. https://www.nytimes.com/2013/07/11/us/boston-bombing-suspect-is-said-to-be-linked-to-2011-triple-murder-case.html.
- Kukstis, James E. "Six of Massachusetts' Most Notorious Serial Killers." Wicked Local, October 6, 2022. https://www.wickedlocal.com/story/regional/2022/10/04/jeffrey-dahmer-serial-killer-boston-strangler-giggler-tony-chop-chop-worst-massachusetts/10459954002/.
- Lambert, Bryan. "Massachusetts Is Shutting down MCI-Concord. These 5 Notable Prisoners Were Once Housed There." Boston 25 News, January 24, 2024. https://www.boston25news.com/news/local/massachusetts-is-shutting-down-mci-concord-these-5-notable-prisoners-were-once-housed-there/UCR2G3FZSRELDP267QXMEOOR6M/.
- Latson, Jennifer. "How an Abortion-Clinic Shooting Led to a 'Wrongful

Life' Lawsuit." Time, December 30, 2014. https://time.com/3648437/ john-salvi-shootings/.

- "Legal Notice for Whispers Pub." Boston Globe, p46, September 19, 1989. https://www.newspapers.com/image/439133400/?terms=whis pers%20pub&match=1.

- Linder, Douglas. "Sir William Phips." Famous-trials.com, Accessed April 23, 2024. https://famous-trials.com/salem/2035-sal-bphi#.

- Liscio, David. "Investigation of Mob Slaying Clouded by Cops' Speculation." The Daily Item, September 25, 1991. https://www. newspapers.com/image/948165664/.

- "List of Criminals from Massachusetts." FamousFix.com, Accessed April 23, 2024. https://www.famousfix.com/list/criminals-from-mas sachusetts.

- Lister, Tim, and Paul Cruickshank. "Dead Boston Bomb Suspect Posted Video of Jihadist, Analysis Shows." CNN, April 20, 2013. https://editi on.cnn.com/2013/04/20/us/brother-religious-language.

- "Listing of Museums and Galleries Located in Massachusetts." Visit-massachusetts.com, Accessed April 23, 2024. https://www.visit-mass achusetts.com/state/museums-and-galleries/.

- Mahoney, Melissa. "Stay Overnight in the 284-Year-Old New Boston Inn, an Allegedly Haunted Spot in Massachusetts." OnlyInYourState®, September 21, 2021. https://www.onlyinyourstate.com/massachusett s/new-boston-inn-ma/.

- Malmborg, Donna. "The Ghost of the Historic Knox Trail Inn – New England Legends." New England Legends, October 2, 2020. https://ou rnewenglandlegends.com/the-ghost-of-the-historic-knox-trail-inn/.

- Margetta, Rob. "Jacob Robida: Final Days of a Killer." New Bedford Standard-Times, March 2, 2007. https://www.southcoasttoday.com/s tory/news/2006/02/19/jacob-robida-final-days-killer/52957726007 /.

- Martin, Philip. "Is the Waltham Triple Murder Investigation at a Dead End?" WGBH, April 13, 2018. https://www.wgbh.org/news/2018-04-12/is-the-waltham-triple-murder-investigation-at-a-dead-end.

- Martinez, Edecio. "Philip Markoff, Alleged 'Craigslist Killer,' Found Dead in Cell after Apparent Suicide." www.cbsnews.com, August 16, 2010. https://www.cbsnews.com/news/philip-markoff-alleged-craig slist-killer-found-dead-in-cell-after-apparent-suicide/.
- Mashberg, Tom. "Meet the Suspects: Mobster Bobby Donati." Boston Herald, March 29, 2008. https://www.bostonherald.com/2008/03/29 /meet-the-suspects-mobster-bobby-donati/.
- "Mass. V. Leahy: Rest Stop Murder." Court TV, Accessed April 24, 2024. http://www.courttv.com/trials/taped/leahy/background.html.
- "Massachusetts' Most Notorious Crimes." WCVB, December 25, 2016. https://www.wcvb.com/article/massachusetts-most-notorious-crime s/8115052.
- "Massachusetts State Prison, Charlestown." Charlestown Historical Society, Accessed April 24, 2024. https://charlestownhistoricalsociety. org/chs_events/massachusetts-state-prison-charlestown/.
- McGovern, Bob, Chris Villani, Jennifer Miller, and Laurel J. Sweet. "'Shocked' Defense Team to Conduct Own Probe of Aaron Hernandez Death." Boston Herald, April 19, 2017. https://www.bostonherald.co m/2017/04/19/shocked-defense-team-to-conduct-own-probe-of-aa ron-hernandez-death/.
- McReynolds, Marcus. "The Crimes Committed by Jolly Jane." Robert J. DeBry and Associates, June 5, 2022. https://robertdebry.com/jollyja nelifeandcrimes/.
- Medeiros, Dan. "The Lizzie Borden House Was Named One of the World's Best Haunted Hotels. How Scary Is It?" Fall River Herald News, October 26, 2021. https://www.heraldnews.com/story/lifestyl e/travel/2021/10/26/lizzie-borden-house-fall-river-best-haunted-h otel-ghost-paranormal/8546497002/.
- Mehren, Elizabeth. "Killer of 2 at Abortion Clinics Commits Suicide." Los Angeles Times, November 30, 1996. https://www.newspapers.co m/image/158035100/.
- Mike1989. "Christa Worthington's House in Truro, MA (Google Maps)." Virtual Globetrotting, September 2, 2013. https://virtual

globetrotting.com/map/christa-worthingtons-house/view/google/.

- Milne, Andrew. "Kristen Gilbert: The Suburban Soccer Mom and Nurse That No One Suspected Was a Serial Killer." All That's Interesting, February 20, 2019. https://allthatsinteresting.com/kristen-gilbert.

- Morning Sentinel. "5th Black Woman's Murder in Boston Triggers Calls for More Police." February 23, 1979. https://www.newspapers.com/image/855313336/.

- Morsberger, Cameron. "Local Author Pens Novel on Infamous Needham Bank Robbery." Needham Local, April 19, 2024. https://needhamlocal.org/2024/02/local-author-pens-novel-on-infamous-needham-bank-robbery/.

- Myers, Jennifer. "For 10 Years, 'Jolly Jane' Poured Her Poison." Lowell Sun, November 2, 2011. https://www.lowellsun.com/2011/11/02/for-10-years-jolly-jane-poured-her-poison/.

- Noble, Janis DiLoreto. "Decision in the Matter of Kenneth Seguin." Commonwealth of Massachusetts Executive Office of Public Safety Parole Board, May 15, 2013. https://www.mass.gov/doc/kenneth-seguin-life-sentence-decision-october-26-2022/download.

- Papadopoulos, Maria. "Keith Luke's Organs Donated after Death." WCVB5-ABC, May 21, 2014. https://www.wcvb.com/article/keith-luke-s-organs-donated-after-death/8201703.

- Papadopoulos, Maria. "Witnesses Take Turns Staring down Keith Luke." Enterprise News, May 26, 2013. https://www.enterprisenews.com/story/news/crime/2013/05/26/witnesses-take-turns-staring-down/37365290007/.

- Park, Madison. "Massachusetts Man Indicted on 52 Charges after 3 Bodies Found at His Home." CNN, August 17, 2018. https://www.cnn.com/2018/08/17/us/massachusetts-indictment-murder-kidnap-women/index.html.

- Patmore, Neil. "'The Devil Incarnate': Inside the Chilling Crimes of Serial Killer Tony Costa, the 'Cape Cod Vampire.'" All That's Interesting, October 4, 2022. https://allthatsinteresting.com/tony

-costa.

- Patmore, Neil. "How a Troubled 14-Year-Old Murdered His Math Teacher in a School Bathroom — Then Carted Her Corpse Away in a Trash Can." All That's Interesting, December 6, 2022. https://allthatsinteresting.com/philip-chism.
- "Poison Her Passion." The Clinton Morning Age, July 27, 1902. https://news.google.com/newspapers?nid=2267&dat=19020727&id=6ncmAAAAIBAJ&sjid=CgEGAAAAIBAJ&pg=4194.
- "Police Grill Boy Slay Suspect." Boston Globe, January 7, 1970. https://www.newspapers.com/article/the-boston-globe-kenneth-harison/104403597/.
- "Police Identify 11th Murder Victim." Daily Evening Item, May 8, 1979. https://www.newspapers.com/image/947776473/.
- Pollard, Gayle, Carmen Fields, and Viola Osgood. "Six Slain Women and Those Who Loved Them." Boston Globe, April 1, 1979. https://www.newspapers.com/image/436716094/.
- Potts, Michael. "Jane Toppan: A Greed, Power, and Lust Serial Killer." Www.academia.edu, Accessed April 24, 2024. https://www.academia.edu/15686136/Jane_Toppan_A_Greed_Power_and_Lust_Serial_Killer.
- Powers, Richard. "Snow Threatens Cape Search." Boston Globe, March 7, 1969. https://www.newspapers.com/image/434634437/.
- "Prosecutor after Serial Killer Sentenced: Weldon Will Never Be Free to Hunt in Springfield Again." WWLP, October 1, 2021. https://www.wwlp.com/news/local-news/hampden-county/prosecutor-after-serial-killer-sentenced-weldon-will-never-be-free-to-hunt-in-springfield-again/.
- "Revere Man Found Slain in Trunk of His Car-High Beam Research." Boston Globe. October 8, 2016. https://web.archive.org/web/20161008201903/https://www.highbeam.com/doc/1P2-7678780.html.
- Richard, Barry. "After 35 Years, New Bedford Highway Killings Remain Unresolved." WBSM 1420, March 20, 2023. https://wbsm.com/new-bedford-highway-killings-remain-unsolved/.

- Riley, Neal. "'Philip Chism Is a Monster,' Detention Center Attack Victim Says about Murderer of Danvers Math Teacher." www.cbsnews.com, April 26, 2024. https://www.cbsnews.com/boston/news/philip-chism-change-of-plea-victim/.
- Ryan, Andrew, Todd Wallack, and Beth Healy. "Aaron Hernandez, Infamous Ex-Patriots Star, Sounded Upbeat in Final Prison Calls before Suicide." WBUR, March 27, 2023. https://www.wbur.org/news/2023/03/27/new-england-patriots-prison-aaron-hernandez-suicide-murder-nfl-phone-calls.
- "Sacco & Vanzetti: Justice on Trial." Mass.gov, 2019. https://www.mass.gov/info-details/sacco-vanzetti-justice-on-trial.
- Sacks, Ethan, and Julmary Zambrano. "3 Bodies Found at Home of Massachusetts Man Accused of Kidnapping, Torture." NBC News, June 2, 2018. https://www.nbcnews.com/news/crime-courts/3-bodies-found-home-massachusetts-man-accused-kidnapping-torture-n879236.
- "Search for More Bodies in Gruesome Cape Killings." Finchburg Sentinel, March 7, 1969. https://www.newspapers.com/image/45348786/.
- Setterlund, Chris. "Truro Cemetery Holds Dark Secrets." CapeCod.com, October 19, 2015. https://www.capecod.com/community/truro-cemetery-holds-dark-secrets/.
- "Seven Dead in Mass. Office Shooting." ABC News, December 26, 2000. https://abcnews.go.com/US/story?id=94595&page=1.
- Smith, Benjamin H. "Serial Killer Nurse Who Liked 'Thrill' of Emergencies Murdered Patients to Impress Boyfriend." Oxygen Official Site, May 11, 2018. https://www.oxygen.com/snapped/crime-time/serial-killer-nurse-murdered-patients-kristen-gilbert.
- Snow, Mary, and Jason Kessler. "Med Student Held without Bail in Possible Craigslist Killing." CNN, April 2, 2009. https://www.cnn.com/2009/CRIME/04/21/mass.killing.craigslist/index.html.
- Sophia. "These 10 Famous Homicides in Massachusetts Will Never Be Forgotten." OnlyInYourState, March 12, 2016. https://www.onlyinyo

urstate.com/massachusetts/famous-murders-ma/.

- Spencer, Buffy. "Serial Killer Alfred Gaynor Pleads Guilty to Three New Murder Charges." masslive, October 26, 2010. https://www.mas slive.com/news/2010/10/serial_killer_alfred_gaynor_pl.html.
- "Suspect, 2 Victims Dead after Stabbing Spree in Taunton." CBSNews.com, May 10, 2016. https://www.cbsnews.com/boston/n ews/taunton-police-silver-city-galleria-shooting/.
- Sweet, Laurel J. "35 Years after Horton Murder, Victim's Kin Carry on His Memory." Boston Herald, October 26, 2009. https://www.boston herald.com/2009/10/26/35-years-after-horton-murder-victims-kin-carry-on-his-memory/.
- "Taunton Rampage Attacker Had Psychiatric Issues, Family Says." CBSNews.com, May 11, 2016. https://www.cbsnews.com/boston /news/taunton-mall-stabbing-rampage-arthur-darosa-silver-city-gall eria-massachusetts/.
- Tenser, Phil. "Mass. Mansion Once Owned by Namesake of Ponzi Scheme on the Market for $4.3M." WCVB, September 22, 2023. https://www.wcvb.com/article/charles-ponzi-lexington-massachuset ts-19-slocum-road/45262421.
- Tenser, Phil. "Solemn Memorials on Boylston Street Before, during Boston Marathon." WCVB, April 15, 2024. https://www.wcvb.com/a rticle/boston-marathon-memorial-boylston-street-2024/60496620.
- "The ALLY Foundation | About." The ALLY Foundation, Accessed April 23, 2024. https://www.theallyfoundation.org/about/history/.
- The Editors of Encyclopaedia Britannica. "Sacco and Vanzetti | Definition, Background, Verdict, & Facts." Encyclopædia Britannica, 2019. https://www.britannica.com/biography/Sacco-and-Vanzetti.
- "The Gardner Museum Case: Bobby Donati." ArtTheft blog, Accessed April 27, 2024. https://arttheft.weebly.com/bobby-donati.html.
- "The Giggler, Boston Serial Killer." Celebrateboston.com, Accessed May 2, 2024. http://www.celebrateboston.com/crime/giggler-serial-killer.htm.
- "'The Giggler': The Horrific Serial Killer from Boston Whose Calling

Card Was 'Laughter.'" Dangerous Minds, January 24, 2017. https://da ngerousminds.net/comments/the_giggler_the_horrific_serial_killer_ from_boston_whose_calling_card_was_l.

- "The Haunted Club Quarters Boston | Haunted Hotel in Boston." Ghost City Tours, Accessed April 24, 2024. https://ghostcitytours.com/bost on/haunted-places/club-quarters/.
- "The Haunted Hotel of Concord, MA." Concord's Colonial Inn, October 21, 2019. https://www.concordscolonialinn.com/haunted-hotel/.
- "The Tony Costa Cape Cod Murders." Cape Cod Today, July 21, 2011. https://web.archive.org/web/20110721094654/http://www.capecod today.com/blogs/index.php/2007/09/11/the_tony_costa_cape_cod_ murders?blog=149.
- "These Are 10 Haunted Restaurants You Can Eat at in Mass. For a Good Scare." Mass Live, October 27, 2022. https://www.masslive.co m/entertainment/2022/10/these-are-10-haunted-restaurants-you-ca n-eat-at-in-mass-for-a-good-scare.html.
- Townsend, Catherine. "Serial Killer Tony Costa's Garden of Horrors." The-line-up.com, September 14, 2017. https://the-line-up.com/tony-costa-garden-of-horror.
- Trex, Ethan. "Who Was Ponzi — What the Heck Was His Scheme?" CNN. Accessed April 24, 2024. https://edition.cnn.com/2008/LIVIN G/wayoflife/12/23/mf.ponzi.scheme/.
- Voss, Gretchen. "Last Exit." Boston Magazine, May 15, 2006. https://w ww.bostonmagazine.com/2006/05/15/last-exit/.
- "Watertown Man Who Found Boston Marathon Bomber in His Boat Dies." CBSNews.com. September 29, 2017. https://www.cbsnews.co m/boston/news/david-henneberry-boston-marathon-bombings-wat ertown-boat-owner-dzhokhar-tsarnaev-captured/.
- Wetzel, Dan. "Aaron Hernandez's 2015 Murder Conviction Reinstated, Which Could Have Ramifications for His Family." Yahoo Sports, March 13, 2019.
- "What We Know about the Boston Bombing and Its Aftermath." CNN, April 18, 2013. https://edition.cnn.com/2013/04/18/us/boston-mara

thon-things-we-know.

- "Whitey Bulger and the Lancaster Street Garage ." The West End Museum, July 29, 2022. https://thewestendmuseum.org/history/era/new-boston/whitey-bulger-and-the-lancaster-street-garage/.
- Williams, Michelle. "Who Is Stewart Weldon? A Closer Look at the Man Who Had Bodies of Missing Persons at His Home." Mass Live, June 5, 2018. https://www.masslive.com/news/erry-2018/06/3c8d65d31d1748/who_is_stewart_weldon_the_man.html#.
- Withers, Rachel. "George H.W. Bush's 'Willie Horton' Ad Defined Dog-Whistle Politics." Vox, December 2018. https://www.vox.com/2018/12/1/18121221/george-hw-bush-willie-horton-dog-whistle-politics.
- "Woman Identified in 12th Murder." Boston Globe, May 9, 1978. https://www.newspapers.com/image/437000935/.
- Wood, Dave. "Cathedral High School Student Found Slain." Boston Globe, January 31, 1979. https://www.newspapers.com/image/436680534/.
- Yan, Eric Levenson, Holly. "Aaron Hernandez's Murder Conviction Cleared after Suicide." CNN, May 9, 2017. https://www.cnn.com/2017/05/09/us/aaron-hernandez-murder-conviction-abated.
- Zitner, Aaron, and John Laidler. "Holliston Mother, Children Are Mourned and Buried." Boston Globe, May 9, 1002. https://www.newspapers.com/search/?query=Mary%20Ann%20Seguin&p_province=us-ma&dr_year=1992-1992.

Chapter 4: New Hampshire

- "10 Most Dangerous Cities in New Hampshire." Travel Safe - Abroad, February 24, 2023. https://www.travelsafe-abroad.com/most-dangerous-cities-in-new-hampshire/.
- Associated Press. "Alton Man Held for Killing of Laconia Boy." Portsmouth Herald and Times, September 15, 1937. https://www.newspapers.com/image/12358016/.

- Bastoni, Mark. "Isles of Shoals Murders-Horror on Smuttynose Island." New England, March 9, 2022. https://newengland.com/yankee/histo ry/smuttynose-murders/.
- "Bernice Courtemanche | Cold Case Unit | NH Department of Justice." DOJ. Nh.gov, 2024. https://www.doj.nh.gov/criminal/cold-case/victi m-list/bernice-courtemanche.htm.
- Billin, Dan. "State's Case Details Anatomy of Two Slayings." Concord Monitor, April 6, 2002. https://www.newspapers.com/image/925256 934/.
- Boehm, Connor and Jacob H. Parker. "The Dartmouth Murders Twenty Years Later." The Dartmouth Review, January 27, 2021, https://dartreview.com/the-dartmouth-murders-twenty-years-lat er/.
- Bookman, Todd. "NH Recorded 27 Homicides in 2023, Including Four Police Shootings, according to Attorney General." New Hampshire Public Radio, January 3, 2024. https://www.nhpr.org/nh-news/2024-01-03/nh-recorded-27-homicides-in-2023-including-four-police-sh ootings-according-to-attorney-general.
- Bradford, Alina. "New Hampshire's Safest Cities of 2024." www.safe-wise.com, March 18, 2024. https://www.safewise.com/blog/safest-cit ies-new-hampshire.
- "Carl Drega." Murderpedia.org, Accessed April 10, 2024. https://murd erpedia.org/male.D/d/drega-carl.htm.
- "Comery Held in Wife's Death." The Boston Daily Globe, January 3, 1915. https://www.newspapers.com/article/the-boston-daily-globe-boston-globejan/8807067/.
- Dandrea, Alyssia. "A Killer's Trail." Concord Monitor, January 27, 2017. https://www.newspapers.com/image/838840085/.
- Downs, John W. "I Met the Smuttynose Murderer." www.sea-coastnh.com. Accessed May 4, 2024. https://www.seacoastnh.co m/i-met-the-smuttynose-murderer/?showall=1.
- "Eliphas Dow." Murderpedia.org, Accessed April 16, 2024. https://mu rderpedia.org/male.D/d/dow-eliphas.htm.

- "Eliphaz Dow." Freepages.rootsweb.com, Accessed April 16, 2024. https://freepages.rootsweb.com/~laplante/genealogy/PS36/PS36_41 4.HTM.
- "Eva Morse | Cold Case Unit | NH Department of Justice." DOJ.nh.gov, Accessed April 15, 2024. https://www.doj.nh.gov/criminal/cold-case/ victim-list/eva-morse.htm#.
- Ferland, Dr. David. *Historic Crimes & Justice in Portsmouth, New Hampshire.* Arcadia Publishing, 2014.
- Finney, Douglas. "Josie Langmaid Historical Marker." www.hmdb.org, April 16, 2019. https://www.hmdb.org/m.asp?m=132249.
- Gatollari, Mustafa. "Serial Killer Terry Rasmussen Died from Cancer While Locked up in Prison." Distractify, February 20, 2021. https://w ww.distractify.com/p/how-did-terry-rasmussen-die.
- Geake, Robert A. *Death in Early New England: Rites, Rituals and Remembrance.* Google Books. Arcadia Publishing, 2023.
- Gualtieri, Jacqueline. "Dine with Ghosts at the 11 Most Haunted Restaurants in New England." Spoon University, September 1, 2016, https://spoonuniversity.com/place/dine-with-ghosts-at-the-11-most -haunted-restaurants-in-new-england.
- Gutierrez, Michael Kennan. "The Trial and Execution of Ruth Blay." We're History, June 12, 2015. https://werehistory.org/ruth-blay/.
- Holm, Ashley. Letter to Dawn Barclay. "Question about Oscar Comery." Email from aholm@manchesterhistoric.org, March 2, 2024.
- "James Parker, Convicted of Murdering 2 Dartmouth College Professors in 2001, Granted Parole." CBSNews.com, April 18, 2024. https://www.cbsnews.com/boston/news/james-parker-parole-ha lf-susanne-zantop-murder-dartmouth-college-new-hampshire/.
- Jansen, Sharon L. "Ruth Blay and the Crime of Concealing the Birth of a 'Bastard' Child." The Monstrous Regiment of Women, December 15, 2015. https://www.monstrousregimentofwomen.com/2015/12/ruth-blay-and-crime-of-concealing-birth.html.
- "John Walter Bardgett." Murderpedia.org, Accessed April 15, 2024. https://murderpedia.org/male.B/b/bardgett-john-walter.htm.

- "Julianne McCrery." Murderpedia.org, Accessed April 15, 2024. https://murderpedia.org/female.M/m/mccrery-julianne.htm.
- Kerr, Jan Bouchard. "Sex, Lies & Murder: The Pamela Smart Case — Misty Morning Drive." www.crimelibrary.org, May 1, 1990. https://www.crimelibrary.org/notorious_murders/family/smart/1.html.
- Landrigan, Leslie. "Franklin Evans, New Hampshire's Jack the Ripper." New England Historical Society, January 6, 2023. https://newengland historicalsociety.com/franklin-evans-new-hampshires-jack-the-ripp er/.
- Lynch, Troy. "Homicides in New Hampshire up in 2022 Compared to Last 2 Years." WMUR, December 31, 2022. https://www.wmur.com/ article/new-hampshire-homicides-up-2022-compared-last-2-years/4 2373381.
- Makinen, Karri. Letter to Dawn Barclay. "Question about Carl Drega for Historical Society for Book." KMakinen@bownh.gov, February 27, 2024.
- Marvel, William. "Bluebeard of Ossipee." The Conway Daily Sun, September 21, 2020. https://www.conwaydailysun.com/opinion/col umns/william-marvel-bluebeard-of-ossipee/article_79413b7c-fc04-11ea-aa75-0f708799dce3.html.
- "Mary Elizabeth Critchley | Cold Case Unit | NH Department of Justice." DOJ.nh.gov, Accessed April 15, 2024. https://www.doj.nh.gov/crimin al/cold-case/victim-list/mary-elizabeth-critchley.htm#.
- McCormack, Kathy. "Somber Memories 20 Years after Small-Town Shootings." Portsmouth Herald, August 17, 2017. https://www.seacoa stonline.com/story/news/2017/08/14/somber-memories-20-years-a fter/19739932007/.
- Megan. "Dine with a Ghost at These 13 Haunted New England Restaurants." 97.5 WOKQ, April 6, 2024. https://wokq.com/haun ted-new-england-restaurant/.
- Michelle. "These 4 Famous Homicides in New Hampshire Will Never Be Forgotten." OnlyInYourState, October 16, 2020. https://www.only inyourstate.com/new-hampshire/famous-homicides-nh/.

- Milbouer, Stacy. "These 3 Famous Criminals Have Ties to New Hampshire's History." granitepostnews.com, February 12, 2024. https://granitepostnews.com/2024/02/12/these-3-famous-serial-kill ers-have-ties-to-new-hampshires-history/.
- Mills, Daniel. "The Suncook Town Tragedy (Marietta Ball, Part 2)." These Dark Mountains, October 8, 2019. https://thesedarkmountains. com/episodes/the-suncook-town-tragedy-marietta-ball-part-2.
- "Moonlight Murders." Smuttynose Island Murders, Accessed April 15, 2024. http://www.smuttynosemurders.com/moonlight-murders.htm l.
- Morgan, Amber. "Greggory Smart, the Man Killed by His Wife's Teen Lover." All That's Interesting, September 26, 2024. https://allthatsinte resting.com/greggory-smart.
- "Mother of Mystery Maine Boy Confesses to Killing Son and Dumping Him on Rural Road: Sources." ABC News, May 18, 2011. https://abcn ews.go.com/US/mother-mystery-maine-boy-confesses-killing-son-s ources/story?id=13631248.
- Nielsenhayden.com. "Making Light: Carl Drega, Part III," August 19, 2008. https://nielsenhayden.com/makinglight/archives/010507.html .
- Ocker, JW. "Graves of the Smuttynose Murder Victims." Atlas Obscura, June 4, 2012. https://www.atlasobscura.com/places/graves-smuttyno se-murder-victims.
- Ocker, JW. "Josie Langmaid Monument." Atlas Obscura, August 2, 2010. https://www.atlasobscura.com/places/josie-langmaid-monument.
- "Oscar Comery." Murderpedia.org, Accessed April 16, 2024, https://m urderpedia.org/male.C/c/comery-oscar.htm.
- "Oscar Joseph Comery (1885-1916)." Findagrave.com. Accessed April 15, 2024. https://www.findagrave.com/memorial/109708480/oscar-j oseph-comery.
- "Pamela Smart." Murderpedia.org, Accessed April 20, 2024. https://m urderpedia.org/female.S/s/smart-pamela.htm.
- Parkhurst, Marcia. Letter to Dawn Barclay. "Drega Address." Email

from towncolumbia@myfairpoint.net, February 28, 2024.

- Patmore, Neil. "The Chilling Story of Terry Rasmussen, the 'Chameleon Killer' Who Changed Identities with Every Brutal Slaying." All That's Interesting, September 13, 2022. https://allthatsinteresting.com/terry-rasmussen.
- "People Executed by New Hampshire by Hanging." FamousFix.com, Accessed April 15, 2024. https://m.famousfix.com/list/people-execut ed-by-new-hampshire-by-hanging.
- Pittman, John. "Smuttynose Island." Atlas Obscura, April 20, 2011. https://www.atlasobscura.com/places/smutttynose-island.
- Priolo, Sandy. Letter to Dawn Barclay. "Question for Northwood Historical Society." Email from rockyacres1072@myfairpoint.net, February 25, 2024.
- "Property Crime 2022." Crimestats.dos.nh.gov. Accessed April 15, 2024. https://crimestats.dos.nh.gov/tops/report/property-crimes/ne w-hampshire/2022.
- Rachel. "This Jail in New Hampshire Is Actually a Restaurant and You Need to Visit." OnlyInYourState®, December 22, 2017. https://www.onlyinyourstate.com/new-hampshire/jail-restaurant-nh/.
- "Resources for Homicide Cases." New Hampshire Department of Justice, Accessed September 10, 2024. https://www.doj.nh.gov/burea us/resources-homicide-cases.
- Robinson, J. Dennis. "Hanged in Portsmouth." Portsmouth Herald, October 29, 2018. https://www.seacoastonline.com/story/news/local /portsmouth-herald/2018/10/29/hanged-in-portsmouth/942850800 7/.
- Robinson, J. Dennis. "Ruth Blay Hanged Here in 1768." Sea-coastNH.com, 2008. http://www.seacoastnh.com/history/histor y-matters/ruth-blay-hanged-here-in-1768/.
- Sam. "17 Most Haunted Hotels & Places in New Hampshire You Can Visit." New England Wanderlust, August 21, 2022. https://newenglan dwanderlust.com/haunted-hotels-in-new-hampshire/.
- "Sarah Simpson." Murderpedia.org, Accessed April 15, 2024. https://m

urderpedia.org/female.S/s/simpson-sarah.htm.

- "Serial Killer Terry Rasmussen's Victims, Known and Unknown." ABC News, January 18, 2021. https://abcnews.go.com/US/terry-rasmusse ns-victims-unknown/story?id=69585534.
- Small, Eric to Dawn Barclay, "Question about the Eliphaz Dow Killing of Peter Klough," email from Eric Small enswalton@comcast.net and Beverly Multrie bmutrie@hotmail.com, April 16, 2024.
- Snierson, Lynne. "Dining with Ghosts at the Windham Restaurant." New Hampshire Magazine, October 5, 2014. https://www.nhmagazi ne.com/dining-with-ghosts-at-the-windham-restaurant/.
- "State v. Long, 90 N.H. 103." Casetext.com, Accessed April 16, 2024, https://casetext.com/case/state-v-long-246.
- "Steven Spader." Murderpedia.org, Accessed April 20, 2024. https://m urderpedia.org/male.S/s/spader-steven.htm.
- Sweeney, Lois. "Small Murder." Email from Sweeney Sweeney, lmsween@roadrunner.com, February 28, 2024.
- SYFY Official Site. "Episode Recap: Ghost of Christmas Past." December 16, 2014. https://www.syfy.com/ghost-hunters/season-6/ blogs/episode-recap-ghost-of-christmas-past.
- "Teen Who Killed Pamela Smart's Husband Freed 25 Years Later." Chicago Tribune, June 4, 2015. https://www.chicagotribune.com/ 2015/06/04/teen-who-killed-pamela-smarts-husband-freed-25-year s-later/.
- "Testify as to Their Opinion of Long's Sanity," Portsmouth Herald and Times, December 10, 1937. https://www.newspapers.com/image/12 973699/.
- "The Hontvet Murder House." Seacoastnh.com, Accessed April 15, 2024. http://www.seacoastnh.com/the-hontvet-murder-house/?sho wall=1.
- "The Most Haunted Hotels in New Hampshire." Hauntedrooms.com, January 29, 2020. https://www.hauntedrooms.com/new-hampshire/ haunted-places/haunted-hotels.
- "The Northwood Murderer." American Hauntings. Accessed May 4,

2024. https://www.americanhauntingsink.com/northwood.

- "The Victims." Smuttynose Island Murders, Accessed April 16, 2024. http://www.smuttynosemurders.com/the-victims.html.

- "Timeline of Serial Killer Terry Rasmussen's Terror in New Hampshire, California." ABC News, March 18, 2020. https://abcnews.go.com/US /timeline-serial-killer-terry-rasmussens-terror-hampshire-california /story?id=69505755.

- "Timeline of Terry Peder Rasmussen and Marlyse Elizabeth Honey-church." DOJ.nh.gov, June 5, 2019. https://www.doj.nh.gov/news/20 19/documents/20190605-allenstown-timeline.pdf.

- True Crime New England. "Episode 98: The Connecticut River Valley Killer." Accessed May 3, 2024. https://www.truecrimene.com/episod es/asyjv4wu01nw81ce7vusl4qri7fywl.

- "Unemployed Truck Driver Arraigned in Slayings of Wife, 3 Children." UPI, October 21, 1991. https://www.upi.com/Archives/1991/10/21/ Unemployed-truck-driver-arraigned-in-slayings-of-wife-3-children/ 5374688017600/.

- "Violent Crime 2022," Crimestats.dos.nh.gov. Accessed April 15, 2024. https://crimestats.dos.nh.gov/tops/report/violent-crimes/new-hamp shire/2022.

Chapter 5: Rhode Island

- "9 Fire Marshal 2b." Quahog Annex. August 16, 2011. https://quahog annex.wordpress.com/tag/brendel-murders/nest%20Brendel&match =1_epics/providence_mob/9.html.

- "10 Most Dangerous Cities in Rhode Island." TravelSafe-Abroad.com, January 24, 2024. https://www.travelsafe-abroad.com/most-dangero us-cities-in-rhode-island/.

- "A Maid Who Worked for Oil Heiress Carolyn Skelly." UPI, August 20, 1984. https://www.upi.com/Archives/1984/08/20/A-maid-who-wor ked-for-oil-heiress-Carolyn-Skelly/5646461822400/.

- "Adam Emery." Unsolved Mysteries Wiki, Accessed April 13, 2024.

https://unsolvedmysteries.fandom.com/wiki/Adam_Emery.

- Allen, Christopher. "The Mysterious Case of Adam Emery." Newport This Week, August 27, 2020. https://www.newportthisweek.com/arti cles/the-mysterious-case-of-adam-emery/.
- "Amasa Sprague." 2024. Wikipedia. March 23, 2024. https://en.wikip edia.org/wiki/Amasa_Sprague.
- "Arthur Daddy Black," Newport Mercury, September 30, 1932. https://www.newspapers.com/article/newport-mercury-arthur-daddy-black/14139178/
- Barry, Dan. "In Rhode Island, an Old Mobster Lets Go of a Long-Kept Secret." The New York Times, December 21, 2008. https://www.nyti mes.com/2008/12/22/us/22land.html.
- "Beavertail State Park | Rhode Island State Parks." Riparks.ri.gov, Accessed April 10, 2024. https://riparks.ri.gov/parks/beavertail-s tate-park.
- Bell, Michael E. & Meri R. Kennedy. "Ghostly Happenings: Haunted History of Sprague Mansion." Cranston Herald, October 18, 2017. https://cranstononline.com/stories/haunted-history-of-sprague-man sion,128592.
- Bell, Rachael. "Craig Price: Confessions of a Teenage Serial Killer." Crime Library. Accessed April 10, 2024. https://www.crimelibrary.or g/serial_killers/predators/craig_price/index.html.
- Blanco, Juan Ignacio. "Katherine Bunnell." Murderpedia.org, Accessed April 8, 2024. https://murderpedia.org/female.B/b/bunnell-katherin e.htm.
- Blanco, Juan Ignacio. "James DeBardeleben," Murderpedia.org, Accessed April 8, 2024. https://murderpedia.org/male.D/d/debardelebe n-james.htm.
- Blanco, Juan Ignacio. "Jeffrey Mailhot." Murderpedia.org, Accessed April 8, 2024. https://murderpedia.org/male.M/m/mailhot-jeffrey-p hotos.htm.
- Breton, Tracy, and Wayne Miller. "How Billy Sarmento Fell through the Cracks State Missed Its Chances to Stop 2 Killings." Providence

Journal, March 19, 1989. https://groups.google.com/g/alt.rhode_isla nd/c/4kszhczXjs0?pli=1.

- Brunelle, Bethany. "Former Newport Home of Claus and Sunny von Bülow Sold for $30 Million; Could Be RI Record." Newport Daily News, September 9, 2021. https://www.newportri.com/story/busine ss/real-estate/2021/09/09/clarendon-court-newport-estate-once-ow ned-sunny-and-claus-von-bülow-sold-30-million/8262755002.
- Carlsen, John. "Rhode Island's Safest Cities of 2024." SafeWise, March 18, 2024. https://www.safewise.com/blog/safest-cities-rhode-island/ #.
- Cherrygarden, Fred. "Gravelly Point." Atlas Obscura, April 2, 2024. https://www.atlasobscura.com/places/gravelly-point.
- "Claus von Bülow, Socialite Cleared of Trying to Murder Wife, Dies Aged 92." The Guardian, May 31, 2019, https://www.theguardian.co m/us-news/2019/may/31/claus-von-bülow-socialite-cleared-wife-m urder-dies-aged-92.
- Clem, Lauren. "Inside the Original Rhode Island State Prison." Rhode Island Monthly. April 25, 2023. https://www.rimonthly.com/inside-t he-original-rhode-island-state-prison.
- "Cold Case Files." Quahog.Org, Accessed 4/14/2024. https://quahog. org/index.php/FactsFolklore/Trivia/Limelight/TV/Cold_Case_Files
- Coletta, Sue. "True Crime Story: A Bizarre Coincidence." Suecoletta.com, April 28, 2022, https://www.suecoletta.com/true-crime-sto ry-a-bizarre-coincidence/.
- Confino, Arielle. "A Look Back at the Early History of Violence on Federal Hill." GoLocal Prov, August 15, 2014. https://www.golocalpr ov.com/news/a-look-back-at-the-early-history-of-violence-on-feder al-hill1.
- Connelly, Richard. "Police in R.I. Wonder Why Man Slain Near Home and on Patriarca's Turf." The Boston Globe, Sep 26, 1982. https://ww w.newspapers.com/image/437237758/.
- Corey, Katie and Liz King. "Episode 79: The Brendel Family Murders." True Crime New England, January 21, 2024. https://www.truecrimen

e.com/episodes/episode-79-the-brendel-family-murders.

- Corey, Katie and Liz King. "Episode 109: William Sarmento." True Crime New England, Accessed April 10, 2024. https://www.truecrim ene.com/episodes/episode-109-william-sarmento.

- Corey, Katie and Liz King. "Episode 118: James Soares Jr." True Crime New England, November 9, 2023. https://www.truecrimene.com/epi sodes/zcnkq4rjme4ct4dseiqn2olezwz7to

- "Craig Price." Murderpedia.org, accessed April 12, 2024, https://murd erpedia.org/male.P/p/price-craig.htm

- "Crime Rates for Rhode Island." Neighborhoodscout.com, Accessed April 10, 2024. https://www.neighborhoodscout.com/ri/crime.

- "Detective Seeking Closure for Family of Woman Killed in 1985." WPRI.com. March 15, 2019. https://www.wpri.com/news/local-news/northwest/detective-seeking-closure-for-family-of-woman-kil led-in-1985.

- DiBiase, Thomas A. (Tad). *No-Body Homicide Cases: A Practical Guide to Investigating, Prosecuting, and Winning Cases When the Victim Is Missing.* CRC Press, 2014.

- Doiron, Sarah, and Kim Kalunian. "'We Were Wordless': Family of Man Found Executed in Lincoln Desperate for Justice." WPRI.com, May 21, 2021. https://www.wpri.com/news/local-news/blackstone-valley/we-were-wordless-family-of-man-found-executed-in-lincoln-desperate-for-justice/.

- "Edna Therrel 'Terry' Boody Macdonald (1919-1971)." 2020. Finda-grave.com. 2020. https://www.findagrave.com/memorial/23006252 7/edna-therrel-macdonaldmes.htm.

- Fenton, Josh. "On Federal Hill Mobsters Used to Kill Mobsters, Now Tourists Get Shot." GoLocalProv, Accessed April 15, 2024. https://ww w.golocalprov.com/news/on-federal-hill-mobsters-used-to-kill-mob sters-now-tourists-get-shot.

- Fuqua, Lisa Marie "The Vanishing Killer Act." True Crime Addiction, February 12, 2020, https://medium.com/true-crime-addiction/the-va nishing-killer-act-true-crime-5a1bdfeb134b.

- Gaines, Judith. "Did Financial Woes Lead to Family Being Killed? Richmond Times-Dispatch, November 12, 1991. https://www.newsp apers.com/image/831985916/.
- "Going Inside the Crime Lab for a 25-Year-Old Cold Case." WPRI.com, May 30, 2019. https://www.wpri.com/news/local-news/blackstone-valley/going-inside-the-crime-lab-for-a-25-year-old-cold-case/.
- GoLocal Prov News Team. "Review of Newport's Most Infamous Crimes —Mob Murders to Ice Cream Schemes." GoLocal Prov, June 2, 2019. https://www.golocalprov.com/news/newports-most-infamous -crimes-mob-murders-to-ice-cream-schemes#.
- GoLocalProv News Team. "Review of Wyatt Finally Releases Infor-mation about Detainee's Death." GoLocal Prov, August 26, 2019. https://www.golocalprov.com/news/Wyatt-Finally-Releases-Info rmation-About-Detainees-Death#.
- Hamlin, Suzanne. "The DeBardeleben Case: A Shocking Story of a Counterfeiter, Killer, Kidnapper, and Serial Rapist," True Crime Docket, January 9, 2023, https://truecrimedocket.com/2023/01/09/t he-debardeleben-case-a-shocking-story-of-a-counterfeiter-killer-kid napper-and-serial-rapist/.
- Hill, John. "Notorious R.I. Killer Hightower Imprisoned in Illinois." The Providence Journal, December 23, 2017. www.providencejournal. com/story/news/2017/12/23/where-are-they-now-notorious-ri-kill er-christopher-hightower-imprisoned-in-illinois/16733655007/.
- "John Gordon (Convict)." Wikipedia, Accessed April 2, 2024. https://e n.wikipedia.org/wiki/John_Gordon_(convict).
- "Kimberly Sue Morse Knew Her Killer." Murder She Told, Accessed April 10, 2024. https://www.murdershetold.com/episodes/kimberly-morse.
- Lance, Peter. "Read the International Media Coverage for HOMICIDE at ROUGH POINT: The True Crime Story of How Billionaire Doris Duke Got Away with the Murder of Gay Designer, Art Curator and War Hero Eduardo Tirella in 1966." Peter Lance Blog, Accessed April 12, 2024. peterlance.com/wordpress/?p=10975.

- Landeck, Katie. "Rebellion? Murders? Here Are Four of the Most Haunted Restaurants in Rhode Island." The Providence Journal, October 10, 2023. https://www.providencejournal.com/story/lifestyl e/food/2023/10/10/haunted-ri-restaurants-tavern-on-main-valley-i nn-white-horse-tavern-tavern-on-main-carriage-inn/71057870007/.
- Larrabee, John and Russ Olivo, "An Ordinary Guy," Rhode Island Monthly, April 17, 2007, https://www.rimonthly.com/an-ordinar y-guy/.
- Martin, Paul. "Death Trip." The Shreveport Journal, August 6, 1984. https://www.newspapers.com/image/601626947/.
- "Mashapaug Pond." UPP Arts, Accessed May 5, 2024. http://www.upp arts.org/mashapaug-pond.html.
- May, Allan. The Providence Mob. CrimeLibrary.org, Accessed April 10, 2024. https://www.crimelibrary.org/gangsters_outlaws/family_e pics/providence_mob/1.html.
- "Mike DeBardeleben." Criminal Minds Wiki, Accessed April 15, 2024. https://criminalminds.fandom.com/wiki/Mike_DeBardeleben.
- Miller, G. Wayne. "R.I.'s Community Mental Health System Became a Victim of Its Own Success." The Providence Journal, October 26, 2014. https://www.providencejournal.com/story/lifestyle/health-fitness/2 014/10/27/20141026-r-i-s-community-mental-health-system-beca me-a-victim-of-its-own-success-ece/33827084007/.
- Mulvaney, Katie and. Mark Reynolds. "Aftermath of Shooting in Washington Park: 9 Injured, All Expected to Recover." The Providence Journal, May 14, 2021. https://www.providencejournal.com/story/ne ws/crime/2021/05/14/providence-washington-park-shooting-after math-all-expected-recover/5091442001/.
- Nemy, Enid. "Claus von Bülow, Society Figure in High-Profile Case, Dies at 92." The New York Times, May 30, 2019. https://www.nytime s.com/2019/05/30/obituaries/claus-von-bülow-dead.html.
- "New England Cold Case Project: Megeann Paul." Facebook, December 16, 2020. https://www.facebook.com/NewEnglandColdCases/ph otos/a.101844861853571/102620488442675/.

- Newsweek Staff. "Mystery: A Double Suicide Smacks of a Scam." Newsweek. December 19, 1993. https://www.newsweek.com/myster y-double-suicide-smacks-scam-190584.
- "Old Washington County Jail." South County, Rhode Island, Accessed April 13, 2024. https://www.southcountyri.com/listing/old-washingt on-county-jail/81/.
- Pelletiere, Bella. "Former Woonsocket Hone of Rhode Island Ripper Posted for Sale." The Valley Breeze, December 7, 2023. https://www.v alleybreeze.com/news/former-woonsocket-home-of-rhode-island-ri pper-posted-for-sale/article_e16c29d6-9216-11ee-b21c-5b0835cbd1 98.html.
- Phaneuf, Sandy. "Second Suspect Arrested in Sayles Street Shooting." Woonsocket, RI Patch, August 24, 2011. https://patch.com/rhode-isla nd/woonsocket/second-suspect-arrested-in-sayles-street-shooting.
- "Public Enemy #1 was her Patient | Photos." Newport Daily News. June 1, 2019. Accessed April 11, 2024. https://www.newportri.com/picture -gallery/news/2019/05/31/public-enemy-1-was-her/68659505007/.
- "Read the International Media Coverage for Homicide at Rough Point: The True Crime Story of How Billionaire Doris Duke Got Away with the Murder of Gay Designer, Art Curator and War Hero Eduardo Tirella in 1966 | Peter Lance," n.d. https://peterlance.com/wordpress/ ?p=10975.
- "Rebecca Spencer; Joan, Jennifer and Melissa Heaton," National Organization of Victims of Juvenile Murderers, October 16, 2020. https://teenkillers.org/memorials/rhode-island-victims/rebecca-spe ncer-joan-jennifer-melissa-heaton/.
- "Remains of Joseph 'Joe Onion' Scanlon Identified." Youtube.com. Accessed April 11, 2024. https://www.youtube.com/watch?v=un-EqHGE_jU.
- "Rhode Island Cold Case." Department, Rhode Island Cold Case by Pawtucket Police. Accessed April 11, 2024. https://coldcaseri.com/m edia.
- "Providence Man Sentenced to Serve 14 Years in State Prison for Role

in May 2021 Shootout in Providence That Wounded Nine." Riag.ri.gov. August 2, 2022. https://riag.ri.gov/press-releases/providence-man-se ntenced-serve-14-years-state-prison-role-may-2021-shootout.

- "Rudy Marfeo." The Tombstone Tourist. Accessed April 11, 2024. https://thetombstonetourist.com/graves/rudy-marfeo/.
- "Safest States in the U.S.," Wisevoter.com, May 5, 2024. https://wisevo ter.com/state-rankings/safest-states-in-the-us/#.
- Shorey, Ethan. "Six Years after Stowik Murder, Mutter Says Victim's Family Deserves Better." The Valley Breeze, October 21, 2021. https://www.valleybreeze.com/news/six-years-after-stowik-murder-mutter-says-victim-s-family-deserves-better/article_b02dc668-30ca-11ec-8fa9-ab0785f481ba.html.
- Shorey, Ethan. "Stowik Case Makes 'Cold Case' Cards. but Chief Says It's Not a Cold Case." The Valley Breeze, January 9, 2019. https://ww w.valleybreeze.com/news/stowik-case-makes-cold-case-cards-but-c hief-says-it-s-not-a-cold-case/article_bdd689c9-1abd-5139-a648-06 2e433babb5.html.
- "Sockanosset Boys Training School," ArtInRuins, March 24, 2024. https://artinruins.com/property/s.kanosset-boys-school/.
- "State v. Carpio (2012)." Findlaw. Accessed April 9, 2024. https://casel aw.findlaw.com/court/ri-supreme-court/1601003.html.
- "State v. Hightower." Justia Law. Accessed April 11, 2024. https://law. justia.com/cases/rhode-island/supreme-court/1995/661-a-2d-948.ht ml.
- "The 10 Most Haunted Hotels in Rhode Island." Haunted Rooms America. Accessed April 10, 2024. https://www.hauntedrooms.c om/rhode-island/haunted-places/haunted-hotels.
- "The Chicago Syndicate: Joseph 'Joe Onions' Scanlon's Remains Are Confirmed." www.thechicagosyndicate.com, Accessed April 11, 2024. https://www.thechicagosyndicate.com/2009/07/joseph-joe-onions-s canlons-remains-are.html.
- "The Mysterious Disappearance of Adam Emery," Unsolved Mysteries, accessed April 12, 2024, https://unsolved.com/gallery/adam-emery/.

- Tucker, Eric, and The Associated Press. "RI Man Gets Life Sentence in Child's Beating Death." San Diego Union-Tribune. February 18, 2009. https://www.sandiegouniontribune.com/sdut-toddler-killed-021809-2009feb18-story.html#..
- "Updated: Lincoln Woods Body Identified." ABC6 News, Providence Now, August 10, 2011. https://www.abc6.com/state-police-investigating-body-found-at-lincoln-woods/.
- Waddle, Ray. "Realtor Found Slain in Vacant Bossier Home." The Times, April 29, 1982. https://www.newspapers.com/image/2201866 70/?match=1&terms=Jean%20McPhaul.
- Wanjala, Lilian. "Esteban Carpio's Story: What Really Happened and Latest Updates." Tuko.co.ke - Kenya news, November 21, 2023. https://www.tuko.co.ke/facts-lifehacks/celebrity-biographies/52851 4-esteban-carpios-story-what-happened-latest-updates/.
- "Wanted by FBI: Man in Murder Case Who May Be in Florida." CBS News, January 2, 2017, https://www.cbsnews.com/miami/news/wan ted-by-fbi-man-in-murder-case-who-may-be-in-florida/.
- White, Tim. "Some of RI's Most Notorious Criminals Shipped out of State." WPRI.com12, July 15, 10AD. https://www.wpri.com/news/so me-of-ris-most-notorious-criminals-shipped-out-of-state/

Chapter 6: Vermont

- Alexander, William. "Curses, UFOs, and the Mystery of 'Bennington Triangle.'" Vermont's Very Best - Haunted Vermont, Folklore & much more…, July 1, 2014. https://www.vermonter.com/bennington-trian gle/.
- Alexander, William. "Resident Ghosts of the Back Inn Time – Fact or Fantasy?" Vermont's Very Best - Haunted Vermont, Folklore & much more…, August 4, 2011. https://www.vermonter.com/lora-resident-ghost/.
- Alexander, William. "Spend the Night with Ghosts at Vermont's White House Inn." Vermont's Very Best - Haunted Vermont, Folklore & much

more…, October 24, 2023. https://www.vermonter.com/haunted-wh ite-house-inn/.

- "Almon and Emeline (Alice Meaker, Part 3)," These Dark Mountains, March 13, 2020. https://thesedarkmountains.com/episodes/almon-a nd-emeline-alice-meaker-part-3.

- Associated Press. "Couple Faces Arkansas Charges for Baby's Death." The Bangor Daily News, May 5, 2002. https://www.newspapers.com/ image/664242062/.

- Associated Press. "Vermont Woman Who Killed 4 Sentenced." www.boston.com, November 15, 2017. https://www.boston.com /news/local-news/2017/11/15/vermont-jody-herring-sentence/.

- "Barbara Agnew." Vsp.vermont.gov, January 10, 1987. https://vsp.ver mont.gov/unsolved/homicide/agnew.

- Becker, Kaitlin McKinley. "Police Investigating Suspicious Death in Vt. Hotel Room." NECN, November 23, 2020. https://www.necn.co m/news/local/police-investigating-suspicious-death-in-vt-hotel-roo m/2355508/.

- "Brian Rooney." Murderpedia.org, Accessed April 18, 2024. https://m urderpedia.org/male.R/r/rooney-brian.htm.

- Callahan, Maureen. "How a Vermont Couple Ended up in a Serial Killer's Gruesome Chain of Carnage." New York Post, July 2019. https://nypost.com/2019/06/30/how-a-vermont-couple-ended-u p-in-a-serial-killers-gruesome-chain-of-carnage/.

- Carlsen, John. "Vermont's Safest Cities of 2024." www.safewise.com, March 18, 2024. https://www.safewise.com/blog/safest-cities-vermo nt/.

- "Catherine C. Richards," Rutland Daily Herald, April 12, 1983. https://www.newspapers.com/image/534628344/.

- Chase, Stacey. "Shooting Spree Detailed in Court Filing." Rutland Herald, July 16, 2001. https://www.newspapers.com/image/5352836 47/?terms=Bishop&match=1.

- "Christine Billis." Murderpedia.org, Accessed April 18, 2024. https://m urderpedia.org/female.B/b/billis-christine.htm.

- Coletta, Sue. "Killing Mary Mabel Rogers." Suecoletta.com, May 9, 2020. https://www.suecoletta.com/killing-mary-mabel-rogers/.
- Conroy, J. Oliver. "Vermont Police Use Cigarette DNA to Solve Woman's Murder, 52 Years On." The Guardian, February 23, 2023. https://www.theguardian.com/us-news/2023/feb/23/vermont-rita-c urran-murder-police-dna-cigarette.
- D'Ambrosio, Dan. "What Do We Know about Jason Eaton, Man Accused of Shooting 3 Palestinian Students." USA Today, December 1, 2023. https://www.usatoday.com/story/news/nation/2023/12/01/ja son-eaton-vermont-shooting-accused-palestinian-students/7176850 7007/.
- "Death Recommended for 'Serial Baby Killer." CBSnews.com, December 19, 2013. https://www.cbsnews.com/losangeles/news/death-rec ommended-for-serial-baby-killer/.
- "Detective Story Archives." New England Historical Society, Accessed May 6, 2024. https://newenglandhistoricalsociety.com/tag/detective-story/.
- Dobrick, Mariessa. "Virtual Speaker Series: True Crime Vermont: Intrigue in the Archives." Vermont Historical Society, January 18, 2024. https://vermonthistory.org/calendar/virtual-speaker-series-tr ue-crime-vermont-intrigue-in-the-archives.
- "Donald DeMag." Murderpedia.org, Accessed April 18, 2024. https://m urderpedia.org/male.D/d/demag-donald.htm.
- Donnelly, John. "Suspect in Slaying of Girl, 11, Pleads Innocent to Kidnap." The Burlington Free Press. April 12, 1983. https://www.ne wspapers.com/article/the-burlington-free-press-schaefer-plead/418 90498/.
- Elder-Collins, Liam, and Henry Epp. "Jody Herring Sentenced to Life without Parole." Vermont Public, November 15, 2017. https://www.v ermontpublic.org/vpr-news/2017-11-15/jody-herring-sentenced-to-life-without-parole.
- "Emeline Meaker." Murderpedia.org, Accessed April 18, 2024. https://murderpedia.org/female.M/m/meaker-emeline.htm.

- "Estranged Husband Arrested in Death of His Wife 31 Years Ago in Vermont." APNews.com, September 20, 2024. https://apnews.com/article/murder-carroll-peters-cheryl-peters-morrisville-vermont-b0dbd62a01ff30b1e6a138144b57719e.
- Farrow, Libbi. "Mystery in the Mountains: Who Shot Cheryl Peters?" ABC22 & FOX44, September 7, 2021. https://www.mychamplainvalley.com/mystery-in-the-mountains/mystery-in-the-mountains-we-want-a-jury-trial/.
- Farrow, Libbi. "Mystery in the Mountains: Who Stabbed Lynda Moore to Death in 1986?" ABC22 & FOX44, September 20, 2021. https://www.mychamplainvalley.com/mystery-in-the-mountains/mystery-in-the-mountains-who-stabbed-lynda-moore/.
- "Gary Lee Schaefer, Episode 10" True Crime New England, Accessed April 18, 2024. https://www.truecrimene.com/episodes/episode-10-gary-lee-schaefer.
- "Gary Lee Schaefer." Murderpedia.org, Accessed April 18, 2024. https://murderpedia.org/male.S/s/schaefer-gary-lee.htm.
- "George Long." Murderpedia.org, Accessed April 18, 2024. https://murderpedia.org/male.L/l/long-george-r.htm.
- "Grace and Gracie Reapp." Cold Case New England, July 17, 2023. https://coldcasene.org/f/grace-and-gracie-reapp.
- "Grace M. & Grace Nicole Reapp." Vsp.vermont.gov, June 7, 1978. https://vsp.vermont.gov/unsolved/missing/a/reapp.
- Grimes, Kristin. "9 of the Most Dangerous Places in Vermont." OnlyInYourState, October 24, 2022. https://www.onlyinyourstate.com/vermont/dangerous-vt/.
- Grimes, Kristin. "These 9 Haunted Hotels in Vermont Will Make Your Stay a Nightmare." OnlyInYourState, May 20, 2022. https://www.onlyinyourstate.com/vermont/haunted-hotels-vt/.
- Hall, Joseph. "Mary Robers." Email from jm_hall@comcast.net, May 21, 2024.
- Hallenbeck, Brent. "48 Vermont-Centric Books That Could Make for Perfect Holiday Gifts." Burlington Free Press, December 2, 2018.

https://www.burlingtonfreepress.com/story/entertainment/2018/12/02/vermont-authors-books-holiday-gift-list/2160447002/.

- Hearn, Daniel Allen. "Vermont Historical Society Stores Windsor State Prison's Electric Chair." Springfield Vermont News, August 8, 2017. https://springfieldvt.blogspot.com/2017/08/vermont-historical-society-stores.html.

- Heintz, Paul. "Vermont Prison Probe Finds 'Disturbing' Number of Sexual Misconduct Allegations." Seven Days, December 23, 2020. https://www.sevendaysvt.com/OffMessage/archives/2020/12/23/vermont-prison-probe-finds-disturbing-number-of-sexual-misconduct-allegations.

- "Isabelle 'Belle' Haskins Parker (1850-1922)." Findagrave.com. Accessed April 18, 2024. https://www.findagrave.com/memorial/117349251/isabelle-parker.

- "Israel Keyes." Murderpedia.org, Accessed April 18, 2024. https://murderpedia.org/male.K/k/keyes-israel.htm.Kinsman, Betty. Letter to Dawn Barclay. "Contact-New Submission." Email from sahs@vermon-tel.ne, March 8, 2024.

- "Jason Hann." Murderpedia.org, Accessed April 18, 2024. https://murderpedia.org/male.H/h/hann-jason.htm.

- Lakritz, Talia. "The Most Notorious Unsolved Crime in Every State." Business Insider, October 28, 2022. https://www.businessinsider.com/us-cold-cases-true-crime-2018-4#vermont-between-1920-and-1950-as-many-as-10-people-disappeared-in-the-bennington-triangle-in-southwestern-vermont-45.

- Levitt, Alice. "Exploring Vermont's Haunted Restaurants." Seven Days, October 30, 2013. https://www.sevendaysvt.com/food-drink/exploring-vermonts-haunted-restaurants-2266453.

- Lewis, Thea. *True Crime Stories of Burlington, Vermont*. Arcadia Publishing, 2023.

- "Local Child Killer Changes Gender While on Death Row." KESQ, March 15, 2019. https://kesq.com/news/2019/03/15/local-child-killer-changes-gender-while-on-death-row/.

- "Mary Rogers, Episode 86" True Crime New England, Accessed April 18, 2024. https://www.truecrimene.com/episodes/episode-86-mary-rogers.
- "Mary Mabel Rogers." Murderpedia.org, Accessed April 19, 2024. https://murderpedia.org/female.R/r/rogers-mary-mabel.htm.
- "Missing Person / NamUs #MP4031." Namus.nij.ojp.gov, Accessed April 18, 2024. https://namus.nij.ojp.gov/case/MP4031.
- Monroe, Scott. "Provost Verdict Tossed; Killer Still Gets Life." Vermont Community Newspaper Group, December 29, 2005. https://www.vtcng.com/stowereporter/archives/provost-verdict-tossed-killer-still-gets-life/article_848e8066-b114-5cb3-ae18-155923ff2efb.html#.
- "More than a Century Ago, the Rogers Murder Made National Headlines." Vermont Country Magazine, July 20, 2022. https://vermontcountry.com/2022/07/20/more-than-a-century-ago-the-rogers-murder-made-national-headlines/.
- Muras, Chris. "Here Are the 15 Absolute Best Places to Visit in April across the United States." OnlyInYourState, September 21, 2023. https://www.onlyinyourstate.com/usa/best-places-to-visit-usa-april/.
- O'Grady, Patrick. "End of a Long Chapter in Windsor as Prison Closes." Valley News, November 1, 2017. https://www.vnews.com/Only-staff-remains-and-Windsor-prison-closes-down-208-years-after-the-first-prison-opened-on-State-Street-in-1809-13432197.
- Pierce, Tracy Davis. "Billis Returned to Prison." Barton Chronicle Newspaper, October 21, 2020. https://bartonchronicle.com/billis-returned-to-prison/.
- "Police: Man Found in Vermont Hotel Room Shot to Death," WPTZ, November 23, 2020. https://www.mynbc5.com/article/police-man-found-in-vermont-hotel-room-shot-to-death/34762795.
- Porche, Verandah. "Question for Book Research." Email from at the Guilford Historical Society., May 9, 2024.
- "Provost Convicted of Four Murder Counts," Rutland Daily Herald, November 1, 2003. https://www.rutlandherald.com/news/provost-c

onvicted-of-four-murder-counts/article_6c3f1f3c-eb4d-5409-9461-457442edc4dc.html.

• "Quadruple Homicide Suspect Caught after Vermont State Police Traffic Stop." www.newson6.com, July 16, 2001. https://www.newson6.com/story/5e3681892f69d76f62095de1/quadruple-homicide-suspect-caught-after-vermont-state-police-traffic-stop.

• Ramos, Nestor, "Perplexing Death Still Troubles Vt. Town, Decades Later." Boston Globe, July 6, 2015. https://www.bostonglobe.com/metro/2015/07/06/farmer-mysterious-death-nearly-years-ago-still-troubles-newbury/nwbywhBbvU88JXhFSo8tGN/story.html.

• Rathke, Lisa. "Vermont, Usually One of the Safest States, Saw a 185% Rise in Firearms Homicides Last Year." Press Herald, December 15, 2023. https://www.pressherald.com/2023/12/15/vermont-usually-one-of-the-safest-states-saw-a-185-rise-in-firearms-homicides-last-year/.

• Ropek, Lucas. "18 Years Later, Vermont Police Still Looking for Clues in Slaying of Springfield Woman Found alongside I-91." masslive, March 5, 2017. https://www.masslive.com/news/2017/03/years_later_police_still_looki.html.

• Schiller, Dr. Andrew. "Vermont Crime." Neighborhoodscout.com. NeighborhoodScout, March 29, 2019. https://www.neighborhoodscout.com/vt/crime.

• Schroder, Jan. "11 Hotels and Breweries That Used to Be Prisons." Fodors Travel Guide, December 27, 2017. https://www.fodors.com/news/photos/from-prisons-to-pints-and-pillows-11-former-jails-where-youll-want-to-serve-time.

• Seling, Megan. "10 True Crime Landmarks Every Murderino Needs to Visit." Livability, August 23, 2019. https://livability.com/vt/experiences-adventures/10-true-crime-landmarks-every-murderino-needs-to-visit/.

• Shea, Mary Catherine. "Barre Bank Robbery Collection" Vermont Historical Society, 2016. chrome-extension://efaidnbmnnnibpcajpcglclefindmkaj/https://vermonthistory.org/ documents/findaid/BarreB ankRobbery.pdf.

- "Slain Woman's Husband Arrested in Puerto Rico," Burlington Free Press, March 19, 1999. https://www.newspapers.com/image/202607 607/.

- Smallheer, Susan. "Vermont Convicted Murderer, Kidnapper Dies in Kentucky Prison." Brattleboro Reformer, November 28, 2023. https://www.reformer.com/local-news/vermont-convicted-murd erer-kidnapper-dies-in-kentucky-prison/article_ec3d2b9c-8dfe-11e e-a2f9-77f7c5811a85.html.

- Smith, Gene X. "In Windsor Prison." American Heritage, May 1996. https://www.americanheritage.com/windsor-prison.

- Solochek, Jeffrey S. "Third Victim Dies in Murder-Suicide." Tampa Bay Times, January 2, 2006. https://www.newspapers.com/image/33 1416977/.

- Sophia. "The Puzzling Unsolved Murder in Vermont That Still Haunts One Small Town." OnlyInYourState, June 9, 2019. https://www.onlyi nyourstate.com/vermont/unsolved-murder-vt/.

- "State vs. Blair." Supreme Court of Vermont Windsor, October 6, 1953. https://law.justia.com/cases/vermont/supreme-court/1953/1260-0.h tml.

- "The Briefest of Histories." Magic Hat Brewing Company, Accessed April 18, 2024. https://www.magichat.net/about/.

- "The Farmhouse Where Israel Keyes Murdered Bill and Lorraine Currier." Oddstops.com, Accessed May 9, 2024. https://oddstops. com/location.php?id=405.

- "The House Where Brianna Maitland's Car Was Found." Oddstops.com, Accessed May 9, 2024. https://oddstops.com/location.php?id=544.

- "The Most Haunted Hotels in Vermont," Hauntedrooms.com, January 29, 2020. https://www.hauntedrooms.com/vermont/haunted-places/ haunted-hotels.

- "The Murder of Alice Meaker." Waterbury-history-vt, Accessed May 6, 2024. https://www.waterburyhistoricalsociety.org/fall-meeting-prog ram.

- "Two Murders in Hardwick," Hardwick Gazette, July 19, 1977. https://www.newspapers.com/image/845013202/.
- "Unsolved Missing and Murder Cases in Vermont, Uncovered." The Citizen Detective, Accessed April 18, 2024. https://uncovered.com/states/vermont-cold-cases.
- Valley News. "Man Shot at White River Junction Hotel." VTDigger, October 7, 2022. https://vtdigger.org/2022/10/07/man-shot-at-white-river-junction-hotel/.
- "Vermont Cases," Savagewatch - Unsolved Crime. "February 4, 2018. https://savagewatch.com/vermont-cases/.
- "Vermont Ex-Con Back Behind Bars for Domestic Assault." WCAX, June 8, 2019. https://www.wcax.com/content/news/Billis-back-behind-bars-511026301.html.
- "Vermont Murder Most Foul." Suncommunitynews.com, May 11, 2011. https://suncommunitynews.com/news/18230/vermont-murder-most-foul/.
- "Windsor Village Apartments." Banwell Architects, Accessed April 18, 2024. https://www.banwellarchitects.com/portfolio/windsor-village-apartments/.
- Wolfe, Elisabeth, Sara Smart, Celina Tebor, and John Miller. "Suspect in Shooting of 3 Palestinian College Students in Vermont Pleads Not Guilty." WBAL, November 28, 2023. https://www.wbaltv.com/article/vermont-shooting-suspect-3-palestinian-college-students-not-guilty-plea/45957321#.
- "Wrisley Discharged?" The Brattleboro Reformer, October 13, 1913. https://www.newspapers.com/article/the-brattleboro-reformer-wrisley-dischar/116921944/.

Acknowledgements

I want to shout out thanks to the people who were instrumental in helping this book come to life. Specifically, thanks to Shawn Reilly Simmons, Verena Rose, and Deb Well at Level Best Books for believing in the concept and enduring my unending emails.

Thanks to all of the librarians at the historical societies that researched addresses that I could not find on my own. Much appreciation to Barbara and Keith Noyes, who provided books on haunted destinations and assassination travel that I might not have found otherwise. Also, to Daphne Dennis for her extraordinary research prowess. Special thanks (and apologies) to Maria Kriesel, Lia and Tom Ioannou, and Liz Benuscak for turning a blind eye when I used their real estate office for writing and editing instead of concentrating on selling real estate.

Big hugs to amazing author Elf Ahearn, who is my biggest cheerleader and makes a mean turkey sandwich during our writing sprints, and to everyone at Hudson Valley Scribes who inspired my swag and also admonished me whenever my writing fell short. And to my fellow authors at Sisters in Crime and Mystery Writers of America, who are my constant inspiration.

And finally, to my long-suffering husband Josh and my children, Justin and Maki, who understand that magic happens when you ignore cooking and cleaning in favor of creating.

About the Author

Dawn M. Barclay (who writes fiction as D.M. Barr) has been writing in the travel field for decades, first as a travel trade journalist and later as a book author. She is the 2023 Lowell Thomas Gold-award-winning author of the autism travel bible, *Traveling Different: Vacation Strategies for Parents of the Anxious, the Inflexible, and the Neurodiverse* (Rowman & Littlefield, 2022). Dawn also won the First Prize-Other Writing award from the Society of Professional Journalists in 1992 for a story on travel law.

Vacations Can Be Murder, her multi-volume true crime travel series with Level Best Books, combines the two things she loves best (after chocolate and dogs): travel and crime. Along with being an author of psychological suspense, she is a member of the Society of American Travel Writers, the American Society of Journalists and Authors, the New York Travel Writers Association, and several mystery writers organizations.

AUTHOR WEBSITE:
 www.VacationsCanBeMurder.com

SOCIAL MEDIA HANDLES:
 https://www.facebook.com/vacationscanbemurder
 https://www.instagram.com/vacations_can_be_murder/

Also by Dawn M. Barclay

As Dawn M. Barclay:

Traveling Different: Vacation Strategies for Parents of the Anxious, the Inflexible, and the Neurodiverse

As D.M. Barr:

Expired Listings: Revenge Begins at Home

Murder Worth the Weight

Saving Grace: A Psychological Thriller

The Queen of Second Chances

Simple Tryst of Fate

Deadly When Disturbed

New York State of Crime: Murder New York Style 6 (co-editor and author)

Justice for All: Murder New York Style 5 (co-editor and author)

Index

ACCOMMODATIONS, ATTRACTIONS & SITES

MUSEUMS & MEMORIALS

PRISONS & CORRECTIONAL FACILITIES

TOURS

RESTAURANTS & BARS

CEMETERIES